HAZARDS
OF LEARNING

HAZARDS OF LEARNING

An International Symposium
on the Crisis of the University

G. R. Urban

with an Introduction by Seymour Martin Lipset

Open Court
La Salle, Illinois

030230

Acknowledgments

This symposium consists of edited versions of conversations originally broadcast, in 1973 and 1974, by Radio Free Europe, with whose kind cooperation it is here published.

Library of Congress Cataloguing in Publication Data
Main entry under title:

Hazards of learning.

"Thirteen dialogues ... originally commissioned and broadcast by Radio Free Europe in 1973 and 1974."
  1. Universities and colleges—Congresses. I. Urban, Geroge R. II. Radio Free Europe.
LB2301.H34   378.1   76-3094
ISBN 0-87548-339-9

Contents

Preface

The thirteen dialogues assembled in this volume were originally commissioned and broadcast by Radio Free Europe in
1973 and 1974. The reader will note (to his dismay or delight)
that they were not conducted in the spirit of entirely disinterested inquiry. The interrogative method itself is a subtle way of
loading any discussion, for the assumptions built into the
questioning inevitably set the framework in which the answers
are elicited, and even where the questioner's frame of reference is rejected, the discussion tends to move in step, negative
step, with it.

But I must also admit to a thematic, and indeed philosophical, predilection. The question which surfaces in these dialogues, now under this, now under that heading, is whether
the modern university's functions are exhausted by the creation, conservation, and transmission of knowledge, or

whether the university must also be, as it always has been, a custodian—if not *the* custodian—of high culture and moral education. In other words: Is learning enough; and if it is not, how does the hazardous (as I see it) activity of amassing information pass into the relatively hazard-free, though still very disturbing, state of being educated? If it is true that education is what is left when what has been learned is forgotten, what is the kind of learning that we can, having absorbed it, afford to forget and yet claim to be educated? A similar question may be detected behind my curiosity to know whether scientific inquiry, or technology, carries a transmittable and universal ethos of its own; and if it does, whether such an ethos might successfully replace that elusive yet manifestly cohesive cluster of traditions, sensitivity, and critical method that we loosely call humanistic culture, and that is now said to be in a state of decline and, indeed, collapse.

The ensuing discussion of the crisis of the university in the late 1960s and early 1970s is important in its own right, but I also regard it as a profitable way of addressing ourselves to the perennial problem of whether knowledge and morality are comprehended in the same circle.

The most this symposium attempts to do is to append an informed footnote to these questions.

Brighton, England   G. R. URBAN
June 1976

The editor feels a sense of gratitude for encouragement and scholarly help generously given by Rex Littleboy, who has not lived to see the publication of this symposium.

Introduction

This is a book about the "crisis of the university." But as will be evident to all readers, the participants in this symposium do not agree as to what the crisis is about. For some, such as G. R. Urban and Richard Löwenthal, it is the challenge to scholarship, to free inquiry, posed by the recent wave of student activism. As Urban notes, "Idealism and despair at the universities go hand in hand with a strong current of irrationalism and anti-intellectualism which often extends to a straightforward rejection of knowledge." Two contributors, Alain Touraine and Richard Hoggart, proudly report, however, that they supported the student revolt of the 1960s at their universities, Nanterre and Birmingham. Hoggart says, "I spent much of my time on the side of the students in the battle that developed at Birmingham in 1967-68." Touraine notes that during the May Days in 1968 in France, "I did not negotiate with the authorities—I was physically on the barricades. . . . I said at the time, and I have maintained since, that the only intelligent attitude was to try to accept the dual orientation of the student movement—that is to say, to encourage the social conflict aspect of it and limit the consequences of the institutional crisis to the university."

Not surprisingly, the participants also disagree strongly as to the reasons for the emergence of widespread student protest in the late sixties. They differ as to whether they see it as a response of youth to strains in the larger society or polity, or as reaction to changes within the university world which have a negative impact on the education and life of students.

Those who address themselves to the political sources of the revolt point to specific events, particularly the Vietnam War, which encouraged a revival of radical protest. De-Stalinization and the revolts in East Germany, Hungary, and Czechoslovakia weakened the strength of Cold War ideology. Conversely, revolutionary hopes revived as a result of events in the Third World, Cuba, and China. Yet for the most part, the participants in the symposium who stress extramural causes are inclined to emphasize basic structurally induced tensions more than purely political factors. Those cited include:

1. A rate of social change that produced sharply different conceptions of the world for different age groups (MacRae). But it should be noted that Mann explicitly denies that a significant generation gap exists.

2. Technological developments, particularly television, that make everything seem possible to young people. But MacRae, who suggests this hypothesis, also notes that student protest "was not a revolt against technology or against the G.N.P."

3. Demythologization, an elaboration of Max Weber's thesis that the rational justifications for the modern materialistic world do not sustain faith in the system. Young people do not see Western society as fulfilling any important social ideals (MacRae).

   Löwenthal notes "the emptiness—the lack of meaning . . . of life in a competitive consumer society." Hersch also points to "a loss of any sense that the world has meaning. . . . There are no signposts left, civilization isn't going in any particular direction. . . . " But Beloff rejects these explanations and suggests that the voiced student complaint against the aimlessness of modern society "is artificial" and ideological, that it is not a real source of the students' malaise.

4. Another cause of the negative feelings of young people, suggested by Jeanne Hersch, is the decline of close affective personal relations, a "lack of love," which is blamed in part on the emancipation of sexual life, on the separation of the sex act from love.

5. Resentment against "the increasing bureaucratic remoteness of the forms of Western representative democracy" (Löwenthal).

6. Changes in the labor market for university students resulting from the growth of the mass university, which has made a "growing number of students realize that they were not going to spend their working lives in the academy or professional world but that they were much more likely to end up as employees of large organizations" (Touraine).

7. The increased emphasis on competitive meritocracy has heightened tensions, particularly for young people. A meritocratic society is "one made up of large numbers of isolated, itemized, ambitious individuals." When "you reward power-pushing intellectual merit to the exclusion of all else, you create a world more naked and brutal than the world you are replacing." Meritocracy has drained the "residual sense of community" (Hoggart).

Those participants who emphasize factors stemming from changes within the university also present a variety of disparate, sometimes contradictory, sources of student discontent. Among these are:

1. The decline of faculty involvement in teaching. MacRae suggests Berkeley erupted first because its faculty was more involved than those at any other school with "serious concerns elsewhere that took them away all the time. . . . They were more airborne than any other

group of professionals I'd ever known or heard of." Beloff also stresses that "the reasons that students are discontented is that their teachers are not with them, or if they are with them in the flesh, they are not with them in the spirit, because they are busy consulting the timetable for the next plane to Brussels. The model for restoring learning to universities is a ban on air travel."

Ashby stresses the growth of the emphasis on research, which means that the university is no longer concerned with whether a faculty member "teaches . . . well, but whether he publishes papers that his peers . . . will appreciate and will regard as good enough to elect him to an academy." Faculty increasingly behave as "though they were workers in a research institute," and "star" professors often "opt out of undergraduate teaching altogether." Student discontent, therefore, is in part a reaction to "the impression that, in many universities, the undergraduate is no longer the primary interest of the university."

Löwenthal notes that in Germany and some other European countries, the increased numbers of students who flooded the universities were short-changed because there was no corresponding increase in the professorial ranks. As a result, a large part of the actual teaching was taken over by teaching assistants who had low incomes and little status, and who were themselves often disgruntled.

2. The growth in size and differentiation of function turned universities from communities into bureaucracies with a consequent "remoteness and impersonality" (MacRae). Beloff emphasizes that university expansion placed students "in the hands of large impersonal forces with which they are psychologically unsuited to cope."

Mann also insists that the postwar expanded university no longer provided students with the sense of "protection and psychological security which European settlements of the past did." The new schools particularly are a "concrete desert—lonely and impersonal."

3. Some of the participants blame the policy of expanding the numbers going to university for bringing in students

who are unqualified to benefit from higher education and hence resent and turn against the university. Thus Lord James stresses that "in higher education we often tend to feed rather second-rate minds with ideas they are not competent to digest." He notes "the very real danger of educating people beyond their capacity, and this has created social troubles in the United States, Germany, and France. . . . " He is unequivocal in his belief that the university "is an elite institution and must remain so."

Alexander King also sees the crisis of the university as resulting in some part from the fact that the "enormous increase in enrollment is motivated by the desire for better jobs," rather than an interest in knowledge and culture. When university enrollment in a country moves from 2 to 3 percent of the relevant age cohort to 20 to 40 percent, its scholarly purpose is inevitably "diluted." The attachment of the new students to learning "is from zero to something very small." It is "wholly wrong to put them in the university."

Jeanne Hersch also calls for rigorous selection of the students on the basis of academic qualifications. "Otherwise you are creating a mass university with elite pretensions, which is a sure prescription for social trouble. This is what happened in some American universities, which have really ceased to be universities." Beloff makes the same points, arguing that the expansion of American universities brought "an intake of large numbers of young people who were unfit for university study. It was discovered that this made them unhappy and discontented." He states that "first-rate students, unless psychologically disturbed, are never involved in student politics."

Not surprisingly, Beloff, Hersch, and King advocate intensified programs of "general," broad, cultural education and deplore the incorporation within the university of specialized vocationally oriented training as destructive of its scholarly and culture-preserving purpose. King suggests the need to keep separate universities concerned with academic work from those involved in specialized professional education.

4. Yet another group of participants reaches almost diamet-

rically opposite conclusions. They argue that the increase in numbers is good and necessary. Insofar as expansion is a source of unrest, it results from the failure of higher education to provide the kind of education students desire.

Paul Seabury of Berkeley suggests that the large American state universities show real vitality because they have admitted many students from class backgrounds not previously associated with university attendance. Touraine, who was at Nanterre when the French student revolt began, contends that student protest was directed against the "antiquated academic setting" of the French university: the fact that the greatly enlarged system continued to prepare students "first and foremost for academic succession," that it did not modify its curriculum to deal with the needs of the students. General cultural education, to him, is a reactionary elitist system invented "to counteract the first attempts to give the public a mass elementary and, later, technological education." Löwenthal calls attention to a similar lack of response by the elitist German system to the mass intake of students who sought training for professions.

The variety of hypotheses put forth by distinguished academics from a number of countries points up the difficulty of trying to find a "solution." Thus some, Ashby, Beloff, and King, seek to enlarge the role of general education in the modern specialized university. Touraine, on the other hand, views it as a "reactionary idea," seeking to make "us all gratuitous heirs to a so-called Christian civilization and Western culture."

5. They differ also in their evaluations of the impact of the traditional hierarchical structure of university governance on the activities of the university. Hoggart argues that "the students had a very good case" in demanding the "democratization of the university structure, student participation and so on."

Alain Touraine, like Hoggart, was a sympathetic participant in the protest of the 1960s and also thought that the universities should allow students considerable influence. He, however, rejects the particular form of student participation introduced in French universities by Edgar Faure after the 1968 rebellion. Touraine's opposition stems from the fact that he identifies participation in operating the institutions of an "alienated" society as a form of co-optation that, while "giving us the outward trappings of independence," in fact "is just another word for incorporating people in a social order." As he sees it, the government legislated increased participation as a way of avoiding having to deal with the basic problems of the university; "let the professors and the students fight it out in their participatory bodies—this was the latent idea."

Beloff, now the head of the new British independent (nongovernmental) University College at Buckingham, strongly rejects the notion that students should participate in running the university. He argues incisively:

The university is a community which is necessarily hierarchical because the functions which it performs are performed at different levels according to different ranges of qualification and experience. . . . There can be basically no similarity between the responsibilities of a professor, a junior teacher, a graduate student, an undergraduate, a laboratory assistant, and so on. The correct analogy is not with society but with other hierarchically organized communities—an ocean liner, for example, . . . an aircraft—no one suggests that the passengers take part in flying it. . . . The university conceived as a model of democracy is outright rubbish.

For Beloff, the emphasis on "treating universities as democratic assemblies" has produced a crisis, "the steady lowering of university teaching and research."

Richard Löwenthal, speaking from his experience at the Free University of Berlin, also strongly rejects the efforts to "democratize the universities" on the model of the civil polity as the application of a false analogy, "which has resulted in the politicization of higher education, in the appointment of faculty for their left-wing political views."

Not all the participants, however, explain student revolt as a response to particular malfunctions of society or higher education. Two, the anarchist Mick Farren and the sociologist Donald MacRae, point up factors inherent in the social situation of the studentry as encouraging them to engage in political protest. Speaking specifically of the modern university, Farren notes:

The Western campuses . . . are an unreal world which lends itself, as no other institution does, to revolutionary game situations: You play cowboys and Indians with the administration, with the police department and the National Guard. . . . And it is certainly true that if you are a university student, the campus is all-enclosing: You get your food, shelter, education, and entertainment at the university, so the idea that you change the world when you change the university becomes quite overpowering. But the unreality comes through: You believe in the heroic act of dying on the barricades because in the last moment you really expect someone to blow a whistle—it is all over and everybody can go home for tea.

Donald MacRae brings in the sociological dimension, noting that "young people are to some extent in revolt because they have to make their own lives in their own way and assume responsibility. The phenomenon of the generational revolt is not a university phenomenon and not a novel phenomenon. It is a constant feature of history." More specific to university-based events, however, is the fact that "the role of the student has always been a rather peculiar one. A student is a person who is isolated from society, isolated from the ordinary daily economic work of the world, who is supposed to be devoted to the world of learning and abstract intelligence precisely at an age of maximum physical vigor, maximum passion and desire in all fields of life." Students have always been allowed "a good deal of internal license to make room for the passions and desires of their age and to compensate for the university's intellectual and moral pressures." As a result, universities from the Middle Ages on have been "extraordinarily turbulent places" noted for their record of violence, of support for bohemian, revolutionary, and nationalist movements. And MacRae argues, therefore, that "we might think of the situation of comparative quiescence following the Second World War as being extremely unusual, and that it lasted for almost twenty years is itself something that needs explanation."

Unfortunately, none of the other participants in this symposium takes up the implications of the assumption that the social situation of the studentry makes them the most protest-prone of all social strata (a theme I must confess to having analyzed in my book *Rebellion in the University*). Clearly, it challenges their efforts to use the recent protest wave to justify particular sets of social and educational arrangements or reforms.

This book, then, should be read not so much as an effort to describe and explain the sources of the "crisis of the university" as a document illustrating the fact that we are dealing with a "divided academy," one which harbors a wide range of political and educational opinion. Each participant gives expression to his own ideology, his own particular set of beliefs about the university and society. The editor and convener, G. R. Urban, is to be complimented for having brought together such a disparate set of people, varying from Farren, Hoggart, and Touraine on the left to Beloff, James, and King on the conservative side. Each in his own way points up some of the positive and negative aspects of the modern university existing in a rapidly changing, troubled world. It is hoped that this book will help to educate people within and outside the university about the nature of the institution.

SEYMOUR MARTIN LIPSET

Lord James of Rusholme

When Is Higher Education an Education?

Lord James of Rusholme is a former Vice-Chancellor of the University of York and a former High Master of Manchester Grammar School. He was chairman of the British official inquiry on teacher training (1972), and some of the recommendations of his committee's report ("The James Report") have been incorporated in the British Government's White Paper *Education: A Framework for Expansion, 1972.*

Urban In an earlier series of discussions ("Alienation and Participation in Industrial Society")* we tried to identify the roots of a public sentiment which is as difficult to describe as it

---

*Radio Free Europe, 1971-72. Part 4, a discussion by Ota Sik and G. R. Urban of egalitarianism and self-fulfillment, was published in *Survey*, Spring 1973.

is real and worrying. It has to do with a feeling that we are no longer at home in the world we have created; that our mental horizons are global while our ability to deal with them is not; that we are driftwood in a sea of technological change and bureaucratic controls; that we are isolated from our fellow men and alienated from the fruits of our labor.

We found that one of the most important causes of this alienation is the dull, repetitive, and dehumanizing nature of work. There were other factors—population growth, urbanization, standardization—but the one that hammers our sensibilities most insistently and most irresistibly is work. Work, we found, is still considered as punishment, even though punishment of a subtle kind. It is still true that by the sweat of his brow shall man live. Trade union leaders told us how very far we were from realizing Bernard Shaw's vision of a balanced life: a commonwealth in which work is play and play is life.

There is a conception of higher education which holds that dehumanizing work should be suffused with some intellectual and moral vision so as to stop it from being dehumanizing. One of its protagonists, Alfred North Whitehead, said: "The early Benedictine monks rejoiced in their labors because they conceived themselves as thereby made fellow workers with Christ." Whitehead went on to argue that it was the task of teachers—especially technical teachers—so to mold their students that they may overcome the frustrations and weariness of modern work—overcome it, as he hoped, in the spirit of the Benedictine monks.

This is clearly a desirable concept of education, both at the higher and the secondary levels, but I wonder whether it is not assigning to education the task of anesthetizing us for a life we would otherwise find less bearable. I also wonder whether those who are involved in higher education feel it to be their job to do the anesthetizing. And if neutralizing the alienation that is stirring in the modern worker's heart *is* one of the things education is supposed to do, could we object if another type of society offered an *ideology* as an alternative anesthetic? This leads us to the related question: Is work-satisfaction an end in itself? And if one believes that it is, does it much matter

Hazards of Learning

whether it is achieved in the fellowship of Christ or under Marxist dispensation?

Lord James   Ideally students should like the work they do, and I do not think that any idea of anesthetizing is involved. Looking back forty years to the time when I went to university, I can say I positively enjoyed my studies. I loved coming into contact with the great men in my subject, which was chemistry, and enlarging my horizons. It may be true that we have to some extent lost this, and it is a very important question for higher education why we have lost it. But the extent of the loss should not be exaggerated: I do not think we have lost it nearly as much as it is often alleged. The majority of students positively enjoy their work; they like reading medieval history (or whatever it may be), and this is fundamental. But there is another point here: The modern student demands that his studies be "relevant." "Relevance" is a key word in education today; it deserves to be more closely examined than it often is.

"Relevance" is sometimes interpreted as being immediately applicable to current social or industrial situations and the like, and one of the important points students make when they criticize education is that much of it is "irrelevant." So anyone engaged in higher education today, whether as student or teacher, has to sit down and ask himself, "What do we mean by relevance?" Too often "relevance" is interpreted with frivolous superficiality. If the study of society is not immediately related to life in East London or the working-class areas of the Paris suburbs, we are told it is irrelevant. This is very wrong. It may be that for some people—not all—to read Thucydides about power, or to read St. Augustine about the development of the soul, or to read Plato on the organization of society, or Aristotle about the nature of politics is not only as relevant as some sociological or psychological study dealing with a precise contemporary situation, but much more relevant because they force us to ask more fundamental questions.

We have in this country (I'm speaking as an Englishman) recently had a White Paper on education setting out the government's plans for educational advance for the next ten years—

Urban —A great deal of it based on your own report on teacher education—

Lord James —Some of it, yes, related to my report, but one part that is not based on my report is fundamentally based on Plato, although there is no acknowledgment. What has happened is that British educationists and the British government have begun to realize the importance of what are called the "nursery years," that is to say the ages of three and four (we in this country begin compulsory education at the age of five). In Plato's *Republic* the importance of these early years is clearly spelled out. Plato says the early years are all important, and he wrote that in the fourth century B.C. Now we in this country, having spent thousands of pounds on research and a great deal of time and effort, have just got round to saying in a government document what Plato said a very long time ago. I am not making the point that Plato was a great man who thought of it first; what I am saying is that if one reads and discusses intelligently things that seem totally remote from our world, one is forced to ask the right questions, and it is this questioning that I regard as one of the keys of education. It is not necessary that you should provide the answers, because the answers will change, but it is very necessary that you should learn to ask the right questions. And this is why I say that a relevant study is one that makes you ask the right questions.

Urban If so obvious a teaching of Plato's could go unheeded for more than two thousand years—and it isn't that there have not been revivals of Platonism in the intellectual history of Europe—would a critic of university education not be justified in saying that the universities have not done their job very well, or, possibly, that the human material is less educable than we generally assume?

Lord James The universities have done their job, but unfortunately the philosophy of education has always been concerned with the highly educated, upper age groups. It is a combination of social awareness and educational awareness in our time that has made us realize what Plato realized twenty-three hundred years ago, namely that one's preparedness to take difficult ideas in later life, which is what Montesquieu, for example, is concerned with, is conditioned by the early years. But this simple truth has been obscured by the class structure of society, in which a great deal of what Plato said about the early years has been, as it were, taken for granted and therefore not thought worthy of the philosopher's and the educationist's attention. Today we are dealing with a society which we want to see grow more egalitarian, and we realize that this cannot be done unless the problem of the equality of opportunity is attacked at its roots, that is to say, in the early years.

But to return to your main question—the alienation of the individual in our society: I think it is possible to overemphasize the problem. I do not think it happens nearly as much as we say it does. But there is a problem, and there are two practical ways to tackle it. One is the provision of increased opportunities for further education; I think the next twenty years will see a great advance in the possibilities of further education for people who want it. There is already a great deal going on (the amount of further education in Britain would surprise you if you really went into it). The possibilities for classes in French, or the modern novel, or flower arranging are there, but obviously much more has to be done. Our aim must be an education that does not stop with school or with the university, but goes on until we are gray.

The second influence that we can turn to good account—and which has to some extent already been turned to good account—is television. Almost every child and adult in the land is subject to the cultural influence of television. Here you have a new medium, far the greatest discovery since printing. Unfortunately our educational planners have not been entirely alive to its possibilities, in spite of the efforts of some radio and television people. They impose enormous responsibility on those who run the media and, in England at any rate, good beginnings have been made. Our television for schools has always been superb, but we are still groping toward the proper realization of the impact of television on the adult.

Here I must say a few words about the Open University. This is a series of programs, of university standard, in various subjects for people who either did not go to the university or who want to refresh their knowledge. The association we have, in the Open University, between the actual programs, a number of tutors to whom you send essays, and the courses you attend during vacation, seems to me to be an opportunity for adult education on an unprecedented scale. Education can thus become a lifelong process.

There are two aspects of this continuing education. One is the general education of the person to make him a more civilized and sensitive member of the democratic community, and to some extent this is what the Open University is doing. But in addition to this there is an aspect I myself care very deeply about. Any professional man, whether he is a lawyer, a doctor, or, above all, a teacher, has got periodically to have a chance for refreshment and new knowledge. Both the cultural needs and the professional aspirations of the individual for further education throughout his professional life have to be met, and I believe trying to meet them will be one of the great challenges of the coming years.

Urban Aren't you, with respect, slightly overestimating the disinterested curiosity and educability of the ordinary man? University expansion has not been greeted with universal enthusiasm. I have heard it said even in this city of York that higher education, without the jobs to go with it, will create social tensions, and the American example has been quoted as evidence. It seems to me that even within the university the ambition to enlarge one's horizons beyond the examination requirements is limited to a very small number. When I was a postgraduate student at London University, intercollegiate lectures on general topics had just been introduced. These were lectures given by very eminent people on intellectually challenging interdisciplinary problems. Yet they were extremely poorly attended because, I discovered, they were not directly related to examinations, or so it was thought by the great majority.

Lord James Lack of interest in interdisciplinary topics—which is now forcefully discouraged at some of the new British universities—is another aspect of the mistaken notion of relevance. Of course honors course requirements at British universities are very demanding, yet a university education must do more than equip the student with a body of knowledge—it must stimulate his imagination. This, too, is relevant. How does the individual or society benefit from a university education if the graduate is in command of certain facts but cannot make relevant judgments or discriminate among values? In what sense can we call him educated if we have left his emotions uneducated? As Mark Pattison, one of the nineteenth-century Oxford reformers, rightly said: The fruit of learning is "not a book, but a man."

We are passing through a phase from an elite education to a mass higher education. Inevitably, when you get a lot of young people together, some will seem layabouts. That is the price you have to pay for educating a larger proportion of the population to a higher level than ever before. But there is, in this country, no great evidence that graduate unemployment has become a real problem, and what there is is due to the fact that we have not yet adjusted our economy to our new system of higher education.

Now your first point was this: Am I not being hopelessly starry-eyed in thinking that every worker on the bench wants to improve himself educationally—that eventually all are going to read Henry James and enjoy the Beethoven quartets?

I am not assuming that at all—the vast majority will always prefer to look at *Miss World* or *Coronation Street*,* and I doubt whether these people are especially disturbed by the dullness of their work. My guess is that they would not regard themselves as being "alienated." What we are trying to do is to make it possible for a higher proportion of intelligent and sensitive people than have hitherto had the chance to be introduced to Henry James, or Proust, or Cezanne, or whatever. We want to make sure that there aren't any people who are debarred from recognizing the highest things because they have not been given the opportunity.

Take the example of the television series *Civilisation* by Lord

*British television programs.

Clark (Kenneth Clark). This was a magnificent history of the seminal beliefs and ideas of Western civilization, made visible and audible through the medium of art, and Lord Clark made it into a personal and most stimulating search into the sources and development of our civilization. The programs were received with great enthusiasm. They attracted audiences very much larger than anyone thought possible. The series had to be repeated in Britain and was shown in America with equal success. It had to be put into a book. My point is that without that series there would be tens of thousands of people deprived of any chance to encounter the men who gave new energy to our civilization and the works of genius—in architecture, painting, music, philosophy—with which they enriched our world. I am concerned that we should use every medium to make this sort of experience available to people. I'm not expecting everybody to respond to that kind of thing, but neither do I want there to be anybody who could respond but who is denied the chance.

Urban You mentioned Plato in support of the extension of education to the nursery years. But Plato's purpose was far from being "liberal." Indeed, he feared that certain types of artistic experience—dramatic poetry and music—might interfere with the education of the guardians, in the sense of undermining their loyalty to the state. This is a totalitarian idea with which one would not wish to go along. Nevertheless it is true that thought and artistic experience are "high-risk" activities. Hegel said: "All real thought is tragic," for we never know where thinking may take us. There is no guarantee that guidelines for the good life, or wisdom, or even some coherent picture of the world will emerge at the end of a university education. Some of the unrest among American students is probably due to the spread of undigested knowledge and to the unfounded expectation that education has the power to "solve" problems. In Britain the problem is less acute because university admission has always been subject to a *numerus clausus*, and those admitted are put through a rigorous curriculum. There is also the fact that British universities provide one teacher for every eight or nine students, which is an extremely favorable ratio. But when you throw the whole spectrum of artistic and intellectual experiences open to anyone who feels he wants to expose himself to it, the semieducated, clueless, wondering, disturbed element in society is bound to increase and the social and spiritual stability of society to decrease. The egalitarian ethos of our time may make it inevitable for us to do as we are doing, but we should, I think, be prepared for the consequences.

Lord James There is a certain truth in this, but a very partial one. There is, of course, the very real danger of educating people beyond their capacity, and this has created social troubles in the United States, Germany, and France, but not nearly so much, as you rightly say, in this country. I would be very reluctant to see the principle of further education questioned; what I would like to see questioned is the kind of further education we give. There we have to improve our techniques of teaching so that we cause people to question and to answer much more than we have done.

In higher education we often tend to feed rather second-rate minds with ideas they are not competent to digest. For a large number of people our orthodox higher education is too tall an order. I would rather see them have a shorter period of higher education with a much larger general education component so that they can meet some of the great ideas, share some of the great intellectual and esthetic experiences. A general education of this kind is much to be preferred to feeding students with chunks of difficult ideas in politics or sociology. And by general education I mean a liberal education: one which frees the mind from received ideas and false sentiments and stresses man's rationality.

The question is: How does one achieve these things? Do we make a scientist generally educated if we impose on him some rudimentary Latin? Or vice versa? Surely, no; and that is incidentally why I think that the German *Abitur*, with its great spread of subjects, all of them studied as inert information, is fundamentally misguided. I would let people specialize in what they care about at the age of sixteen, but around that specialization I would build two zones. Zone One to concern itself with useful knowledge: scientists in England learning German and Germans learning English as tools, and so on. Zone Two—the more important—would be a zone of stimulus. Here one would try to make the chemist expand his interest to something outside his subject: to lead him to read for himself. And if, in the long run, we can get him to do so, not because he is taught but because he is stimulated, then we have won the battle. By exciting his curiosity and then giving him access to a course of general education, we can produce a man who can look at Piero della Francesca, read Homer in translation, and listen to the Mozart G Minor quintet, even though his great interest and passion in life is organic chemistry.

General education is our answer to that menacing phenomenon, the *Fachidiot*—the man who is a fool and a danger in all things outside his speciality. It is not that we want to build hastily assembled bridges between Lord Snow's "two cultures." It is rather that, having encouraged the student to master the methods of inquiry in his special field, we would also induce him to develop an interest in and understanding of the principles of description and argument in other fields too. Thus we could assist the classical scholar or the historian toward some understanding of how mathematicians or physicists argue and arrive at their judgments and, conversely, by what criteria historians, for instance, determine what are facts in history and what questions can be asked of them. This would require imaginative insights into new areas of thought and feeling, and equip the student to distinguish authentic voices of reason and sentiment from those that are not.

Urban There is another concept of general education far removed from the one you have just described, the polytechnical kind of education developed by Marxist theorists in Eastern Europe. In the perceptive words of A. D. C. Peterson, Director of the Institute of Education, Oxford University, this polytechnical education

is firmly based on a Marxist theory of knowledge which relates genuine learning to problem-solving arising out of the processes of economic production, and it sees the fulfillment of the individual in the development of his capacity to serve the economic needs of society. It is general in the sense that an attempt is made to introduce pupils to an understanding of the structure of the main industrial processes on which society is based—agriculture, petrochemicals, heavy engineering, etc. In this respect it is not dissimilar in principle from the "encyclopedic" approach to general education as general knowledge which was prevalent in the West up till the end of the Second World War. . . . It also makes its own fundamental assumption, which is the exact mirror-image of the Western liberal one, that is that the process of learning to serve society will also lead to the best development of the individual.

Lord James This is indeed, as Peterson says, an encyclopedic and by now very old-fashioned kind of general education, which merits neither to be described as "general" nor as "education." It is a form of training, a conditioning of the student for the tasks a particular society expects him to perform later in life. The emphasis on certain skills it imparts compounds its one-sidedness. This is precisely what we are trying to get away from with our concept of a liberal general education. But I am not convinced that either this kind of indirect conditioning, or even the direct teaching of one particular creed, can ultimately be effective.

Urban But the evidence is pretty conclusive—both from the Soviet Union and Nazi Germany—that indoctrination has been much more effective among scientists and technologists than in the humane branches of learning. There are, of course, outstanding exceptions, such as the physicist Andrei Sakharov and the biologist Zhores Medvedev, but, by and large, in the Soviet Union, Czechoslovakia, Poland, and Hungary the initiators of reform and revolution have been writers, poets, philosophers, historians, and journalists. The case of the wartime German rocket experts, some of whom now serve in Cape Kennedy and others at Soviet space stations, is perhaps the best example that when a totalitarian state emphasizes the education of technologists to the detriment of historians, classicists, political scientists, and the like, it knows what it is doing. Technologists are a politically safer investment.

Lord James This is a curious phenomenon which I find very hard to understand. In this country the scientist or technologist is as likely to be a dissident, in so far as we have dissidents, as any other person. It may be that our educational system is freer. In some ways, the way you teach is more important than what you teach. If you teach chemistry in an authoritarian way and say, "This is what the textbook says, learn it"—you are not imparting any wisdom. I have no hesitation in saying that, and I have taught chemistry for many years. The right way to teach is to say, "Look, the textbook says this. Is it right? Let's go and find out."

I remember an excellent textbook on organic chemistry that I taught from, but it had one "fact" in it that was demonstrably wrong, and I'd say: "Never accept authority unless you prove it to be right. You cannot, of course, prove every scientific fact for yourself, but you can have the attitude that makes you want to."

In other words, you cannot produce liberal minds by a curriculum; you can produce liberal minds by an attitude. Every teacher, whatever he teaches, has got to be open to argument, discussion, and questioning. The ideal lesson is not a lecture but a discussion.

Now in order to speed things up, of course, you have to tell your students certain things—you cannot wait for them to find out that water is H_2O. But at a later stage I'd rather set them a series of problems. It is more challenging, and for that reason the students enjoy it more.

Urban I am impressed by the difficulty of making general education both wide and intellectually firm. It is so easy to dismiss it as a soft option, and so difficult to define its proper scope. Karl Jaspers, for example, who has written extensively on university education, would agree with two of the points you have just made. First, that a Socratic " 'midwifery,' in which the student is helped to give birth to his abilities and powers," is much to be preferred to scholastic instruction. Second, he would also agree that general education has to be an integral part of a university education. "The university deteriorates,"

Jaspers wrote, "if it becomes an aggregate of specialized schools alongside of which it tolerates the so-called 'general education' as mere window dressing."

But Jaspers's claims for what the university can do by way of pushing the student's awareness beyond the frontiers of his discipline would seem to be more demanding than yours. Jaspers talks of a "philosophical attitude" which students ought to be able to derive from the whole of knowledge, of an "intellectual aristocracy" and "cosmic outlook." What he probably means is that when a student leaves the university, he should not leave it as a mere chemist or historian, nor even just as a generally educated person, but as one who has been through a great adventure of learning and is capable of holding ideas and facts imaginatively together.

Lord James To me much of this is airy-fairy. I wish Jaspers had been more successful in making his theory work in his own country (Germany). Only a very small minority are capable of understanding and living up to Jaspers's synthetic vision of the university. No educational system is going to produce a generation of Jasperses. What I am talking about is a much more limited concept: We must not fall into the error of wanting to teach everybody everything. There is an erroneous tendency in many paper systems of education to believe that if you put x items on a timetable you are thereby educating people. My aim would be to educate them to a special subject, to teach them to be masters of one thing, but, at the same time, to teach them to care about truth wherever it may be, to go away and look for knowledge and to question accepted knowledge. It is, as I said earlier, in this zone of stimulus and opportunity that a person can educate himself outside the core of his specialization. The acquisition of certain ancillary skills is less important. You must have some mathematics if you are a chemist or an economist, but that is not part of education—it is a skill like riding a bicycle.

Urban In some respects you are perhaps more in agreement with Jaspers than would at first appear. Jaspers is very emphatic that the methods of secondary education—the teaching of skills, the close supervision of studies, the rules and regulations—must not be allowed to hamper the university student

Lord James Perfectly true; I'd go a long way with Jaspers. The distinction between schooling and education is quite fundamental, and it is too seldom made. Our universities may too easily become schools in a bad sense, and some of the schools in this country are more truly educational institutions than the universities are, because they de-emphasize the narrow concept of schooling, whereas some of our universities tend to emphasize it. I also agree with Jaspers when he decries the need of compulsory study plans, because with such plans university study is liable to end up being straitjacketed and turned into schooling in order to achieve certain statistical results that may have little to do with genuine education. It is terribly important to bear in mind that university education is nothing if it does not instill in the student some flair for wresting from an elusive reality a few grains of order and meaning. "Know-how," testable information, skills, are at best mere aids to that ability, which can only flourish if the passionate pursuit of knowledge in some special area is surrounded by a penumbra of educative influences that point beyond it.

Urban This brings us to the "high" conception of the university—one which stresses the importance of the university as a repository of high culture, a trustee of the spiritual component in human affairs, rather than a source of professional training although it allows for that too. It seems to me that with the retreat of religion, more and more of our spiritual energies are being channeled into art, especially music, and into a conception of the university as a place for retreat for the contemplative life. That "in the absence or recession of religious belief . . . music seems to gather, to harvest us to ourselves' was recently shown by George Steiner (*In Bluebeard's Castle*) and Lord Annan, Provost of University College, London University, reminded us in his Reith Television Lecture of 1973 that the university may well become the last refuge for those who want to practice contemplation. He said: "How much did England invest between the twelfth and fifteenth centuries in that form of capital equipment called cathedrals and churches? How much manpower did England employ in the form of priests, monks, and friars? Probably far more of the gross national product than was reasonable. But in those days the Exchequer wasn't so damned silly as to demand that theologians calculate the cost benefit. Of all that effort of prayer and praise of God little remains, but what does remain is the glory of that age." And later: "For centuries there have been institutions (in the Middle Ages they were called monasteries) which provide a refuge for those who practice contemplation. . . . That's what universities exist to provide."

Lord James   I agree with Annan in a great deal that he says. I once described the university, in a long sentence, as a place where teachers and taught discuss and evaluate difficult and sometimes original ideas of considerable generality in an educative environment. I believe, like Lord Annan, that the university is an elite institution and must remain so, but I would put a little more emphasis on the university's role as a pioneer of new knowledge—a place where teaching *and* research advance together by a process of cross fertilization. When we talk of preserving tradition, of the university as a successor to the medieval monasteries, we tend to focus on the body of existing knowledge, knowledge ready to be handed down. This is of course a fundamental task of the university, but over and above that the university must evaluate and take in new areas of study.

Having said that, I must underline my agreement with the importance Lord Annan attaches to the teaching functions of the university. The university is not only a place of scholarship but an elite institution producing teachers for every other kind of institution devoted to the pursuit of knowledge. But this teaching function is best exercised if teaching is conceived in the broadest sense, as a pastoral activity. The universities have to be concerned not only with the intellectual development but also with the moral development of the young people who come to them. And this is where they are often in danger of falling down. Too often an unconcern with teaching is over-compensated by an undue preoccupation with research, in which case the experience of being at a university may not be the enriching experience it ought to be.

Urban This brings us back to one of the first points raised in this discussion: What kind of values, what kind of outlook do we want this enriching experience to impart? Christian educationists like Sir Walter Moberly would insist that the university's pastoral duties have to be thought of as Christian duties. Whitehead speaks of the Benedictine ideal. On the other hand a Communist educationist might well argue that moral vision, a reliable community ethic, work-orientation, self-sacrifice, and the like are precisely the things a Marxist ethos is most likely to give to society. It seems to me that whatever name we append to the pastoral guidance we expect from the universities, it will, in fact, have more and more to replace the fading voice of the Christian churches.

Lord James We cannot base our universities on a Christian ideology because there is no universal acceptance of Christian ideas. But even if there were, Christian educationists would have to defend themselves against the charge that for centuries the Church had controlled the universities and misused its chances. The clergy, the critic would say, had monopolized the teaching posts and channeled all thought within narrow limits sanctioned by the Church. It was only by throwing off this yoke that the revival of learning and the advance of science have been made possible. Now these are points we would find it very difficult to counter, even assuming that there were certain Christian insights which might enable the university to be the university more fully than it is without them.

So I do not think it would be wise, or indeed viable, to base the pastoral role of the universities on a purely Christian ideal. Nevertheless we live in a liberal society, and there are still enough shared moral attitudes among us to make a moral education a practical proposition. Of course, the only way a moral education can be transmitted is by example: by teachers who believe in it. There are still enough teachers who believe in tolerance, in the avoidance of cruelty, in the value of the individual as an individual, to make a moral education possible. You may call these Christian values; someone else may say they are humanist values. Whatever you call them, whatever they are based on, these fundamental beliefs in the individual as a free object of care and tolerance, of kindness, or what an Englishman would call—a word that is almost untranslatable—decency, are the guidelines we *have* and must do our utmost to transmit.

The essential point is surely this: that the function of universities transcends simple teaching and research. They must not only respond to social needs but transform them, for they exist not simply to give the community or the individual what they want, but to try to show them what they ought to want. For, at their best, places of higher education in the modern world, a world where religion has lost its universal authority, are the chief custodians and interpreters of value in society. It is these great tasks that justify their authority and their liberties; it is in the light of them that we must judge their curricula, their methods, and their organization.

Donald G. MacRae

Students in Orbit

Donald G. MacRae is Professor of Sociology at the London School of Economics and Political Science. His past appointments include: Visiting Professor at the University of California at Berkeley and Fellow of the Institute for Advanced Studies, Stanford University. He has published *Ideology and Society* and is a member of the British Council for National Academic Awards and chairman of its Committee for Arts and Social Sciences.

Urban   It has been often observed of the student rebellion of the late 1960s that in its renunciation of any concern with power and wealth, it is more like a religious heresy reminiscent of the millennial creeds of the Middle Ages than a political movement. It was said to be setting out not only to overthrow technological society by irrational rebellion, but also to undermine the influence of scientific modes of thinking over our political system: in other words, to undermine the institutionalization of rationality. As the twentieth-century university is one of the seats of rational inquiry, it follows that any assault on rationality is also an attack on the university, whether in Western society or in Eastern Europe.

It seems to me that the student rebellion's unconcern with rationality has to do with the fact that the student movement is perhaps the first radical movement in modern times that has not set material progress as its aim. It claims to reject technology as a worthy goal of endeavor or even as a means of improving the welfare of the poor and disadvantaged. For three centuries, revolutionary leaders worked on the assumption that science would make us both better and more comfortable. Since Francis Bacon, the equation mark between science and political progress has never been disturbed. Now the student revolutionaries have erased it. They dispute the claims and ethos of science, which, they say, has become an inhumane mode of activity and which has made us over into servants of the industrial, bureaucratic state. Idealism and despair at the universities go hand in hand with a strong current of irrationalism and anti-intellectualism which often extends to a straightforward rejection of knowledge.

Of course there have always been fanatics in academic life, but until about 1967 they were small groups moving in private orbits. It is only since 1967 that protest has taken the form of direct action. "A few short years ago," Sidney Hook wrote in 1971, "anti-intellectualism was an epithet of derogation. Today it is an expression of revolutionary virility."

How did the romantic primitivism of the student rebellion come out of the conformism of the 1950s? Why has it taken the form it has? One thing is fairly clear: Students are indifferent to purely educational matters. Their quarrel is with the state of modern society, of which they dispute the fundamental principles. I'm reminded of the words of John Stuart Mill: "When the questioning of these fundamental principles is not an occasional disease, but the habitual condition of the body politic . . . the state is virtually in a position of civil war."

030230

MacRae Let me first look at the question whether what has happened at the universities is to be defined in terms of irrationality or perhaps in other terms. I'd like to start with the very odd history of universities in society. Since the first universities were established in Italy, Paris, and Oxford in the twelfth and thirteenth centuries, the role of the student has always been a rather peculiar one. A student is a person who is isolated from society, isolated from the ordinary daily economic work of the world, who is supposed to be devoted to the world of learning and abstract intelligence precisely at an age of maximum physical vigor, maximum passion and desire in all fields of life. Universities in the Middle Ages were extraordinarily turbulent places, and people, in fact, got killed in them. Very often university unrests had to be put down by the civil power, even though, in medieval Paris or Bologna, students were allowed a particular degree of license which was officially or tacitly recognized and was necessary as a safety valve.

In the period following the French Revolution, a new tradition established itself: The university student came to be associated with bohemian ways of behavior and with movements that were essentially revolutionary, either socially or (in the great days of nineteenth-century romanticism) in the nationalistic sense. In the 1830s and in 1848 students were notoriously dangerous animals throughout Europe, and, of course, throughout the history of the universities in czarist Russia. This was, it is true, not a feature of the nineteenth-century student movement in Britain, the United States, and Canada, where the universities were small elite bodies, most of them situated away from the main centers of population, which is not an unimportant point. Here, too, students were allowed a good deal of internal license to make room for the passions and desires of their age and to compensate for the university's intellectual and moral pressures. So in one sense we might think of the situation of comparative quiescence following the Second World War as being extremely unusual, and that it lasted for almost twenty years is itself something that needs explanation. One might turn your question around and ask: Why were students in a specific decade, in the 1950s, so extraordinarily quiescent, at least in the Western countries?

Urban In Britain and America, for instance, they were quiescent between the two world wars too.

MacRae They were certainly not quiescent in Italy, Germany, and France; particularly the Right-wing students were very far from being quiescent. In Britain radicalism on the Left took the form of polarization, on the one hand, around the Russian revolution—Soviet Communism—and on the other around the actual condition of the Western world in a period of economic crisis and the rise of Fascism, which characterizes so much of the 1930s. British universities, even such elite universities as Oxford and Cambridge, did produce a remarkable number of Communist party members and fellow travelers in that period. Indeed, despite the Ribbentrop-Molotov Pact, in the early years of the war too, down to 1941, many involved themselves passionately not only in political education but also in street demonstrations, agitation, and propaganda. But their protest was not usually directed toward university authorities, but to the larger world of which the universities and the students were a part. Many students saw themselves as fulfilling a traditional, messianic, world-transforming role, just as students had seen themselves performing such a role in the days of the *Göttinger Sieben* or in the days of Kossuth in Hungary. Therefore I do think it is the 1950s that require some explanation.

Students in the early 1950s were certainly an older body of people because some of them had long service during the war and most of them had undergone some period of National Service. (Other factors were involved, but these I can describe more clearly when I turn to those that define and shape the student revolts between, say, 1965 and the mid-1970s, although since 1973 things seem to be changing once again.)

One of the factors was the enormous expansion of the number of students at universities. This meant that the university system throughout the Western world was being administratively strained, particularly by the late fifties and early sixties. Birth rates had risen, the proportion of people of university age was much higher, and remains much higher, than at any previous period in the history of the industrialized countries. (As a result of a general fall in the birth rates of the Western industrialized countries in the 1950s and 1960s, this period may be coming to an end, but will continue into the 1980s.) There was also a new demand for university education, so that not merely were there more young folk around, but more of them wanted to go to university, and those who wanted to do so were from backgrounds that were not the traditional ones of university students.

Urban Students with a working-class background?

MacRae There are great disputes over the exact degree to which there was an increase of students from working-class backgrounds in different countries. I'm not sure if the question is properly posed. The proportion did not increase as much as many people perceive it, because—certainly in Britain and the United States—many of the newcomers were not working class and had not been in the working class in family terms for many generations. They were coming from families who were sending their children to university for the first time. It is much more important to ask what proportion of the new group of students came from families with no tradition of higher education. But there is no dispute that the number of people in universities whose family traditions were not of higher education did enormously increase. And these young people were different. I sometimes get laughed at for saying that one of the important differences was a physical one. However, young people were certainly healthier; they were bigger and more vigorous. It sounds terribly simple-minded, but there is plenty of medical and physiological evidence that this was so. In those countries that keep physical statistics of conscription, we can measure the physical qualities of the postwar student generation, and these statistics show that students in the 1960s were larger and heavier, with bigger hands and feet.

What is perhaps even more important, though for reasons physiologists don't understand, was the falling age of sexual maturity, so that these young people found themselves confronted by all the problems and passions of sexuality at a much less experienced stage of life than had been the case with previous generations. We have one fairly precise source of data—the onset of first menstruation in girls. This fell steadily in postwar years. (There are now signs that the age of sexual maturity is beginning to cease to fall—obviously it could not go on beyond certain limits.) Physiologists are not clear whether it has to do with better diet or whether there are other causes, but the fact is undoubted.

These young men and women found themselves in a world of full employment. The old fears of the 1920s and 1930s, the old impulses of the Protestant ethic leading to dedicated hard work and subjection, or at least deference, to one's superior, seemed much less relevant in a world full of economic opportunity, where the economic risks were not very great because everybody was employed and no one was doing badly. One of the great features of industrialization is that all industrial societies have built into them—despite recurrent trade cycles and economic crises—a momentum of growing prosperity. If we take a 3 percent growth of gross national product, then a country will double its real wealth in only twenty-four years. Most Western countries were, in the 1950s, in fact proceeding at a far higher rate of GNP, so it seemed that the world was going to be a never-ending cornucopia of economic security, of more goods and more benefits. This meant that young people were freed from the tyranny of a perceived economically difficult situation, and could exercise their minds, their fantasies, their loves and hatreds with a new independence.

Urban I should have thought intellectual unrest and passionate commitment were the consequences of stress situations of various kinds—economic hardship, emotional strain, war—rather than of the kind of factors you have just listed. Could one not take the meaning of *plenus venter non studet libenter* (it is difficult to study on a full belly) a step further and say that it is also unreasonable to expect people to make revolution on a full belly? What you are saying is that the students were rebelling *because* their bellies were full.

MacRae Well, I can give you a partly slick answer and a partly real answer, but even the former has some truth in it. The American sociologist W. I. Thomas said some fifty-five years ago that if people perceive things to be real, whether they are real or not, they will act in terms of those things and thus make them real. Perceived realities have real consequences, and in the 1950s the world was (to use a rather grandiloquent phrase) being conceived as somehow contingent—as being a very dangerous place. However threatened one was by war in previous times, however threatened one was even by hunger in earlier times, one could hope to be a survivor. It seemed in the apocalyptic atmosphere of the nuclear age that the world itself could come to a halt. Therefore you had, on the one hand, the curiosity and freedom to experiment without too much risk—the animal vitality of which I have just spoken— and on the other hand the feeling that, well, it's all going to end, not, as T. S. Eliot said, "with a whimper" but in fact with a great, loud bang. Therefore something had to be done to stop this.

Urban I find your phrase "the world conceived as contingent" extremely expressive, but I would perhaps give it a larger meaning than that associated with an atomic holocaust. I should have thought the contingency of the world would cover perceptions such as the precariousness of civilization, the fragility of rationality in human affairs, the philosophical implications of the role of accident in biology and uncertainty in physics—in short, a feeling that human survival is a tightrope act which is bound to be increasingly accident prone as technology advances.

MacRae All this is implied, but the wider interpretation of contingency is a product of the 1960s; the 1950s were a period of the narrower interpretation centered on the bomb. The universal anxiety, the devaluation of politics, the identity crises came later. There was also a fear in Europe that somehow or other, even if there were no atomic war, Soviet tyranny might take over, and that was seen as another sort of apocalypse which increased the feeling that the world was contingent.

But coming back to the more serious part of my answer to your question: It does seem to me psychologically quite normal that young people are to some extent in revolt because they have to make their own lives in their own way and assume responsibility. The phenomenon of the generational revolt is not a university phenomenon and not a novel phenomenon. It is a constant feature of history. I am told by Chinese historians that even in Chinese society, which tried most to eliminate generational revolt by cultivating respect for parents and ancestors, there was still—especially at times of dynastic change—a clear element of generational revolt.

Again I would mention something here as being very important but controversial. It does seem to me that, leaving the radical Right aside, the radical Left among young people in general, and students in particular, has been (as I said earlier) polarized around Russia, around Soviet orthodoxy and the Communist parties. Even those people who were on the radical Left, but were in revolt against the Communist parties, tended to move in step, even if it was counterstep, with Communist party lines and adopt something of what they believed to be discipline within Communist parties. There was the belief that a good Communist student, particularly in a capitalist country, had first of all to be a good student in order that he might be a better Communist, that is, learn as much as possible, master as much of the world of the enemy as possible in order the better to overthrow it and help forward a new system of life. On the other hand, Communist party programs, and especially the manipulation of the individual and his subservience to Soviet policy, antagonized a great many people, so that Communism both polarized and limited the area of political revolt.

After the war, old-line Communism lost its credibility in the Western world (that it still had any left in the 1960s is to me extraordinary). Certainly after East Berlin in 1953 and Czechoslovakia in 1968, and above all Hungary in 1956, it seemed impossible for a long time to come that Communists should have any serious influence within the university world. So you had a diffusion of radical Left-wing extremism which could go in any direction—cults of fantasy, long forgotten hopes of

Hazards of Learning

workers' control, of syndicalism, and apocalyptic visions of all kinds were spawned. The phrase I heard used in Berkeley, and again in Columbia, was that the universities could be the fulcrum on which the lever of revolution could rest. This was, of course, a most un-Communist thought, but all these ideas could now come into full play. There was a transformation of the possibilities of radical extremism on the Left, and it was felt that the new departures would not be contaminated by the crimes, the narrowness, and the stupidity of any Communist order.

Urban Isn't there a slight exaggeration here of the importance which Communism played as a catalyst? The vast majority of students at the universities were never involved or even radically inclined. A reliable survey I saw of Italian student attitudes in the very "hot" days of 1968 shows that 94 percent of students were against all forms of violence, 84 percent wanted reform, not revolution, and, even more interesting, only 15 percent thought that Italian society was authoritarian. On the confidence list, the leaders of the student movement were at the bottom with 3.2 percent. Only trade unionists—at 2.1 percent—and, inevitably, members of Parliament at 0.5 percent did worse. Mothers topped the confidence list with 70 percent. I should imagine the figures for the late 1950s would have been more conservative still.

MacRae Students are by definition at an impressionable age, and so they should be; one of the reasons they go to university is to gather impressions and sort them out. People who could exercise different forms of leadership on the Left were either repelled by the servile obedience demanded by Communist parties or they were held in them as in an iron cage, and the result was that a good deal of the natural, spontaneous leadership was, in one way or another, taken out of the student situation by Stalinism, even though the numbers involved for or against Stalinism were very small indeed. This is not a factor to be underestimated in any understanding of what was to happen in the 1960s.

Furthermore there was a great fuss, in the 1950s, about the discovery—or rediscovery, because it was much more a rediscovery than a discovery—of the young Marx, the non-Stalinist Marx, if one might put it like that. Marxism could now be seen as a much more viable, much more plausible, much more open, and much more plastic theory which could be exploited in different ways. And the exploiters were of course much more likely to be found among students of history, sociology, and philosophy than among dentists or engineers. And this was true for the whole of the student crisis. New affinity groups could be identified that consisted predominantly of students from the social sciences and humanities but excluded the majority of technologists and even students of medicine.

Urban I'm told by sociologists of the developing world that there, too, students divide on almost exactly the same lines, students of management studies, commerce, and agriculture being even more quiescent than those in the applied sciences.

MacRae This is in fact so, and a great many explanations have been put forward to account for it. I don't think we have to look for terribly sophisticated reasons. Students who have chosen to study human affairs, human cultures, human values are much more likely to take the culture and values of their own society seriously, and to want to have an immediate influence on shaping them, than, say, students of computer science or soil mechanics. In fact, the social sciences do not offer the expected comforts, and those who do not want to learn what the social sciences genuinely have to give, repudiate them for passionate commitments and falsifying abridgments of reality.

Now all the factors I have listed came increasingly into play in the fifties and became important factors in the sixties. They were colored by yet another influence—the perceived image of the romantic revolutionary. The 1950s saw the Hungarian freedom fighters as romantic figures. In the Third World many of the leaders of nationalist movements were romantic figures. In America—I was in Berkeley at the time (1958-59)—Castro was an immensely romantic figure. The revolutionary hero was restored to credibility because revolutions were apparently being made successfully and were also restored to respectability. The romantic revolutionary was becoming a possible model of behavior.

Urban How do you explain the fact that the East European models of revolutionary romanticism did not catch on? Certainly the East Berliners and Hungarians fought back, the Poles came very close to fighting back, and the Czechs and Slovaks fought another type of battle against great odds. When Czechoslovakia was invaded in August 1968, the Italian revolutionary students accepted the Chinese explanation that the whole incident was only a rift between two revisionist cliques. When Jan Palach burned himself, "Down with Palach!" was to be seen inscribed on the front of the Commercio Hotel in Milan, which was then occupied by students. This may not have been typical, but it was one significant strain in Italian student behavior.

MacRae The Hungarians were in fact seen as romantic figures but their function was to blow away the last cobwebs of Stalinism and therefore the impetus of their impact was largely, though not entirely, lost. The Czechoslovaks in 1968 were not identified as romantic resisters. The occupation of their country was looked upon as general defeat—one, mind you, which would prove temporary, but, more important, also one which could not bear comparison with the May 1968 events in Paris. It was extraordinarily wrong to believe that, but this was popular feeling among students at the time, both in Europe and in the United States.

Nineteen sixty-eight was a year of messianic hopes, messianic achievements, and messianic failures, and one form of messianism took its inspiration from the Third World. This was the time when the exotic revolutionaries came into their own—men who could be associated with Rousseau's idea of the noble savage, of the first man coming back to redeem the world. You didn't have the disadvantage of knowing too much about exotic revolutionaries or even of the conditions in which they operated, so these exotic models became symbols and idols very much more easily than the models in the more familiar European cultures. Maoism was another and very important form of this uninformed exoticism, as it is indeed the background to everything I'm talking about. Naturally, as the developing countries attained their nationalist revolutionary goals and inevitably reverted to administrative necessity and political power by new elites, the romantic image began to fade. You could not make a romantic figure out of Salvador Allende while he was alive. Nevertheless some of the myth persists. I found among Dutch students, for instance, that quite a bit of their idealism survives.

Another factor that seems to me very important is the degree to which the world of the young people became unfamiliar to their elders: It was a world in which language had changed its role (and I am now speaking especially of North America and Britain, which I know best). Language undoubtedly became more demotic and less precise; the whole role of language as a vehicle of high culture and understanding was devalued. The "approved" languages were the languages of what was believed to be the proletariat, particularly the more hip section of it, and of racial minorities, especially if the minority languages were not well understood. Therefore a good deal of the force of verbal argument, the prescriptive power of language and logic, began to be lost, and the exotic images I have talked about helped this process. Slogans, visual images, posters became of immense importance, and so did the predominantly musical strain in pop culture with its great emphasis on nonverbal communication. This was an entirely new phenomenon.

Down to the fifties the lyrics of popular music are very deft and witty. In the thirties leading poets like Auden actually wrote music-hall songs, blues, to be precise, some of which are still sung in London. In the 1950s all this began to disappear. In pop music you have an enormous amplification of sound which blots meaning out of the music, and at the opposite extreme of amplification is the low definition of sound, the quiet source being the transistor, which is a very inadequate source because the reproduction is poor. So either way, language and meaning are grossly devalued in so far as they are not blotted out altogether.

Hazards of Learning

Urban   Does the influence of television come into this picture?

MacRae   Television, I am convinced, is the biggest issue of all. I am not thinking of the simple-minded relationships that people tend to perceive between television and, say, violence, where the child sees too many shoot-outs between cowboys and sheriffs and therefore everyone is frightened that he'll go out and do in his sister or his poor old mum. I am talking of something rather more profound: the very nature of the box to reduce the size of the world and at the same time to extend its dimensions.

Urban   McLuhan's "global village"?

MacRae   Not quite. My point is that television erodes personality and causality because it is incapable of devoting the time that is needed for developing either. To show what causes what, socially, psychologically, or physically, needs time. It cannot be packed into fifteen minutes. The result is that you show a world that is both very large and very small and completely magical. Anything seems possible. Time loses its significance, with the consequence that, in a world perceived as contingent, apocalyptic expectations assume a dimension of reality. Personal identity becomes imprecise because real people are little more than their representations and dwell in a similarly illusory time and space. For abstract images one need feel no compunction, or, if one desires, one can feel and express an abstract compassion. This sense of unreality is conducive to wild and apparently motiveless action. It permits insensitive behavior to others and identification with causes one does not need to understand. It was this tendency to identify realities with their visual images and the confusion arising from it that began to erupt in the 1960s.

Urban   Where would you put the beginnings of the student crisis?

MacRae   The first date that is normally taken here is the

Berkeley "free speech" movement in 1964. Now I do not want to say anything unduly critical of what was undoubtedly one of the great university achievements in the modern world: the building of Berkeley, between 1940 and 1955, although the foundations of Berkeley go back to 1863. However, I did teach in Berkeley, and I was very conscious of certain features in the life of the university that were not common to all universities. The remoteness and impersonality of the Berkeley bureaucracy was beyond anything I have encountered anywhere else, including other American universities. The distinguished professors were extraordinarily hard-working, but precisely because they had been brought in on the strength of their distinguished records, they had roots and connections elsewhere. They were more airborne than any other group of professionals I'd ever known or heard of—not in any wicked or frivolous sense: they had serious concerns elsewhere that took them away all the time. The student body of twenty-seven thousand had a four-hundred-acre campus, but that is not as big as it sounds. Most of those acres were crammed with research establishments or were occupied by buildings of one kind or another. A lot of ground had been given over for ceremonial uses or rendered unsuitable to human beings in other ways. I was very conscious that there would be some trouble at Berkeley, and I wrote about it in 1959. When Berkeley blew up in 1964 on the so-called free speech issue, the debate about what was really at stake was curiously unfocused. This was the first major upheaval in a leading university in modern times, and the question that was raked up to create an issue was the non-issue of whether you could use obscene language in public discussion—whether you could use words that were traditionally defined as blasphemous. It was extraordinary that this could have been perceived as an issue, but it served to release other forces, and when you have a large and dissatisfied body of students on a crammed campus with an aloof bureaucracy, small causes can very easily have large effects.

On the whole, the unrest spread comparatively slowly and sporadically. At first Berkeley was seen—in the United States and in the rest of the world—as a special case, just as events in

German universities were also seen as being special cases of limited and local interest. It wasn't until 1967 that it was realized that the phenomenon was contagious and that there was also a certain internationalism about it in the sense that the same students cropped up in different places. We had direct experience of this at the London School of Economics, where among the students involved were several who had been involved in Berkeley, or wished they had been involved there, but had, in fact, been on quieter campuses in the United States. Also, the degree to which there was an overlap between the French and German protests and to some extent between the German and British unrest is not accidental. The leaders were veterans. You only needed a small number of graduate students working for higher degrees, and bringing with them a new promise, a new light, and also a certain battle-hardening, for an uneasy situation to explode.

The political background also played an obvious part, especially in America, where from 1965 onward the student protest was getting caught up in the Vietnam war. And that is an issue I hardly need go into, because it created such an obvious matrix for the eruption on the campuses.

In France and in Germany it was precisely the successes of Gaullism and of the Adenauer era which helped to precipitate the events of the late sixties. True, the state of the universities was unsatisfactory enough—there was overcrowding in both countries, there was overcentralization in France and too little federal control in Germany, to name only a few of the legitimate sources of complaint. But in the political, or if you like, ideological, background there was also a vague but very real dissatisfaction with the achievements of our civilization. European civilization has always lived in the hope of progress. Now it was felt that a great deal that the idea of progress had promised had been realized, and yet the world remained, or was even increasingly becoming, a ghastly place to live in. Was this what all the fuss had been about? The huge scale of the achievements was depreciated, and from the denigration of the achievements of civilization noisy affirmations of counter-cultures followed. The world was failing; the promises of progress had been exhausted.

One reassurance was love and the liberation of sex from associations with fear and guilt. But if energies of fear and guilt were now less involved with sex, where would they find an outlet? One answer was in turning from the concentrated life of the passions to the public world, to utopian substitutes of certainty.

Urban This brings us back to the role of the utopian element in the student crisis. The rejection of technological society and the whole rationale of technology has been strong throughout the protests. Do you see that as a cause or one of the expressions of the unrest?

MacRae I do not really think there is a revolt against technology or against the GNP. The protest may be expressed in those terms but this is partly because both the results of technology and the growth of GNP are taken for granted. As I said earlier, students take for granted an abundance of goods and services—the ready availability of all the pleasant material aspects of our culture. They take them so much for granted that they can afford to despise them. They are, as students, more assured than previously of their future status, for the adult world is—or, until recently, was—a world of full employment and therefore a less dangerous place. Indeed, the student can enjoy his relatively untroubled moment of being a student, and he is very likely to abandon his role with great reluctance.

Environmentalism, belief in ecology, vitality, mystical cultism, the drug culture are all interconnected, but I do not think they clearly point to a revolt against technology. They are permissive responses to a perceived world of monstrous deeds, of weapons of mass destruction and incomprehensible and uncontrollable change; in fact, to the contingency of the world of which I talked earlier.

Urban Nevertheless the student critics generally reject the pursuit of technology as a goal, and they urge us to adopt a simpler way of life if only to prepare ourselves for our reduced state after a nuclear or environmental catastrophe. I believe the ideological rejection of technology—even though it may be no more than a slogan—has to be taken seriously, for it is seriously held. I am echoing a point you have just made, quoting W. I. Thomas.

MacRae It must be taken seriously, but we must not, in our own analysis, be taken in by the slogan.

The utopian element—utopianism in the programmatic sense—has deeper roots and a long history. It is not possible to be human without setting beside one's actual experience of the world an ideal alternative, either of oneself and one's own condition, or of a society that offers better conditions. This hope may be transferred to the future, to a vision of heaven after death, to the remote past, to an Eden, a Golden Age, or it may be transferred geographically to some myth about Atlantis or some such place. In the secularized society of our time such a hope was inevitably going to be projected into the actual historic future, because unless you went in for some form of mystical religion, it was much more difficult to put it anywhere else. This, I think, is the major source of utopianism.

Max Weber was in a sense quite right when he said the world was becoming disenchanted—"de-magicked"—as it became economically rational, legalistic, and bureaucratic. He saw this as giving rise to revolutions and storms of emotional political behavior. I don't think his analysis was quite right. It is not so much that secularization and rationalization bring about storms of feeling punctuated by revolts; it is rather that they displace received values and images with alternatives which are better and which have to be placed somewhere outside the actual world, in some form of Utopia. This need to replace is a constant necessity for all of us, and the young could not be expected to do other than try to place Utopia in the immediate future.

Urban Does the behavior of nonstudent youth tie in with your analysis?

MacRae We talked about student youth because they are publicly noticeable and because they are probably the future elite in our society, but also because they are reference groups—as sociologists call those from whom we learn our values, our hopes, and our fears. They are not the only reference groups, but other young people, consciously or unconsciously, tend to model themselves and their attitudes on the student population, partly because it has more time and freedom to experiment and is therefore more likely to manifest novelty and change of fashion. But we should not forget that even in countries with very high proportions of students, three-fifths of the relevant age group are not students, and these three-fifths also contain important *Lumpen*-elements which indeed could and did provide points of reference for the students from time to time. So there is a dialectic, a reciprocity, though it is a very uneven one.

In Britain, for instance, we have seen an extraordinary range of fashion also among nonstudent youth, some of which involved motiveless and pointless violence. In the middle fifties we had the Teddyboy phenomenon: affluent youngsters from the East End adopting, parodying—and therefore destroying—the socially elite clothes of the Guards officers in mufti. Since then there has been a whole succession of gangs and groups—Mods and Rockers, for example, fighting at sea fronts and taking it out on one another and alienating themselves from society. One did so by an interesting parody of bourgeois dress, coupled with an intense exploitation of one aspect of our technology: miniaturization—big men riding small motorcycles and listening to transistor radios. The others went the whole way to proletarian, semi-Fascist symbols, putting themselves into uniform and decking themselves out with the whole paraphernalia of toughness; but again they mainly took it out on one another. They might break shop windows or wreck cafes and terrorize people on the roads, but they were not in revolt against society in the sense of attacking society. They were attacking one another. Later there was a big wave of football hooliganism—the destruction of trains carrying people to and from football matches, the smashing of cars, and other forms of violence became a common sequel to football. Then there was the very transitory phenomenon of the Skinheads—the *Lumpen*-youth, consciously ugly in their chic, who were in fact devoted to attacking other groups rather than fighting among themselves. Now all these things came out of the same set of factors as those I have been talking about in the student body, and they could be paralleled by the *Halbstarke* in Germany at one time, or the Hell's Angels and certain groups of the Black Panthers in the United States. So there is some corroboration, without ideological focus, to be found in what I have been saying in the least privileged, least intelligent, and least educated elements of the youth culture.

Urban What type of man do you see emerging from all this? Do these young people have an ideal image of a human being?

MacRae Yes, they do, or rather they did, because now a new generation is coming along that, even though it may maintain the fashions of the generation of the late 1960s, has different aspirations. I would say the students had an image of man which was extraordinarily naive and simple—and it was an image of man much more than an image of woman, which is also an interesting point. It was the combined image I mentioned earlier: Rousseau's noble savage, the spontaneous, primitive man who was naturally perfect because untrammeled by society and its conventions—a man who knew what life was about because he was good, because he was free, because he was unexploited and unexploiting. (In *Emile*, Rousseau himself modified this ideal.)

This is a picture of man one could see, if it triumphed, yielding place to the most rigorous tyranny, because in its name one could discipline and persecute and mold human beings for dissenting from, or not living up to, this image. However, this man of the students' imagination is not the noble savage in his solitude, he is not (to quote the first use of that phrase in English literature) what Dryden meant when he wrote, "When wild in woods the noble savage ran." Rousseau's noble savage was running alone; the students' ideal man is collective, he is social, but not social in terms of the state or any social organization. He is social in terms of spontaneous cooperation and of consensual feeling because everyone (and this is again one aspect of Rousseau) knows what is good, and hence all must, in their heart, think alike. There is a community of virtue and only a heterogeneity of vice. I find this an extremely dangerous image of man, despite the fact that it has old roots in a certain touching poetry.

Urban Isn't Marcuse embroidering on this theme when he suggests that only the "party of humanity"—those committed to "human society"—have the key to truth? "Truth," he says, "is the end of liberty and liberty must be defined and *confined* by truth. . . . The telos of tolerance is truth." Marcuse is talking about the truth of the perfect society. This truth must, he says, be manifest in our hearts *before* we can permit tolerance.

MacRae The connection is clear enough. Marcuse is too often accused of complexity. I would accuse him of simplicity: He is one of the terrible simplifiers of our time.

Mick Farren

Rebels and Rockers

Mick Farren is the author of *Watch out Kids*. Farren's publishers describe the book and its author in the following words: "The first hippi-yippi-freak political and pointers-to-survival and good-times statement to come out from under this country. A history and statement that reflects in its words and illustrations the whole feeling of where the rock generation's been and where it's going. By the dope fiend political ex-rock and multi-arrested freak leader who don't want to lead no one, Mick Farren."

Urban   If you were to pin an easy label on your subculture, what would that label be?

Farren   I suppose anarchism is the nearest thing to our philosophy in so far as we have one. I often think we have none, for we very largely improvise our ideas as we go along. We are certainly on the left of Marxism, in a "transcendental" no-man's-land. Of course, there are facets of Marxism and Maoism which we find very appealing, but neither seems to deal with the pressing problems of the twentieth century as we encounter them in Western society. Ideologically the people closest to us are the Third World and the black Americans.

Urban   Do you regard yourselves as belonging to the prole-tariat?

Farren   The whole of what I will loosely call the underground is a product of white middle-class affluence and a rejection of white middle-class values. This leaves a large gap between the old-fashioned concept of a working-class proletariat and our-selves. Both in Britain and in America the proletariat is one of the most conservative sections of society—we have seen it reelect Nixon and giving Wallace a heavy vote. In England, trade union leaders—although they may mouth phrases about workers' control in some closed-down shipyard—are, in terms of their personal consciousness, much closer to the employers than to us. The old clear-cut distinctions in the class struggle just do not make sense any more. The consciousness and the values of the two sides, if indeed we can speak of two sides, are the same.

Our affinity with the underprivileged minorities is not con-trived. We started off by rejecting the whole concept of society based on the principle of authority—whether by a party, a group, or an individual. We felt it to be wrong that a group or a party should make decisions for the community and then enforce them by rewards and punishments. We all can see that this authoritarian concept of society is both corrupt and bankrupt—it is unable to solve the pressing problems of the environment, of population, and of technology. We decided to experiment. We asked ourselves whether, as a subculture, we could organize our lives in a nonauthoritarian fashion, giving the individual all the information that was available on what-ever was of concern to him, but then leaving it to him to make up his mind, provided that he respected the rights of others to make up theirs.

For a short time this experiment went on quite happily, but as the outward manifestations of our lifestyle came to be known, we suddenly found that the rest of society reacted to us with great hostility. We were abused for our clothes, for our long hair; we were said to be a bunch of layabouts and homosexuals. Control and respect for authority are so inbred in society that the idea of seeing a group rejecting all concepts of authoritarianism filled a great many people with irrational fear. It was this attitude that pushed us into second-class citizenship, and it was this oppression that moved us toward an alignment with the other oppressed minorities—Red Indians, blacks, and others. At the same time there was a cultural crossover; we were questioning and rejecting the received values of our Western Christian background and trying to immerse ourselves in other religions and cultures—Buddhism, Taoism, etc. Indeed some of us were trying to do without religious ideas altogether. But this rejection in turn made for further conflicts: the moment we began to explore concepts like Zen, we came right up against environmental programming, our parents, and our whole peer group. We would be labeled "no good" and put under pressure to conform.

Urban Wasn't this to be expected? Dissenting minorities have always had a rough time in history.

Farren Yes, in the mid-sixties this counterculture suffered from a great deal of naivety. We felt that if only we could establish a pilot minority culture within the larger structure of society, the unconverted majority would follow our example. This was an amazing piece of naivety, and I personally never quite subscribed to it. However, one could not help being carried away with the expectation.

The old system had run out of ideas. It had no built-in means for coming to grips with any of the urgent problems of our day. So there was a clear case for trying something radically different. People came to us out of sheer desperation. They could see the problems and they could also see that the rest of society was so entrenched in its conventions and prejudices that it was unwilling to open itself to possible alternatives. This brought the conflict out into the open. The emotional reactions on both sides eventually led to the campus flare-ups, to the bombings and shootings in the late 1960s. But we acted out of a sense of despair.

Urban Why did this desperation concentrate on the campuses? Would it not have been a more fitting cause for revolutionaries to occupy the headquarters of IBM, or the telephone exchanges, or the railways?

Farren The Western campuses are a hothouse world—a microcosm of an old-fashioned, bourgeois society. They are an unreal world which lends itself, as no other institution does, to revolutionary game situations: You play cowboys and Indians with the administration, with the police department and the National Guard. At the back of your mind you have romantic images of French or Cuban revolutionaries dying on the barricades and you think you ought to do the same. And it is certainly true that if you are a university student, the campus is all-enclosing: You get your food, shelter, education, and entertainment at the university, so the idea that you change the world when you change the university becomes quite overpowering. But the unreality comes through: You believe in the heroic act of dying on the barricades because in the last moment you really expect someone to blow a whistle—it is all over and everybody can go home for tea. Most student politics in the late sixties were grossly unreal for this kind of reason. Even the 1968 Paris upheavals—and I was there for some days—crumbled when the referee decided to call it a day. The students at the Sorbonne had, in actual fact, overthrown the government, but their grasp of reality was so poor that they didn't realize that they had won. They were splitting hairs over fine points of ideology between Maoists and orthodox Communists while de Gaulle's government eased itself back into power because nobody was filling the empty seats of government. The students overlooked the point that the revolution *had* come, that it had succeeded, and that it was now over.

Urban   The revolutionary student movement hasn't the power of the organized working class, and it is facing a basically hostile Western bourgeoisie which does not accept the leadership the students are offering. Your models of society, your communes, and your ethos have all been rejected and often ridiculed. But you say you have certain affinities with minority groups elsewhere in the world. What are they? Can they be institutionalized?

Farren   Let me first clear away some misconceptions. At one time we labored under the grand illusion that we, as *the* revolutionary class in society, could convene the seventh International and make wide-ranging decisions about how the world ought to be run. This we had to give up early in the game. It became very clear that we just didn't have the means to lead, either in practical or ideological terms.

The various groups and minorities around the world are linked to each other by very subtle ties—rather like the self-regulating tribal connections one finds among Red Indians. It is now widely recognized that a tribal culture provides a very efficient form of democracy provided it is allowed to be self-regulating, that is, that it can design its own restraints and work out its own values. In the seventeenth and eighteenth centuries the American Indians, with no technology, almost worked out a method of harmonious coexistence among themselves. There were, for instance, the Hopis, with their transcendental-metaphysical (almost psychedelic) beliefs, living in close geographic proximity, and in perfect peace, with the Apaches, who were savage nomads. The interlinking took years to develop, and by the time the Europeans moved in there was an almost continental council among the Indian tribes which was able to convey a piece of information from New Mexico to the Great Lakes in a surprisingly short time. Tribal wars were being transformed into harmless rituals, and territorial aggressions reduced to symbolic conflicts in which no one got hurt. All this seemed to work out, but of course it was no match in military terms for the white Anglo-Saxon Protestants.

Urban   What you are saying is that subcultures throughout the world are held together by the sort of links that existed among Indian tribes two centuries ago.

Farren   Yes, and these links are important because I believe Western civilization is going to suffer a serious environmental disaster—it may be a controlled or a total disaster, I don't know—and when that happens, our way of life and our "Red Indian" network will offer a survival model for our culture.

Urban   You regard yourselves, then, as pioneers with a survival kit in your knapsacks. What sort of ideas do you carry in that kit?

Farren   We have a simple ideology, but we are extremely conscious of the need to bend it to the requirements of particular communities. This was one of the things that caused the rift with our parents' generation, who could not think in terms other than ideology: capitalism, socialism, communism, and so on. We're having no truck with any of that.

Urban   What *is* your simple ideology?

Farren   It was summed up at the pop music festival at Woodstock: Do what you like, only remember that the person next to you is your brother and he is just as dependent on you as you are on him. Basically this is saying: Do what you like, but cause no harm by doing it.

Urban   This is an appealing philosophy but I would not be quite happy with a society organized on that principle alone. It could mean all things to all people.

Farren   It is precisely that we don't want to *organize* society. Our ambition is to work out an organic order, a mosaic of autonomous but connected groups. We believe that Western society manipulates the individual by restricting information. If those restrictions are removed, a flood of information comes in. The question then arises, of course, whether the average human being has the faculty to absorb that amount of information and make decisions on it. It is a question, metaphorically speaking, whether you can have three television sets running at once in your room, and whether you can absorb the signals of all three. We don't appear to be able to do so, and that is where the drug culture comes into the picture. Drugs suggest that the human mind is capable of making more intense efforts than are normally asked of it. We have discovered that our minds have been shut down by programming, by conditioning, by our culture, and that we can remove these restrictions. I realize that all these are hopeful assumptions—no more. But what we are definitely saying is that the current system is devoid of solutions, so here is one alternative solution.

Urban Is the drug culture then central to your thinking?

Farren It's not central to it, but it provides both unique thinking methods and new patterns of social behavior. I smoke *cannabis* all the time in exactly the same way as my father has a brandy after dinner. I smoke drugs as a matter of hospitality. Psychedelics are something else again: They fall into the category of being therapeutic because they are mind-expanders. Therefore I don't think psychedelics are necessary for one trained from early childhood to use his mind and not to restrict it.

Urban What then *is* central to your thinking?

Farren Well, we have our communal celebrations. I find almost everything about the way in which the Christian churches operate particularly loathsome; nevertheless it seems very necessary that once a week a community should gather together, exchange information, and go through a communion. It does not matter whether it is a communion with a capital *c*, or whether it is something akin to voodoo or a rock concert.

We believe the word "God" stands for the sum total of the tribe, and by tribe we understand any manageable group—any number of people who can personally relate to one another. It can be ten people or two hundred, but if you go beyond manageable size, bureaucracy enters the situation. When a group puts itself together and celebrates the energy it produces, the ethos that emerges has to do with God in a very vague sense of the word. I call it God for it is a handy word to use, but all it means for me is creating a focus in which a community can invest its feelings. The nature of the symbolism is of very secondary importance.

Last summer, in Ladbroke Grove, in London, where I live—it is a ghetto neighborhood—we found a vacant lot near the new motorway, and there we laid on some rock and roll for our people. We had a couple of fights with the police before our right to the lot was silently established, but now we run a small festival most Saturday afternoons. There is an immensely good feeling among the people there, and if you ask them why they have come, they will say they came to hear rock and roll music, but in actual fact they came because they knew that the music would draw in the rest of the community, that people would be introduced to each other, contacts made, and business taken care of for the coming week.

Urban   This is nice but vague. What *is* to be done? At the end of your book *Watch out Kids* there is a "White Panther Party Ten Point Program" with its sweeping demands for freedom: a free world economy, a clean planet, a free educational system, the freedom of all people, free land, free food, free clothing, free technology, free bodies, free time, free space, and so on.

Farren   These demands are a very transitory program. People need such pieces of paper. They reinforce their feeling of community, just as the Hell's Angels' jackboots satisfy a definite need of those who feel that they have to walk around with tough symbols of their faith visible. From time to time we have to provide symbols to stiffen our ranks and give them something to hang on to. The Ten Point Program you mention was produced by a poet for very frightened kids who suddenly found themselves facing the police department, complete with machine guns and the whole panoply of United States riot equipment. These kids needed something to bolster their confidence, and the ten points told them in very simple terms what we were aiming at. But that is all it was. We make up programs all the time, sometimes even to satisfy the needs of individuals.

Urban   If this is just a morale booster, where is the essence? Would I be right in saying that your aims cannot be verbalized—that you expect your program to provide a model of living which communicates in its own language?

Farren   It is certainly tough to put our lifestyle into words. We have groups of people actually managing, for a short spell, to exist in a state of happiness and harmony, but we find it very difficult to do verbal justice to what produces that harmony. Many of us have, therefore, thrown away verbalization and a lot of logical thinking and begun to use our bodies instead: a whole generation of whites getting back into their bodies and being amazed by their potential. In rock and roll you express your lifestyle by moving your hips and shaking your shoulders, and this feels much more accurate than trying to make verbal statements about it. There are also other ways of expressing our lifestyle, but putting it into words is the most difficult and most inadequate.

Urban   When you say you can express yourselves through the movements of your bodies, do you regard this as an artistic form of expression? In other words, are you frustrated artists rather than frustrated revolutionaries?

Farren   Artists? Sure. Maybe the revolution is actually about a world designed by artists rather than by soldiers, diplomats, economists, and gangsters. Frustrated? That I'm not so sure about. A great many parallels have been drawn between the sort of human response one saw at the Nürnberg rallies and our rock festivals. But if you look at the two more closely, the resemblances disappear. The dress at our festivals, the colors, the nonexistence of closed formations, the gaiety make our mass gatherings a very different thing from what the Nazis were doing. Of course every mass movement uses certain symbols, certain songs and flags, but the ethos of Nazism was regimentation, racial superiority, and authoritarianism. We represent a way of life which is diametrically opposed to all those things.

Urban The German writer Joachim Fest says that your subculture has mistaken its political allegiance. You are, he claims, young people of the Right who happen to be on the Left. In other words, your irrationalism, your cultism, your aggressiveness are more characteristic of a Fascist type of attitude than of anything we normally find on the Left.

Farren Left and Right—I'm not sure if I agree with these distinctions. George Wallace is, to my mind, a very radical man who works for change. Every radical movement uses the masses, uses satire, marching songs, and visual symbols of all kinds to put pressure on societies and governments. It puts people together so that they can feel their strength and concretely see how many are standing up to be counted. This was as true of Hitler as it is of Maoism and of our movement. Radical movements naturally share techniques, for they are creating change in basically conservative societies. Hitler perfected some of these techniques, and we are using them. In some ways we are moving on parallel lines with Hitler, in others we are going in the opposite direction. In his early ideology, Hitler was—according to his own ethics—acting perfectly morally; he was doing what he thought was best for the German people, and most Germans agreed with him. Later his rampant racism left a lot to be desired. But we must recognize the sincerity of his purpose even though we may not agree with the purpose itself, for the Nazis reveled in dark Indo-Germanic images: death, destruction, the twilight of the gods, and so on. Such symbols are abhorrent to us, but, as I say, as far as techniques of radicalism are concerned, these have to be identical or very similar, for there aren't so many to choose from. Germans and Americans are made of the same human material; therefore radical reformers work on the same human needs and frustrations wherever conservative society is in for a fundamental shake-up.

Coming back to your question whether we are frustrated artists: Yes, the subculture grew out of a group of artists, mainly musicians. It was only later that the drug addicts and sexual misfits showed up. Then came the psychopaths, the Hell's Angels, the Californian strain of which was more Right wing than Wallace, and everybody's first reaction was to have nothing to do with them. These people were just as much outside the normal flow of America as the rest of the under-ground was, but they had taken their television seriously: They were dirty, some were rapists, others had blood on their hands.

In other words, around 1967 the social rejects began to pour in, and if you were attempting to organize them as a commu-nity, you couldn't begin to say to them: We'll select the ones we want and discard the rest. We had to deal with what had turned up. When the Hell's Angels showed up, Allen Ginsberg did a lot of work with them trying to civilize them and to get them to talk metaphysics rather than beating up people.

The same thing happened with the people I was working with here in England. We were presented with them and we had to deal with them as best we could. Every misfit in creation came to us: psychotics, the Angry Brigade, and a lot of mid-dle-class kids who were moving into some weird, romantic, old-fashioned anarchy. We tried to, and did, change some of them round into a positive social force from being a potentially antisocial one. You had to make sure never to allow any of the extremists to stay herded together and left to their own de-vices—this always resulted in trouble.

At one festival we harnessed the strong-arm boys to tough physical jobs such as hauling wood, pulling cars out of the mud, and the like. They were translated from being soldiers into lumberjacks. Certainly they were rough and rowdy, and if you were an unprotected girl hanging around their camp you had to expect to get raped. But unprotected girls would stay away from their camp—those that didn't were consciously or subconsciously prepared for an accident. But, by and large, we tamed the aggressive element by giving them heavy jobs to work out their aggressions. For instance, we had very unsatis-

Rebels and Rockers   49

factory catering, so we set up a "Robin Hood" role for them: They stole food from the caterers, which we distributed to the kids. These strong-arm guys were really pleased with what they were doing. They would have been just as pleased if they had gone around knocking people on the head, but we diverted their aggressiveness to constructive targets.

The psychology of these boys was very curious: As soon as they sensed that a reporter was around, they would treat you to tales of rape and pillage. They would take great delight in telling you that they were the most vicious mob since Genghis Khan's. And, of course, some of their violence was real enough, which reinforced the legend. But then, violence is merely an answer to the violence of bourgeois society. These boys believe that the way to be a man, the way to be self-assertive, the way to cancel out your inadequacies is to react violently against other human beings. But, as I say, one can manipulate this aggressive drive into a Maoist kind of duty to the community: "We can fulfill this norm twice as fast as anyone else"; "We can put up this building in a third of the time estimated because we are the toughest guys on earth"; and so on.

Urban Did all this work out at your festival?

Farren It did up to a point. We first tried to maintain law and order by a kind of friendly psychotherapy, but we didn't quite crease [get on] together. The grounds were patrolled by a team of people wearing badges, backed up by a heavy squad of motorcyclists who were kept in the background to deal with any trouble. And we managed to avoid the situation that was most likely to come up and we feared most: authority having to be imposed on the audience by this internal police force. Any such action would have made a mockery of everything we stood for.

Urban Did you put your riot squads into uniform?

Farren We did not have to because they were wearing their own gear, which was unmistakable. Of course there was some fighting; if a bunch of locals came up causing a fight, our guys would go in and quite enjoy the fray.

Urban From what you say, I am not sure that your model of society will find many followers. I am still a little puzzled how mankind is going to be rescued by your example after an ecological disaster.

Farren The question is: If the inequalities and repressions of our present society were removed—and I mean both social and technological repressions of all kinds—what would this liberation free us for? It would free man for a fresh and deeper artistic-religious experience of his destiny, no matter whether the framework of this experience were cybernetics or football. Man has to prove whether he is a self-fulfilling animal, or just bestial and nasty. We believe that man is born good but perverted by society. We believe he is capable of love and cooperation, and when he repudiates these he is being untrue to his nature.

Urban Not an entirely novel thought: "Man is born free, but everywhere he is in chains"—

Farren No, but some old ideas bear reviving, for they tend to be forgotten. We *have* to believe in the goodness of man. If man is, in fact, brutal and loathsome and unprincipled and savage (without being "noble"), we might as well have World War III and get it over with. If Nietzsche was right and Rousseau was wrong, then it is as well to have the holocaust: the sooner the species becomes extinct the better—and let the rats and the ants take over the planet. We believe that man is capable of organizing a nearly perfect society, and if that is proved wrong, well, have we really lost anything?

Urban You realize that the desire to create heaven on earth has been responsible for the worst tyrannies in history. You ask: Would we be losing anything? and my answer is: Yes, we would be losing a great deal, including "repressive tolerance," which makes it possible for you in the present order of society to rage against it and work for its destruction.

Farren The experience of history does not convince me that *our* perfectionism would be irrelevant in those entirely new conditions in which we would have to operate. If the new freedoms we want actually did deteriorate into new forms of slavery, we'd be more or less back where we'd come from, but we would at least have given ourselves a chance to break out of the vicious circle.

Urban "More or less" is a bit vague for comfort. You would feel a very personal difference if you tried to expesss the views you are expressing here today in a future version of Stalin's Russia or even Mussolini's Italy. In Eastern Europe today, Marcuse's "repressive tolerance" would be greeted as an act of profound liberalization. I presume you agree with Marcuse's protest against "repressive tolerance" as a social attitude that is superficially so tolerant of dissent and even revolution that it is, in fact, profoundly intolerant of both?

Farren Yes, I do. You feel the cocoon wrapping round you; you have to keep on breaking out of it.

Urban Don't you then think you are selling your side short by making this recording with me for an American radio station? Isn't the microphone we are speaking into an instrument of "repressive tolerance"? You are, of course, putting your views very strongly, and that is as it should be, but won't the act of broadcasting over a bourgeois network take the thunder out of your message?

Farren You have to choose your moments of protest. There are times when it is better to speak than not to speak at all. There are others when you have to convince the bourgeoisie that you will not be assimilated, that you will not turn up dutifully and behave yourself and that you will not tell them with polite logic all the unpleasant things you want to do to them. A couple of years ago I was one of a group that broke up a [David] Frost television show for that sort of reason: we were determined to give the bourgeois viewing public a taste of the counterculture in the deed. We wanted to show them that we were not just interview material for the media, that the bourgeoisie could not expect us, and the rest of the freaks, to amuse them while they drank their cocoa and got ready for bed. Even clowns have to show their teeth once in a while. If they don't, they lose all vestiges of self-respect.

But there is also a more constructive side to "repressive tolerance." If, as a result of our protest, society begins to move from pedestrian socialism to a more profound form of it—in other words, if the bourgeoisie are silenced by our embrace rather than we by theirs—then we will have achieved something.

Urban A bit of weak-kneed reformism?

Farren You are thinking in bourgeois ideological concepts. Anything that changes conservative society is grist to our mill. I don't agree with the hard-line Leninist who says that everything has to be torn down *before* you can make a fresh beginning. You make fresh starts in many directions while simultaneously putting the broom to work. There is a great deal of hardship and suffering in the world. If you make a start by alleviating some of it, you have made a step in the right direction. If, for example, the skillful use of "repressive tolerance" gave the world a Swedish type of socialism, I for one would not complain. Mind you, this would be very far from our ideal society, but you would at least know that some of the worst problems of hunger, poverty, and suffering were being taken care of.

Urban You have come a long way from your advocacy of a third world war as an act of humanity's self-mortification.

Farren My suggestion for the self-mortification of man by a third world war was based on the assumption that man was brutal and nasty rather than humane and selfless. I happen not to believe that he is brutal and nasty; and if we can move him toward a Swedish model of socialism, his ability to reform himself and society is established. I am not for revolution for the sake of revolution; I want things to get better. I know that you cannot make an omelet without breaking eggs. However, I feel a certain responsibility to the eggs too. Of course there will be pitfalls, but if radical reform gains ground, there will be a slow retreat from conservatism: there will be guaranteed minimum wages; there will be Medicare; and the international poverty line, which now runs roughly along the Mediterranean, may be abolished. So, although I agree that Marcuse's analysis is right, he is not right in thinking that it is impossible to defeat "repressive tolerance" without first reforming the entire consciousness of man. We can, precisely by turning "repressive tolerance" into a weapon of our own, stand society on its head—not by rocking the foundation, but by chipping away at both the foundation and the superstructure.

Urban This sounds like a highly Anglicized version of the radical creed.

Farren It is common sense. Let me give you an example. Up to about 1966 Bob Dylan, the rock singer, produced an intellectually rather taxing, mystical, radical kind of music. Then he suddenly disappeared for about two years. He had a motorcycle accident and he was being put on a drug cure. When he came back into circulation, he started turning out, well, country songs and hillbilly music, and all the radical kids leapt up and down saying, "Dylan has sold out, he's been contained, he's been wrapped around." In fact there was nothing to worry about and a lot to be thankful for because, by producing what was then slightly odd country music, Dylan began to lead the radical youth of America toward a much better understanding of the motivation of ordinary, working-class Americans—or rednecks, of Tennessee truck drivers, and the like. Well, I don't think anyone has the right to rush around the country saying "we're going to change things" and then remain cut off in some cultic ivory tower. If there is going to be a meeting point between student radicals and rednecks, the students will surely have to climb down, and they will surely be contained and seen to be contained and wrapped around. But if we are serious about raising the consciousness of the rednecks, we must see to it that it is raised together with our own. Otherwise what are we on about—another dilettante operation?

Urban The lack of solidarity and even contact between students and workers was very obvious in 1968 both in Berlin and in Paris.

Farren So it was and so it will remain, unless, as I say, the students give up trying to present the workers with some across-the-table ideology. No worker will buy that. And it is no good making a terribly self-conscious effort as students have done in this country. They have to learn to relax when they meet the workers, and relax in the workers' own environment. They will have to start going to football games, hanging around betting shops, and getting drunk in pubs. It is no good going in there with a high moral tone, selling *The Watchtower* [the journal of Jehovah's Witnesses] and not touching a drop. That is the sort of thing the Salvation Army does, but the student radicals, if they are wise, will use another technique. The trouble is that students are not actually prepared to get involved in this kind of situation. The sins of elitism are too deeply embedded in their bones, and that is, incidentally, why I personally don't attach too much importance to campus unrest. It is not going to set the world on fire. True, meshing in with the working guy isn't easy. It is not a question of doing a Communist Party job either—going down to the factory gates and selling *International Socialist* and mouthing slogans. It is a question of enjoying a game of darts at the pub, of getting stoned and sharing a two-way double on some horse. You have to have an actual liking for the factory worker—a personal esteem for him as an individual. But most middle-class college kids—whatever they may say about the virtues of the proletariat—are too lily-livered for that.

That is where the great value of rock music comes in. It sweeps across the class barriers—there is, at a rock concert, only one group, one type of consciousness, one class. It is, like a lot of art, the perfect answer to class hatreds and the class divisions of society. The concept that art is something for the specialist, for the man who has studied it and can write a learned article about it, is one of the most outrageous assumptions of our society. Art, like religion, belongs to us all. It should be a part of our daily lives. In rock the artist and the worker and the man with religious sentiments merge. They celebrate the oneness of humanity through their bodies, in an upsurge of creative freedom. This too is "exchanging experiences" and "learning from the masses," but a very different kind from Lenin's or Mao's.

Urban Nevertheless your subculture has a great deal of affinity with Maoism. Is this a romantic attachment to a faraway creed about which it is easy to wax enthusiastic?

Farren Under modern conditions the classic workers' uprising type of revolution does not work anywhere larger than Cuba. At the time of the Russian revolution, Russia wasn't the superstate she is now. She was a collection of city-states. The curious thing about China is that she has managed to have a sweeping revolution in our own time because the Chinese live culturally in an almost seventeenth-century setting. Now, if you are dealing with a social milieu less complex than ours and if you do make an effort to reduce the bureaucracy, to humanize work, to abolish mandarinism, and create a modern state without putting your country through the ravages of a nineteenth-century type of industrialization, then you are, in fact, working out another model for the survival of man—much larger in scale than anything we have in mind, but not entirely dissimilar from ours. The Chinese ideology, of which we hear so much, is not the end product—it is only a means to an end, a means toward an alternative model of society of a very simple kind.

Urban But the differences between the two are also very striking. Filial piety, respect for age and authority, puritanism in sexual life are not exactly in-words in your subculture. They *are* being strongly upheld by the Chinese.

Farren It is perfectly true that the cultural traditions of the two are very different. As a Westerner, I would be very wary of forfeiting my rights as an individual, and of the antlike group consciousness of the Chinese which attaches an antisocial label to any manifestation of individuality. The Chinese, on their side, would be greatly disturbed by almost anything we do. But with all that, the idea of youth ridding society of a state-capitalistic or state-monopolistic, bureaucratic system is shared and is overpowering.

Urban One heard a very similar formula—youth ridding society of state monopolism and bureaucracy—much nearer home: in Hungary in 1956 and in Czechoslovakia in 1968.

Farren We never got to know enough about those revolutions. They did not make a real impact. We could see that the students in Czechoslovakia were looking for a libertarian, on-going form of socialism, that they were opposed to Brezhnev rather as we've been opposed to Nixon, but Hungary was totally confused in our minds by Western propaganda and Russian propaganda so that the voice of Hungary never really emerged. My personal impression was that the Hungarians indulged themselves in a very old-fashioned, mid-European nationalist movement which then got tied up with Catholicism. It all seemed very distant and entirely nonproductive. I may be wrong, but the information we received added up to this kind of picture. It did not relate to any of our problems.

Urban I suspect these events failed to impress you because they did not set out to revolutionize society from its roots. They merely set out to change the system as it then existed in these two countries. Your personal ambition is permanent revolution, at any rate in theory, for when it comes to practical implementation you seem to be a reformer at heart rather than a revolutionary. But supposing we accept your theory; how would you hope to impart your philosophy without giving it some structure, without making it teachable and therefore inevitably authoritarian? In human affairs it is hard to escape the logic of repetitive consistency. Revolutions tend to create their own orthodoxies. When you have put down the mandarinate four or five times in a row, when you have set the Red Guard on the country's cultural heritage every three or four years, the destruction of tradition itself becomes a tradition.

Farren This is a problem of permanent education. We talk of education, but what in fact we mean is this intense programming which goes on in our schools from the age of five to eighteen or twenty-two. You get a certificate which says you are educated and then you get another which says that you are higher-educated. This is nonsense. I would do away with all that; no bits of paper to show that you are licensed like a car or a dog—no diplomas, no inert information stuffed down your throat, no learning by rote, no examination to test how much information you have managed to retain in your head. That is not what education is about. Education gives you the keys to knowing where the memory banks are actually located— whether in the streets of the East End or the British Museum or at some rock-and-roll hall in Santa Monica—and how you go about using them. This is not a new idea. It has been accepted since Tolstoy but very seldom put into practice.

A child is physically and psychologically able to participate in the life of his community in any manner that is acceptable to that community. His education does not start at any particular time and it should never end. He should absorb, digest, or reject any information that he can find in his environment, whether at school, in the family, among his peers, in nature, or in the streets. The average human being is mentally and physically at his peak at around sixteen to seventeen, and this is precisely the time when he is locked away in some institution which predigests him for a role in society of which he cannot approve—or disapprove—for he is denied any knowledge of the real world. This is a scandalous state of affairs. Permanent education through self-motivation would see to it that the recurrent educational regeneration of society does not degenerate into dogma.

Urban My suspicion persists that the subcultures, if they survive, will, sooner or later, institutionalize themselves. There isn't a single example in history where visionary beginnings did not rigidify into a church or a body of articles of faith.

Farren   The danger is there, but, as I was arguing a minute ago that the Swedish model of socialism should not be rejected on the grounds that it does not give us immediate entry to the perfect society, so I am now saying, in the words of Dutschke, that the march to end institutions has to start with the long march through the institutions. Every time we blow up an institution, it makes other institutions just that much less closed and inhumane. Our generation will perhaps temporarily add another institution to the existing ones, but as time goes on, the rigidity of institutions, and then institutions themselves, will become more and more vestigial. I only hope that the institutions that will arise out of our movement will prove flexible enough to see us through some of the global ecological problems we are facing.

But I share your fear. I have, as an art teacher, a warning example very vividly in the front of my mind. When five-year-olds are first presented with paints and paper and Plasticine, they go for it with enormous fervor—it's all play, it's all uninhibited fun and expression, and they show an amazing freedom in the use of color. Then, about the age of eight, an incredible rigidity enters their work, and by the time they are twelve, the interest in art usually disappears altogether, unless some individual child is thought to have special talent and is encouraged. But what is really frightening is that at about eight or nine children start drawing black lines around every figure; they take some pattern or make up a representational outline, and color it in. Their whole attitude to the graphic medium becomes stultified. Those who later wind up in art schools get this narrow vision knocked out of them, but it usually takes a whole year to remove the blocks and open their eyes to the potentialities of the medium. You can apply all this to social institutions. The insidious pressures to turn creativity into bureaucracy, vision into dogma, are continuous in human nature. In religion, too, those possessed by an innate desire to worship are presented with a restrictive selection: You swallow Catholicism whole or Mohammedanism whole or some other steady-state religion. Similarly, if you want to change society you are expected to adhere to one ideological prescription or another. Whereas for us there is no need to choose between the celebration of drunkenness, the celebration of sex, and the celebration of Christianity. We can embrace Marx, Karl and Groucho, with the same pair of arms.

Urban You have spoken of the celebration of drunkenness and religion at your rock festivals. Where does the celebration of sex come in? Sexual symbolism pervades a good deal of your subculture.

Farren I disagree that sexual symbolism pervades our sub-culture any more than it pervades any culture; sex is such an integral part of human existence, such an amazing motivation, that it's everywhere. Western society is virtually psychotic if you look at the way in which sex has been used as a tool to manipulate individuals. The denial of sex and the rechanneling of male drive into aggression is basic training in the army, but sexual inhibitions go way beyond the army. For us sex is no big deal. It is a means to shock the bourgeoisie, but it is only the first step in removing the sexual fears which still cripple much of our culture.

The drive for women's equality is one of the principal levelers. The new sexual mores are now beginning to affect the individual. For instance, I had a very strong pair-bonding with a young woman, but within that we were both reasonably promiscuous. If this had been an exclusive relationship, it would have collapsed after a couple of months. I know others where the pair-bonding is self-contained—they don't seem to have any needs outside that relationship. Yet others are completely promiscuous both in heterosexual and homosexual relationships. We also have communal groups—five-, six-, seven- or eight-man communes—where partners are continuously exchanged inside the commune but no one looks for outside relationships. It is as broad as that: You work out your sex life for yourself. The essential point to remember is that sex is a form of dialogue—even communion. I need a partner but I am also promiscuous. Given a degree of attraction, I will probably want to sit and talk with somebody all night, but if I do that I will probably want to sleep with them too, maybe once, maybe repeatedly. The difference between sex and conversation is insignificant—it is another medium of expression between people and anything that gets in the way is a vestige of Victorian repression. But, as I say, sex is not central to our concerns.

Urban You have now told us that sex is not central to your thinking and earlier you denied that drugs or even your ten leading principles were central to your thinking. Your message to the world then is summed up in the phrase "Do as you like but don't harm others." If your prime objective is to prepare for the ecological disaster and present the world with a model for survival, can a philosophy which expresses itself only through the rhythmic motion of the body, which refuses to be verbalized, which will have no truck with organization, which relies on a consensus of feelings rather than rational understanding—can such a philosophy give us anything except a self-portrait of a great many highly motivated but horribly frustrated and mixed-up kids?

Farren We believe that the solid citizens of this society have been conditioned to worship consumer capitalism. If you look at the sunshine-breakfast family, with their little house in suburbia, their family car, two or three children, annual holidays, etc., it is clear that to them the alternative society holds no appeal. They cannot understand that their own consumption is the root cause of the trouble, that in a few decades their consumption and the resultant waste will have destroyed the planet or made it unfit for human life. They don't understand that, even supposing we escaped an ecological disaster, we might have to revert to a more primitive standard of living until nondestructive technologies have been worked out.

Now we may be horribly frustrated, but the fact that the culture of the sunshine-breakfast family is a death culture because it steals the remaining raw materials from an exhausted planet, isolating itself more and more from the have-not peoples in Africa, Asia, and Latin America, stares us in the face and is a very legitimate cause for worry.

The alternative society is, if you like, contingency planning of an unconventional kind. It is trying to prepare the world for the consequences of two extremely likely possibilities: an ecological breakdown and the destruction of civilization as we know it by the rising of the world's forgotten poor, who are the majority. I believe that after such a disaster nothing but the simplest of survival models will have the slightest relevance. To save what is worthy of being saved and to destroy what is not is the rebel's philosophy. I can foresee a diaspora of small groups, each leading a nomadic existence, carrying the remains of culture through the ruins of the death culture of the sunshine-breakfast family.

Urban This is your vision.

Farren It is part of the vision.

Urban I must quote to you another part of the vision from the last page of your book *Watch out Kids*:

The awful fact is that it [the vision] will require guns and bombs to defend it against a civilization that, as it falls, would rather destroy everything with it than admit it was wrong.

When we have to fight, we will fight like crazies. Killer-acid-freaks turning up where they are least expected, destroying property and structure but doing their best to save minds.

Clearly this is part of your vision too.

Farren It is part of the vision in the sense that such means may have to be used if we want to attain a better society. But don't forget the words you have just quoted are a postscript to the Ten Point Program we discussed earlier—the one we wrote for frightened kids to stiffen them up in a particular predicament. It is all part of the revolutionary game situation.

Urban So you are really more attracted by playing at revolution than revolution itself?

Farren This is verbalizing a problem that is nonverbal. There is no watertight distinction between the two, as we saw in Paris. The thing to remember is that the rock festivals have already put down roots; we have already seeded a free culture. On the communes and at festivals we are experimenting with methods of survival. These will develop and gain in importance as the cities decay, as the bombs, strikes, and sabotage tear away at the fabric of the old culture and civilization sinks, eroded by its own poisons.

Finally, and this is most important, the very act of this discussion violates my meaning. This conversation elevates my ideas, my psychosis, and my frustrations, a lot of which were created by the society we want to remove, to the level of dogma. In fact, my vision is no more significant than the next man's. The important thing is to find the point where my vision coincides with his. That collective consciousness is the central thing, and I must confess it finds easier expression in nonverbal than verbal articulation. Talk, after all, is just talk.

Paul Seabury
Affirmative Action

Paul Seabury is Professor of Political Science at the University of California at Berkeley and a founding member of the University Center for Rational Alternatives. His publications include *Power, Freedom, and Diplomacy* and *The United States in World Affairs*.

Urban Almost a decade has now passed since the student rebellion shattered the American universities. The sound and fury have died down; a quieter mood has settled on the campuses. Is it here to stay or is it the quiet before another storm?

Seabury I hold no brief for any cyclical theory in human affairs, nor do I believe that one can predict how and why styles, moods, and fashions die or emerge. It is clear, for example, that the 1950s were, in terms of university life, a period of strange complacency which was accompanied, however, by a spirit of growth. Students in the 1950s had no interest in great causes; now that the 1964-70 eruption is over, it is impossible to say whether the 1970s and 1980s will return to something akin to the spirit of the 1950s, or whether they will take another turn.

I can hazard some informed guesses about the 1970s at my own university, Berkeley, and these may well be representative of what is happening at some of those other large universities which are egalitarian in their admission policies, that is to say, where students represent a cross-section of society.

Around 1971-72 the students' mood changed dramatically— and I am now talking of the undergraduate body which is the real bellwether of the student movement. A greatly enhanced sense of self-interest began to show itself and there was a return to privatism of an extraordinarily competitive kind. Student politics became moribund and a great amount of energy started flowing back into purely intellectual activities. Today at Berkeley, enrollments in the hard and interesting courses are again running very high, and student activism of the idealistic kind has sunk to a level commensurate with that of the fifties.

Urban Have you an overall explanation for this great change?

Seabury I have no entirely convincing explanation. There is probably an exhaustion with idealism that can only be attributed to the excesses of the late sixties, where one was looking down the mouth of the volcano and seeing where that form of idealism could lead. There has also been a reaction to the fanatical withdrawalism of the sixties, because one has to remember that in 1964-1970 we had two tendencies running together in the student movement. One was a hyperactive, fanatical involvement in society, and the other a total withdrawal from it. What we have in the late 1970s is a new phenomenon. It is characterized by a mood of hard-headed pragmatism, it is self-centered, it is without illusions and without some of the enduring qualities that had shown themselves in the radicalism of the sixties.

Urban   What then has happened to all the high hopes about the university serving as an ideal type of a future society? Have six years of teach-ins and sit-ins and rampaging on the campuses made no lasting effect on the intellectual history of the universities?

Seabury   The first thing we must realize as political scientists and sociologists is that you can never know all the multifarious ways in which experiences are communicated in society. One factor that may account for the rapidity with which both the hyperidealism and the apathy came to an end at the university may well be the institutionalization of the student culture of the 1960s at the seconday schools. If you live with Eldridge Cleaver all the way through from kindergarten, by the time you get to the university you are yearning for something that can give you a picture of what the real world might be like. The new generation of high school students is sick and tired of social activism and the abstract platitudes that passed for social utopianism in the 1960s. There is an authentic quickening of interest in the more exciting aspects of higher education.

Urban   But the university serving as a microcosm of society was surely an idea that wasn't, on the face of it, unreasonable, and had an appeal beyond the ranks of the student rebels.

Seabury   I am not sure about that. The notion that somehow the university is a microcosm of the society that is to be reformed—that one does not sully oneself too much by direct immersion in the society one hates—the idea of the captured but essentially pure university that can be the instrument of social improvement, simply didn't work. There has been a learning process, and the student militants drew their conclusions both from the second McCarthy era in 1968 and from McGovern's candidacy. We have polling data to show that, very surprisingly, the majority of students voted for Nixon. A lot of young people have also simply got sick of the contemptuous notion that society as a whole is somehow vulgar and wicked.

You notice this contempt in one of the protest songs of the time, "Little Boxes." It describes the character of America in terms of the life of an average American family: the family lives in a house made of "ticky tacky," all their children get a college education, they then go out and get married, move into a house made of "ticky tacky," and so on. The message was that ordinary people are boring, mindless, and beneath contempt—the only people you could identify with were criminals and people who were deprived or depraved in some way. But this rage of the intellectual *manqué* of the 1960s is now coming to an end. The disease of the 1960s was most prevalent among the American upper middle class, and it is interesting to observe that the current vitality of the state universities is owing to their egalitarian admission policies. They are bringing in large numbers of young people from lower-middle-class families, from the blacks and other minorities, who are competing very hard with the upper-middle-class establishment which that particular disease hit hardest.

Urban It is by now one of the standard observations of the university rebellion of the sixties that the leaders of the movement and the language they used came from the social sciences and the humanities, not from the hard sciences or technology. Now that we are witnessing a diversion of the students' energy in other directions, does it still make sense to speak of different grades of militancy between those who have opted for the "soft" and those who have opted for the "hard" disciplines? Have the two interacted under the pressure of the turmoil?

Seabury It was true of America, as it was also true of Europe, that the bulk of student activity came from various disciplines which were concerned with society, and this applied not only to students but also to the faculty. There has been a certain amount of cross-fertilization between the social sciences and the natural sciences, with interesting results. The social sciences have had a powerful humanizing effect on the natural ciences and on technology. For example, a large number of students are now moving into agricultural studies, with certain ecological aspirations. They have a broadened conception of what the social responsibilities of professional schools ought to be. One of the risks now being taken in the professional schools is the dilution of professional content to accommodate the humanistic element. In architecture, to take one example, many students are so concerned with the environment that they pay very secondary attention to the buildings they are designing; or in landscape architecture they are so concerned about the human effect of the configuration of abstract elements that they wouldn't know what a tree was if they saw one, or what an esthetically pleasing effect of a professionally induced creation of landscape architecture would be like. There is always that kind of risk in humanizing a discipline. At the same time there have also been creative consequences. For instance, the old notion that a profession could be isolated as a transmittable skill has been profoundly challenged and can never arise again.

Urban　Aren't there strict limits to the extent to which you can inject human content into the skills of a profession?

Seabury　The whole situation is (to use the words of John Steinbeck) in dubious battle. To me it is perfectly clear that by humanizing a rigorous discipline you may destroy its essential craft character. One would not, for example, think of humanizing an engineering school devoted to the transmission of the skill of building bridges, for the bridges would have to withstand being walked on, being crossed by trucks, and so on. In medicine you have the *narodnik* notion that the old family doctor should be revived. It may well be that the old family doctor was a very powerful and useful social institution in an age when mortality rates were high and a lot of specialized treatments that can now cure people were simply not available. But if the rehabilitation of that old *narodnik* doctor, Lionel Barrymore, with his folksy bedside manner, is to be at the expense of the rigors of a decent medical training, then a lot of

people are going to suffer. You can't humanize medical training without ultimately dehumanizing medicine.

There is another latter-day manifestation of the "cultural
revolution" which is now running through a cycle in American
education. We have a marvelous euphemism for it. We call it
"affirmative action," and it denotes the idea that the university
is negligent in its social responsibility unless the composition
of its faculty as well as its student body reflects the ethnic and
sexual composition of American society as a whole. This powerful tendency began to pick up steam about 1970-71, partly
because of the imposition of affirmative action by the federal
government. In concrete terms this means that the universities
have to exercise discrimination, as it were, in reverse. If, for
example, a university does not have enough women, or blacks,
or Mexicans, or native Americans, then it may be held to be
delinquent in its social behavior. In fact the Department of
Health, Education, and Welfare has been attempting through
its bureaucracy to enforce on the universities and colleges
quota hiring systems on pain of cancellation of government
contracts. The loss of such contracts is a very powerful weapon
because without federal contracts some American universities
simply could not exist. In 1970-71 the University of Michigan,
for instance, depended on federal contract funds for about $60
million. At some major universities, the University of Wisconsin for example, the hiring system is now locked into federal
contracts, and this threatens the autonomy of the university in
the sense that the university can no longer select the best
brains for its vacancies. To remain eligible for federal contracts, universities must devise package proposals stating their
targets for preferential hiring on grounds of race and sex. The
Department of Health, Education, and Welfare may reject
these goals, giving the university thirty days for rectification
even though no charges of discrimination may have been
brought. The University of San Francisco has a policy which
aspires to have an ethnic composition of the faculty of the
university resembling that of the ethnic composition of the
population of the Bay Area, and there are many other universities engaging in do-it-yourself affirmative action. This is a very
grave issue.

Urban Are the ethnic quotas supposed to reflect the ethnic composition of the population served, or that of the state, or of the United States as a whole?

Seabury The standards differ—the criteria of fairness have never been officially established by the federal government, and there are various formulae. Needless to say, each organized minority group tends to get the best formula for its purposes. If you are a black in a predominantly black area, you will want to secure a very high black quota on the faculties as well as in the student body, basing your demands on ethnic ratios in the local population. There are any number of formulae which one can use, but they all basically contradict the conventions of academic hiring—the principle that you look for and engage the best person, irrespective of race, geographical location, or any other irrelevant consideration.

Urban The proportional representation of racial minorities on university faculties arose—in a very different form—in Nazi Germany and other parts of nazified Europe. The racial minority, the Jews, were said to be overrepresented, and the Nazis saw to it that they ended up by being not represented at all.

Seabury In the 1930s and 1940s the quota system was repugnant to all people on the American Left because it was a well-known fact that in many American institutions of higher education—Yale, for instance—there was discrimination against Jews and other minorities. That is why I call "affirmative action" racial discrimination in reverse. You are applying invidious formulae on behalf of groups that appear to you to be deprived.

Urban Is the American Jewish population being considered as an ethnic minority, and are the rules of proportional representation applied to it too?

Seabury Here you have an ironic contrast with the 1930s, for if you were to apply the formula of ethnic representation in universities either on a national or a local basis, the American

Jews would be the first cultural group to suffer from this very greatly, because by that standard they are highly overrepresented. For example, in my department at Berkeley about 40 percent of the faculty is Jewish. The total Jewish population of the United States is about 3-4 percent, so we have, by that token, nine times as many Jews in our department as we are entitled to.

This is one of the reasons why there has been far more activity among American Jews about reverse discrimination than from any other part of our culture. Sidney Hook and I, for example, have been involved in the formation of a group to fight this extraordinary form of racial discrimination, and immediately we were attacked for being Jews. I am not Jewish; I could "prove" (if that weren't distasteful to me) my English ancestry, and I am untainted by that particular self-interest, but it has been the case that the leadership in the fight against the affirmative action program has been taken by Jewish organizations such as the Anti-Defamation League as well as by some deeply concerned scholars.

Urban   Are there enough qualified people among the ethnic minorities to fill the vacancies? Is there any tampering with standards in order to fulfill the racial quotas?

Seabury   Well, this is one of the big problems. The campaign originated on behalf of the American blacks (and then on behalf of women, to whom, for some reason, the same standards of deprivation are applied), and there is simply not enough qualified black manpower to go around. For instance, the quota system demands that so many black economists should be employed by American universities, but there aren't enough black economists to fill the jobs. One of the very immediate bad effects of this has been the lowering of the standards of hiring in some institutions to enable the employer to fulfill his norm. The Labor Department made a very interesting ruling in one of its Executive Orders; it stated that the hiring of disadvantaged (minority) persons ought to be established, in a certain category, on the norm of the least competent person currently employed in that category. For example, in my department this would mean holding a meeting and taking a vote on who was the least competent political scientist among us, so that he or she could be the standard against which one could compare Mr. or Mrs. X from a minority group. The Department of Health, Education, and Welfare insists on hiring minority persons and females even if, in many instances, "it may be necessary to hire unqualified or marginally qualified people." So, as I say, the effect has been that of reducing the criteria by which people are judged, and this is pernicious.

Urban It will surely have the most serious effect on standards throughout American academic life.

Seabury You can control it and you can, frankly, sabotage it in some ways. The really excellent universities are fighting it off. The places that have proved most vulnerable are the second-stream colleges and universities, where the canons of professional excellence were not sufficiently ingrained. This is tragic, because one was hoping that these schools, which have made great strides forward in the past decade, would continually improve. Yet they were the hardest hit by the "cultural revolution."

Urban I'm impressed by the simple-minded egalitarianism that underlies the idea of affirmative action.

Seabury It is a misplaced conception of egalitarianism—Americans are now talking about equality of results as opposed to equality of opportunity. It has been part of the American ethos that everyone has a right to start out in a race and no one is to be judged by invidious standards; but it has always been expected that some people would do better than others in physics or baseball or piano-playing or whatever. What the new egalitarianism is pushing for is equality of results, that is, applying the same criteria at the end of the race as at the beginning. It is impossible to build an excellent or even fair society on that principle.

Now that some insist that the student population should be selected on a quota basis, we have demands for parity of representation on the student bodies that control student admissions. I don't think this ethnically proportional representation on the student body is as pernicious as the quota system in faculty hiring, but it can be very demoralizing, for it means that you have, in effect, a double standard: one applied to students who are judged competitively, that is, according to their scholastic aptitudes, and another applied to people who are said to be deprived—deprived, that is, in terms of some stereotypical criterion of deprivation.

For example, many law schools now have a minority quotient, so that normal standards of admission simply do not apply to, let us say, 30 percent of the incoming class of law students. The same applies in some medical schools.

It seems to me that at some point society has to ask itself: What will be the long-range professional consequences of this double standard? For if it is enforced throughout the United States as a long-term proposition, the time will come when you will have to take a close look at the diploma on the wall of your doctor's office before you decide whether you want to be operated on by him. Certification must mean something to society—it must mean that when you are assigning a socially responsible job to somebody, his credentials are worthy of respect. If you push the notion of reverse discrimination far enough, I fear society will lose its way in a jungle of paper qualifications and its trust in the professional man.

Urban   While this is happening in America, the opposite type of educational policies are being pursued in supposedly egalitarian Russia, where specialized schools cater to outstanding talent in every skill and field of knowledge from a very early age. Soviet musicians, sportsmen, mathematicians are all given a narrow and highly elitist training.

Seabury   The Soviet model, too, with its rigorous specialization, can be pushed to a pernicious extreme. You can lavishly cater to the expert without educating the whole man. In America the virtue of egalitarianism has been turned into a vice, while in Russia specialization has run away with the educators. But at least at the Soviet universities there isn't, to

y knowledge, any rule about the proportional representation
f students and faculty coming from the different Soviet re-
ublics and nationalities, although Jewish admissions to uni-
ersities are said to be unofficially limited by a quota system.

rban   No, Soviet discrimination runs along more old-fash-
oned lines. Sons and daughters of the managerial class and of
nembers of the *apparat* are overrepresented, while the
orkers and peasants are, proportionally, underrepresented.
he differences between, say, the "reactionary" Italian model
nd the "progressive" Soviet model of admissions policy are
ifferences of degree, the "ruling class" being in both cases
he main suppliers of university entrants. But the differences
etween the Soviet model and the American model are dif-
erences of kind. The Americans are the *real* egalitarians. It is
he Russians who have preserved an aristocratic tradition in
heir education system.

How does affirmative action affect the employment oppor-
unities of those unenviable Americans whose skin happens to
e white and their sex male?

eabury   This is a big problem, not without a touch of bitter
rony. The federal government's action, giving preferential
reatment in hiring to deprived groups such as Negroes, Mex-
cans, women, etc., is coming at a time when the job market in
cademic appointments is very tight. The main sufferers in
cademic employment are white males, because it is this
ategory that is, in terms of the discrimination required by
ffirmative action, most heavily handicapped.

Affirmative action is supposed to rectify the injustice done to
he poor, but I know a great many very poor white males who
re, because of their color and sex, being discriminated
gainst, irrespective of what part of society they come from.
One can create new injustices by eradicating old ones.

Naturally, affirmative action does not only hit the universi-
ies; it affects the whole labor market in America, and we can
gauge from the experiences of other countries what the dynamics of this will eventually be.

When I became aware of reverse discrimination based on

race and sex, I began to do some reading and talked to peopl
who had had experience with similar discrimination in di
ferent cultural contexts. I discovered that there was a type c
affirmative action institutionalized in India in the late 1940s an
early 1950s, and with almost identical consequences in th
sense that it led to a ruinous multiplication of the categories c
the deprived. The moment you designate one particular grou
in your culture as being deprived and therefore eligible fc
preferential treatment, you are going to get more than on
group fighting to be included. There was one famous case i
an Indian state in the mid-1960s where things got to a point i
hiring for the civil service that no one could get a job unless h
was officially categorized as a member of a deprived caste. B
now every single caste, except the Brahmins and Lingayats, ha
managed to acquire this new privilege of deprivation. Th
dynamics of the American situation are very similar. In Nev
York City, for example, the categories of deprivation includ
blacks, women, and Puerto Ricans, but now the Italians ar
trying to get classified and the Slavs are also lining up fc
"deprivation." Pushed far enough, this means the retribaliza
tion of American society by government bureaucrats.

Urban Mightn't this be a sign that American society is fallin
apart into its constituent elements? There might come a tim
when only wealthy white Anglo-Saxon Protestants would nc
qualify for the privilege of being underprivileged in some wa\

Seabury It doesn't quite mean that at the moment, but if on
pushes affirmative action to its logical conclusions, it inten
sifies tendencies that are already all too apparent. A lot c
Americans derive a great sense of pride from their biologica
and ethnic identity. This is not simply a recrudescence o
tribalism but a form of direct racism, and to find the federa
government actively institutionalizing and encouraging racisr
is intolerable. Needless to say, it is all done in sound Orwellia
fashion, in the name of the fight *against* racism.

Urban What about the different occupational and behavio
patterns of ethnic groups: Italians who tend to be restaura

teurs, Austrians and Bavarians who go in for mountain farming in Colorado, etc.? Are they also eligible to be classified as deprived for some reason?

Seabury   All societies, including the American, have cultural groups with behavior patterns that have evolved organically. For example, in California, where I come from, there is a very large Portuguese minority—descendants of fishermen who migrated from Portugal at the end of the last century and the early part of the twentieth century. For some reason these Portuguese have remained immune to the enticements of modernization. In terms of living standards they are doing quite well, but they have their own cultural heritage which they try to preserve. One could well say that these people are, because they don't turn up in the statistics, somehow deprived and repressed. But that does not happen to be the case. They are simply different. They have preserved a self-chosen way of life which has served them well for centuries and from which they are reluctant to depart.

Or take a radically different example: Sidney Hook pointed out that almost all the people who run the tugboats in New York harbor are Swedes. Why are they all Swedes? Nobody knows, except that Swedish families happen to have the relevant skills. You could say that here is a signal case of discrimination against all other Americans, for it is a fact that nobody but Swedes does run the tugboats, but the case would be a noncase and nonsense. Or, you might ask, why is it that there are so few Jewish baseball players? It may be true, as some have said, that Jewish mothers like to keep their children at home and teach them to become professional people and rabbis—I don't know, nor does it matter. But the attempt of the state to come in and compel society to adjust to some norm of proportional representation on the grounds that this somehow contributes to the commonweal can be pressed to a point of the most wicked oppression.

Urban   You were saying that there were ways of restricting the effectiveness of affirmative action.

Seabury Yes; "sabotaging" is perhaps a word I should not have used, but there are forms of resistance to this tendency which human nature can devise and which can be effective. For example, the United States Constitution recognizes neither race nor class among American citizens, so in many states local laws still expressly prohibit employers from collecting data on prospective employees with respect to race, religion, and national origin. These laws are being made use of. At the last count, the federal government had only five hundred bureaucrats running the affirmative action program for all American universities. That is, on the face of it, a large number of people, but we have more than five hundred colleges and universities, and therefore the damage that can be done by this Inspector General-type of control is somewhat limited. The inspectors are neither ubiquitous nor omniscient.

But while there are limits to the direct police power of the Department of Health, Education, and Welfare in universities, the trouble now is that most major universities have set up their internal monitoring system to enforce affirmative action, and to do the job the Department of Health, Education, and Welfare wants them to do. These new bureaucracies will be around a long time. Whatever damage they may or may not do, their cost is very high. On the Berkeley campus, for example, it has recently been estimated that the budgetary cost of administering affirmative action programs is equivalent to the cost of hiring eighteen to twenty-four new assistant professors. The gigantic amount of paperwork entailed in monitoring these programs is deemed necessary to satisfy the Department of Health, Education, and Welfare's demand for proof of compliance. But it also signifies a need to satisfy many who want signals of appropriate zeal in realizing the new ethos of discrimination.

Urban I should have thought it would be a blow to the self-respect of any decent scholar to be appointed to a post on the strength of race or sex rather than academic competence.

Seabury A lot of thoughtful people, including minority scholars, are becoming aware of this problem. I remember reading a letter written in some aggravation by a very competent young black economist who had been invited by the Chairman of the Department of Economics at Swarthmore College to take up a post there because he was black. The letter was very nasty and very appropriate. This young black was saying that if he wanted to be advanced in his career, he would want to be taken for what he was as an economist—he did not want to be tainted by second-class citizenship. He found the "advantages" accruing to him because of reverse discrimination patronizing and demeaning.

Urban I suppose minority candidates for admission to the universities are similarly affected. They would carry tremendous chips on their shoulders if they were admitted on the strength of qualifications that were definitely not scholastic.

Seabury The quota system in admissions policy in fact hypersensitizes the whole student body to questions of race. Everybody becomes aware of it. It would be hard to find a better formula for creating instant tensions between the races, because the quota system makes everyone exquisitely conscious of invidious distinctions. And, as I say, the victims of this racial consciousness are the *competent* minority-group students and faculty members who are then tainted—regarded as inferior, when in fact they are not. From a psychological point of view this is a very tough time for a good minority-group scholar to be making his way.

Urban How would a Marxist-Leninist react to affirmative action? He might say that it rests on a failure to recognize the class nature of society, that discrimination on racial lines— even though it may favor some of the downtrodden—is Fascism with the signs reversed, and that the American quota system should, therefore, follow the class divisions of American society, favoring the poor against the rich, the exploited against the exploiters. I don't suppose affirmative action has taken any account of class criteria of this sort *within* the white and black communities—criteria, that is, that run across racial boundaries?

Seabury It is very hard in America for anybody to develop elaborate class distinctions, for the income factor isn't a good index. Some formulae have been worked out—proposals for awarding grants and scholarships to qualified low-income students, and I am all in favor of those. In fact, I think there ought to be many more of them, provided that the criteria of selection are objective and not watered down to fit some preconceived notion of what constitutes deprivation. Otherwise your awards would resemble the objectionable selectivity of some of the so-called socialist countries where discrimination does follow class lines and the goal of discrimination is to eliminate the unwanted classes.

Urban What is the American Communist Party's attitude to affirmative action?

Seabury I recall Earl Browder's remark about the American Communist Party, that it is a subspecies of microbiology that no one takes seriously. If you want the authentic reactions of the Left you have to look to the New Left groups, but these are in a state of confusion because affirmative action was put into effect by Nixon's Republican administration. At the same time I have not heard of a single New Left group that has come out in vocal protest against it.

Urban Ideologically speaking, it isn't something they could favor.

Seabury No, because the ideological New Left would say that affirmative action is a capitalist conspiracy to co-opt the deprived—

Urban —A counterrevolutionary device to take the wind out of the sails of genuine revolutionaries.

Seabury In practice, however, when the New Left were themselves able to exert pressure, they were pushing for the same things. For example, in 1972 in Berkeley we had a strike in the Law School that lasted for about a month. It arose from the demands of New Left militants to establish a 35 percent admission quota for blacks, Indians, and so forth. They managed to have the school closed down, and the faculty capitulated after a month of excruciating disarray.

Urban   You are, clearly, tremendously opposed to affirmative action, and when you say that it is not beyond the wit of man to devise means for controlling it, you are, in fact, advocating the evasion of a directive of the United States government.

Seabury   The United States government is speaking with two voices, and I am convinced that the one imposing reverse discrimination is not the constitutional voice. Let me give you the background to how I personally became aware of this inconsistency in the government's policies.

In 1971 a number of women militants inside the Political Science Department at Berkeley filed a suit with the federal government charging that our department was discriminating against women in its employment policy. So one day two functionaries from the Department of Health, Education, and Welfare turned up and demanded to see the files. Our chairman became upset about this because it was our policy not to reveal confidential information to outsiders, and especially not to government functionaries. It was this reluctance of the Berkeley campus to render unto this particular agent of Caesar what had been denied to previous agents, such as the FBI, that caused the Department of Health, Education, and Welfare to send us an ultimatum of possible contract suspension involving $72 million.

We could smell a rat, and I began, with some friends of mine in California, to look at the directives that were emanating from various bureaucracies in Washington: the Labor Department, the Department of Health, Education, and Welfare, and the Department of Justice. And as I read these documents I began to see to my great astonishment that the federal government was pursuing two wholly contradictory lines in its attempt to establish social justice in higher education. One was the line stipulated by the Civil Rights Act of 1964, which ruled out discrimination in employment on grounds of race, color, and sex, and the other line was that employers must discriminate on the grounds of race, color, and sex in accordance with affirmative action. The essential contradiction lies between the statutory enactments of the Civil Rights Act, which was a well-advised and long-delayed attempt on the part of the federal government to do something about real discrimination, and various enactments coming out of the bureaucracy, especially from the Labor Department, in the form of executive orders which had absolutely no statutory basis. Starting in the mid-1960s, the Department of Health, Education, and Welfare got into the act and began to pressure university employers into discriminating in favor of certain categories designated as minorities. In other words, the conflict lies between the bureaucratic orders and the orders based on the law of the land. That law corresponds to the current constitutional interpretations of the Supreme Court. The orders issued by the Department of Health, Education, and Welfare are therefore not only violating the Civil Rights Act, but they are also violating the Constitution. So when you fight and try to outwit reverse discrimination you are far from acting illegally or unconstitutionally. You are fighting an arbitrary and misconceived interpretation of the law.

Urban The American universities have had more than their fair share of troubles, yet they are recovering from the blows of 1964-1970 with much greater resilience than some of their European counterparts. I find this a surprising development.

Seabury The institutions that first felt the force of the American student rebellion tended to be the large universities like Berkeley, with its twenty-seven thousand students. It was widely assumed in 1964-65 that one of the main reasons for the vulnerability of the United States university was its impersonality—there was the well-known Berkeley slogan "Do not fold, staple, punch, or mutilate either an IBM card or Me." Well, that explanation quickly collapsed. It turned out that institutions far more homelike and congenial to the requirements of community living proved equally vulnerable. The small Eastern liberal arts colleges quickly contracted the infection. In fact, they fared worse than the large institutions, because smallness creates its own weaknesses. You could damage a small college with one blow, especially if the faculty was in an early stage of development. Here you had empty vessels into which you could pour the poisons of dissent and discontent of those critical years. That particular mix has now in many cases frozen into permanent form and the damage is almost irreparable.

My impression is that it is precisely the large universities that have not been damaged in the way in which some European universities have—not, as it is often assumed, because they are mass universities and thus better equipped to deal with numbers and large-scale upheavals. On that showing Paris and Rome ought not to have undergone the malformations and, indeed, the destruction they have.

The reason why the great universities in America are now coming back to a condition of effectiveness, without bearing the marks of any permanent damage, lies in the healthy diversity of the American system. The wave that swept the United States and Europe simply could not take into account the complexity and diversity of United States educational realities. I am reminded of the fable about the resilience of Chinese civilization, which could absorb any number of invaders. Our large universities suffered very heavily from the 1964-1970 intrusions, but they absorbed the invaders without any vital damage. At Berkeley, for instance, there are certain parts of our campus, certain schools and departments, that still bear witness to the upheavals, but, by and large, the structure has sustained itself.

Urban The American universities started from a democratic base which has, until quite recently, not been the case in Europe. The French and Italian universities have never shed the heritage of Napoleonic bureaucracy and centralization, nor have the Germans rid themselves of the rule of the tenured *Ordinarius* and of the institutes within the universities. Thus the European universities presented a single and easily identifiable target. A well-aimed blow could paralyze them. Now there are attempts to make the European universities less authoritarian through a participatory kind of democracy, but America is way ahead of us in this matter.

Seabury I don't think we withstood the trials of the 1960s because there was anything intrinsically democratic about the organization of American universities. The university is not a civic polity. Suggestions that the university should be conceived as one—with representation and decision-making accorded to various elements within the university—do not make for a viable university. The components that make up a university—teachers and taught—are necessarily unequal because their functions are unequal: teaching and the transmission of culture are the teachers' job, and this rules out egalitarianism. Any attempt to institutionalize egalitarianism, as is done by the philosophy of codetermination (*Mitbestimmung*), would prove fatal. Fortunately codetermination has not much caught fire in the major American universities, which are the pacemakers of reform. In some of the smaller colleges it has made headway, and there are many places where you can't even hire a president without a screening by designated student representatives, and sometimes curricula are also determined by joint decision-making between faculty and students. But, as I say, these are the exceptions rather than the rule.

Urban In Europe codetermination is looked upon as the pith and marrow of reform if not indeed of revolution. The model is drawn from labor-management relations, where participation is being rapidly expanded, especially in Germany.

Seabury Yes, you have on the Continent a horizontal misapplication of the doctrine of codetermination from labor-management relations to the universities. Many people in Europe regard the two as being analogous. We have no doctrine of *Mitbestimmung* in the American labor-management experience, but even if we had, I would be strongly opposed to applying it to the university. The German notion that the university should be modeled on industry is wrong. It is also pernicious, because it misrepresents the nature of what the faculty-student relationship should be.

The whole sense of being at a university is that the student is not a worker—if anything, he or she is released from the labor market and temporarily given a most fortunate and privileged position in our culture; and one of the special advantages of that privileged position is that he or she can move through higher education without having to become a cog in the wheel in a depersonalizing, bureaucratic society. This is one of the glories of the whole institution of higher education: for three or four years the student is freed from slavery. Codetermination would reverse this.

Urban If it is neither the size of the American university nor its participatory structure that has saved it from going under, does diversity alone account for its survival? After all, the first university to be gravely damaged was Berkeley, the "multiversity," with its ten thousand courses and untold points of contact with society, industry, and government.

Seabury The heart of the university, the permanent element that guarantees its character and continuity, is the quality of the faculty. If that is crippled, then the university dies, because the heart cannot transmit its vitality to the other parts. This vitality of the intellectual component of the university has been maintained in America. So to the diversity of the system as a factor guaranteeing the university's resilience we have to add the American university's ability to maintain, in the majority of cases, the excellence and continuity of its faculty.

Paradoxically, one of the damaging consequences coming out of the upheavals of the 1960s is the intensification of one of the vices the university was charged with at the time of the student revolution. This is the undue independence and great power of specialized centers and departments within the big universities, the *Fachbereich*, as they are called in Germany, from where the American variant drew its inspiration. The explanation is that under attack from the students the departments closed ranks—the more strongly the students demanded "relevant" courses and participation in the design of curricula and examinations, the more insistently the departments stood on their integrity, and this inevitably meant and means paying less attention to undergraduate work than is desirable. If I were charged with educational reform at the University of California—as happily I am not now—my prime attention would be focused on the undergraduate program: I would seek to satisfy the undergraduate student body's legitimate demand that more attention be paid to their training, and would try to redress the balance of emphasis and authority between research-oriented work, which gets the star billing and teaching, which does not but which is, in the last analysis, the principal reason for the university's existence.

The main victim of the upheavals of the 1960s was the undergraduate program, and the victim was a martyr to those who wished to redeem undergraduate study from the constraints of civilization. But university education is about the transmission of civilization, and that in turn means imparting an element of wisdom, rather than a mere accumulation of skills, to those prepared to make the effort to receive it. Fortunately the great majority of American students are once again keen to make that effort.

Eldon L. Johnson

People's Universities
in the United States

Professor Eldon L. Johnson is Vice-President for Governmental
Relations and Public Service at the University of Illinois and
former President of the University of New Hampshire.

Urban The functions of the university in Europe have traditionally been defined as those of teaching and research, with a
creative tension existing between the two to the benefit of
both teachers and taught. In the United States, starting with
the land-grant colleges about a hundred years ago, the universities acquired another role: that of serving certain public
needs, and especially the needs of the children of farmers and
artisans—the needs, one might say in European terms of reference, of the working class. The relevance of the American
departure for European higher education is twofold. First, it

contrasts significantly with the great difficulty West European universities are experiencing in translating knowledge into application and reconciling the claims of general culture and research. Second, it may well point a way for the East European universities, which are themselves trying to take knowledge to the users of knowledge, and especially to the proletariat.

Johnson The American universities generally are devoted to the idea that there has to be a responsible relationship between the universities and society. Public service—in addition to teaching and research—is a proclaimed part of the mission of most American universities. Before going into the historic background, let me say that "public service," as the phrase is used in the United States, refers to both a clientele that is different from the intake of the traditional universities (including the elitist ones in America) and to a location which does not coincide with the walls of the university. The clientele consists very largely of young men and women outside the normal age for university entry, of others who have, for one reason or another, been by-passed by society and not attained the educational level they would want, and of those who have been out in life, earning a living, but want to come back for study. The location of the service function of the university may be the home of the student or it may be some regional center loosely associated with the university. It is almost always beyond the walls of the university, and the purpose of this extension of the university's work is to put learning in the service of society. Therefore it is a problem-oriented activity that is not confined to a prescribed number of years spent at the university. The idea is to make knowledge useful wherever willing users can be found—in the foundry, in the laboratory, in the fields.

Urban It is an interesting fact that the idea of people's colleges and polytechnical education was born in America half a century before the October Revolution.

Johnson State-supported universities in America, whether they are so-called land-grant colleges or not, have always conceived of themselves, and have always been conceived of by the public, as people's colleges or, more recently, as people's universities. Historically these land-grant colleges, which are in most cases the antecedents of the present large state universities, originated with the Land Grant Act signed by President Lincoln in 1862. The colleges were chartered to apply themselves to reaching the disadvantaged groups, who were being neglected by the elitist institutions of the time. There was originally one land-grant college in each state, founded with the support of the federal government. Implicitly the 1862 Act created a kind of partnership between university and government, a relationship which encouraged the university to look upon itself as an instrument of the state.

Then in the 1880s and 1890s we had the populist parties undergirding it all with a utilitarian attitude—the colleges were to be practical, applied, devoted to "learning by doing." The conception grew that these land-based, working-class, popularly supported institutions were particularly responsive to the needs of the people generally, as they in fact were. They were broadly based, their teaching was relevant to daily needs and problems, so that the public's conception of them as people's colleges was fully justified. And they have been engaged, ever since those early days, in going out to the communities offering a highly valuable service.

Urban   Eighteen sixty-two strikes me as a very early date for an educationally advanced, egalitarian enterprise. In Russia the serfs were emancipated only one year before Lincoln signed the Land Grant Act. Was Marx or were the early French socialists instrumental in creating the climate for this new departure?

Johnson   No one in America at that time would have been well acquainted with Karl Marx. The thinking behind the people's colleges came from an entirely home-based, Western, democratic philosophy, basically the kind of egalitarian attitude that was already widespread in America twenty years earlier, as witnessed by Tocqueville in his writings about American democracy. Tocqueville was impressed by the American drive for equality; he noted the great confidence with which the American people adopted the idea that equal education for the great masses at primary school level would take care of most of America's social problems; and by 1862 this trust in an egalitarian mass education was beginning to express itself at the level of higher education too. But Marx was very distant, and perhaps entirely absent, from American educational thinking. So it was the rural democratic orientation that gave birth to the people's colleges and the state-supported universities with their strong drive to serve the people in all dimensions—not merely instructing their sons and daughters, but also doing research on their problems, having professors go directly out into the field to attack the problems with the people.

Urban It sounds almost like a leaf taken out of the Little Red Book of Chairman Mao.

In fact you were doing in the 1860s what Eastern Europe and China are trying to do—with a Communist rationale—in the 1960s and 1970s, and I wonder whether some of the social problems which the East European countries have encountered in the process were anticipated by the American experience.

A common malaise bedeviling a good deal of the educational advance that has been achieved in Eastern Europe in the last twenty years is the urge of the newly educated to use their degrees as social tickets. They detach themselves from their social habitat the moment they occupy the first white-collar jobs for which their education usually qualifies them. No sooner are they handed their diplomas than rural background, physical work, traditional lifestyles and speech come to be despised and rejected, and fresh "class" divisions are created between the education-based meritocracy and the rest of society. This new class tends to monopolize the system, and while in Eastern Europe—as in America—educational democratization has increased social mobility, it has done so to the disadvantage of the working classes, because the children of the newly educated swell the ranks of applicants for admission to the universities.

Johnson   This is a world-wide problem. I have recently done some consulting in Africa and Asia and I have seen cases where what you lament is the order of the day. You get young men and women at the universities who look upon their pursuit of studies as a way of getting themselves out of work, of getting themselves into a social status the arrival in which is self-justifying. They then relax because they are now removed from the ordinary toils of the society to which they have no intention of contributing further.

But that is not what has happened in America. American society was so egalitarian in its orientation, so opposed to the establishment of classes that a class consciousness of the kind you have in Eastern Europe and the developing world has no chance of taking root here. Instruction in the land-grant colleges was itself so grounded in egalitarianism that in the earliest days these colleges had farms inside the campus where students were expected to do an ordinary day's work. The educational theory was that training on the farm would not only teach students how to farm, but to love the soil, to stick to the land, and to live frugally. This ideological component didn't work, however, for students regarded farm labor on the campus as a sort of enslavement, so the practice was soon abandoned. Nevertheless, even where students were not happy working the soil on the farms, they did stand by the idea that their education was to have practical social application, that it was to be useful to their careers, and that they owed something to society which had seen them through an almost free higher education. Therefore we had no divorce between work and social status.

One of the signal achievements of American higher education has been its ability to handle large numbers, and I would say it was perhaps because such large masses were admitted that we did not get them stratified. The vast intake at the state universities does not lend itself to social elitism; the egalitarian spirit is too strong and it shows through.

Urban   In Europe, learning has always been looked upon as an elite activity, whether universities took their cue from

Wilhelm von Humbolt, dedicated as he was to a fresh concept of humanism, or from the Soviet Union, where ninety percent of students are educated on a narrow front in a variety of technical colleges, with only ten percent going to universities. In both cases, and despite the adaptation to dramatically increased numbers of students, stratification has maintained itself. In Western Europe it has become less pronounced but, as I say, in Eastern Europe it is highly, and in some cases increasingly, visible.

Johnson It is important, though, that we do not leave the impression that one can educate young men and women without changing their values and their preception of their relation to society. I get impatient with some of the attitudes in Africa, where you will find people who say: "The universities are to be blamed for the migration of young men and women from the villages to the cities. They ought to be willing to get a university education and go back to the farms, to stay in the rural areas where eighty-five percent of the people are going to have to live." I think that would be expecting too much and for the wrong reasons. Education does change values. If you have educated young men and women from African villages to university standard and then expect them to go back to their native habitat, that is, to subsistence farming, you would have missed the whole point of a university education. University education should not be faulted on the ground that it has enriched the student with knowledge and impressions and hence altered his outlook. That is what universities are supposed to do. If the American experience is anything to go by—and I think it most likely is—young people with a university degree in their pockets can have it both ways: they can, and do, raise their expectations, exploiting society's social mobility to move up to a higher economic level, and at the same time there is no sense of opposition to useful employment or any attempt to deny that the university is socially accountable to the society which supports it.

Urban The American universities have always been outsize by European standards, and—as you have just shown—many of them never confined themselves to teaching professional skills and doing research. Their doors are open to virtually all. They teach everything society wants to have taught, they provide a sanctuary for the young, a moral training ground, a community center and a social and even matrimonial agency. At the state universities, to all this is added a vast range of activities directly relevant to the daily needs of agriculture, industry, and commerce. In other words, one would have thought that American universities in general, and the mass-based state universities in particular, were ideally equipped to resist, and indeed to forestall, student unrest.

In Berkeley and Yale, we saw that the elite universities were not only unable to forestall the student crisis but were the very begetters of it. I wonder whether the state universities—for example the university of which you are a vice-president—fared any better. No student could complain that the University of Illinois has been out of touch with the needs of the community. If educational problems were at the bottom of student militancy, your type of university should have escaped the crisis unscathed.

Johnson No, we had our share of student disturbances, and I for one can see no distinction, as far as student demonstrations and unrest are concerned, between the public-service-oriented institutions and the more conventional, classical schools such as Harvard, Yale, or Princeton. This is surprising because, as you have just hinted, one would have expected university unrest to be particularly related to the university's concern or unconcern with public service. Some studies made in America would seem to indicate that student militancy was concentrated in those universities which were highly selective in their admission policy and where the student population came from the well-off middle layers of American society. But I can see no *convincing* correlation between the social background of the students and the size and type of the university, or even the so-called relevance of their curricula. Student militancy was just as rife on the state university campuses as in the more affluent private universities. This was not only paradoxical but disturbing because the public service function is one of the most important means by which our institutions get locked onto the problems of society and do provide exactly for the kind of relevance on behalf of which the students are generally demonstrating. And when I say "relevant," I'm thinking of urgent problems of the day that need researching. There are some very distinguished dons who argue that classical studies, for instance, carry their own relevance. I would accept that with the rider that that kind of relevance, important though it may be, acts on a different time scale from the one with which we are normally concerned.

Urban I suspect fashion may have had a lot to do with the indiscriminate spread of campus unrest.

Johnson A few years ago I would have been reluctant to admit this but I now believe fashion did play a part. Back in the forties and fifties, we had the "silent generation," and I said at that time that one day we would get our comeuppance, and we did. That silent generation wasn't completely silent, though. It had somewhere along with it what we called the "fun generation" who were just enjoying themselves, as young people do, while they were getting a college education. They had such fads as swallowing goldfish for sport, or pushing bedsteads down the highway, or seeing how many people could crowd into a telephone booth. When you compare these pastimes with the intellectual concerns of the generation that caused the disturbances a few years ago, I think the rebellious students deserve credit for the seriousness of their motivation. Nevertheless, this protest, too, was, in large part at least, fashion. It was not clearly related to the war in Vietnam, because it was a spent force well before the war ended. There was also a curious love-hate nexus between student extremism on the Left and the Right. The stupendous activism of the Left was feeding on an equally energetic activism of the Right, and the ones who were most active against the war had much more in common with those who were most aggressive on behalf of it than either group had with the mass of students who were somewhere in between and rather indifferent.

Urban   But fashion was surely only the surface manifestation of something that lay deeper in the students' psyche.

Johnson   Yes, and this is a question that has been puzzling us. What gave rise to the original student militancy? For students in France, Germany, Italy, and Japan were all participating in it, although unlike the American students they didn't have Vietnam as a burning issue. Students had different passions and different issues to rally round in different countries, but the militancy and the irrationality of the student programs were universal. The roots of the student malaise have by now been pretty thoroughly laid bare: dissatisfaction with modern industrial society on a whole range of issues, and especially the loss of the individual's ability to assert himself in the face of the restrictions inherent in what he feels to be a highly programmed and mindless bourgeois civilization. The university was being used as a target because it was at hand and extremely vulnerable. But, in America at least, the origins of the petering out of the movement are as interesting as what had given rise to it. The American students' main ideological commitment was opposition to violence. They were opposed to violence in Vietnam, in race relations, in the relations between the rich and the poor, and so on. Having committed themselves to nonviolence, they experienced a traumatic shock when the "Crazies"—as a group of the most extreme students was known in America—began to resort to terrorist attacks on property. The culmination of this terror came at the University of Wisconsin, where a group of students and former students dynamited a building with great damage to property and the loss of a student's life. At that point most of the students who had been willing allies of the "Crazies" were turned off. There was a sudden realization that while the students were nominally fighting violence, here they had violence right in their midst; that they were themselves a party to it and that this could not be tolerated. That, to my mind, was the turning point in America.

Urban   A great deal has been written about the damage done to the American university and to the spirit of democratic institutions by the student rebellion. Has the shock of 1968-70 been an unmitigated disaster, or has the American genius for resilience managed to turn some of it to good account?

Johnson My own view is that the shock has been salutary. The students' drive for relevance, though often naive and misplaced, has made the universities more conscious of the need to reexamine their internal government, to revise their curricula, and to relate their public-service functions more directly and more visibly to the needs of the community. The student disturbances were a net gain in the academic life of the United States. The place where we have arrived is a better place than where we left off in the early 1960s.

People in other countries who live under less liberal institutions than we do must realize that the demonstrations and turmoil on our campuses were a measure of the tolerance we extend—often perhaps too liberally—to everyone in the polity. Our permissiveness toward the students has been especially conspicuous. At the same time we have learned some important lessons about the extent to which the state can, and beyond which it cannot, afford to ignore violent forms of dissent. Clearly, there must be limits. Yet we have also learned sophisticated lessons about the political and potentially explosive meaning of seemingly unpolitical unrest. We can now read the signals, and it is to be hoped that hereafter we can avoid the disruption of the university's essential process of learning and research.

Urban A good deal of the university protest centered precisely on some of the public-service activities of American universities, notably those connected with satisfying the research needs of the so-called American "military-industrial complex." It might, therefore, be useful to take a more detailed look at the way in which public-service functions are initiated and carried out in America. Do industries and the government come forward with certain suggestions that the university is then asked to satisfy, or is the university a kind of intellectual supermarket offering a broad selection of goods to anyone who can afford to pay for them?

Johnson   There is a two-way traffic. We have to have satisfactory communication between the university and society so that public needs are identified and the university can offer competent response measured to them. Naturally, each university has more expertise in some fields than in others, but that does not mean that the faculty goes out and tries to sell what it has or looks for problems to attack. Our universities traditionally respond to outside demand rather than initiate demand.

Let me say another word here about the American university's philosophical commitment to the service role. In our comprehensive universities the faculty is looked upon as a reservoir of talent and competence and therefore as a public resource—not to be tapped indiscriminately but also not to remain inaccessible. Supplying knowledge for problem-solving activities—whether for private groups, the cities, the nation, or international bodies—is, in the American view, revalidating the university's entitlement to public support. The service idea has, in the words of Lord Ashby, become part of the "inner logic" of American higher education and is indeed accorded full, though sometimes grudging, partnership with teaching and research. The present debates are not so much about the service function as about its proper proportion of the total, and your question ties up with the problem of what proportion of the total effort of the university is legitimately channeled into contractual commitments with the outside world. Well, each university has to make its own decisions according to its resources and expertise. Not all American universities are equally engaged in public service as a function, although most of them profess it. The public-service role of the private universities often does not go beyond the utility of producing well-equipped graduates, encouraging professors to perform services through contributions in public life, and institutional research which has public benefits. Public service of the direct kind is, as I indicated earlier in this discussion, strongest in the university which has special accountability to the taxpayer. And it is here that the university has to watch its clients most carefully. The charge implicit in your question can be taken—and is often taken by the public university's critics—beyond the services rendered to the "military-industrial complex." It is often contended that the universities are reaching the wrong clients—the affluent, those already successful, the powerful and established, at the expense of the poor and unorganized.

Urban Do the universities in fact undertake defense-oriented work of the kind against which the students have protested? Have the universities taken fresh thought on this matter since 1968-70?

Johnson The university has its own rationale, its own knowledge-based role which circumscribes the extension activities it can, and should, undertake. If the university gets a contractual request, from private enterprise or the government, which is compatible with the university's conception of its own role, then it would happily cooperate. The critical questions are: How do we ensure the scrupulous restriction of public service to the uses of knowledge and prevent it from being harnessed to the uses of power? What are the outer limits of the university's participation beyond which it is prostituting its purpose? Ideally the university should not put its name to any contractual relationship that violates these limits, but, regrettably, some few do.

Urban If the university receives funds from both private sources and government, how does this affect its autonomy?

Johnson Here again a careful balance must be maintained and justifiable limits set to the kind and amount of work undertaken for private enterprise, voluntary associations, and government. For instance, the university must avoid politicization, but politicization arises the moment the public-service role is confused with policy making. Trafficking in power is alien and damaging to the ethos of the university, which should traffic only in knowledge and its proper application to the problems of society. Bounds can be set with the reasonable agreement of all parties concerned. You can make sure that the sources of support for public-service activities are mixed—both public and private—so that the university's autonomy is not jeopardized by either. You can also insist that the university become involved, by its own free judgment, in a public-service function only when there can be adequate internal feedback to strengthen what is being taught and the uses to which it is being put.

As far as defense and defense-related research relationships are concerned, universities in America are now more sensitized to the delicate balance they must maintain in their nexus with society. They would, for example—and this has not been a consequence of the student upheavals—not enter into any contractual relationship that puts restrictions on the publication of the results of research. They would not go into "classified" research because classified research might give substance to the suspicion that its ends are subordinated solely to the needs of the contractor—usually the government or the military—and are of no benefit to the scientific community or the public. In such cases the university would say, "It is our job to contribute to knowledge which has to be widely shared, and unless you can permit us to communicate the results of the research to the academic community, we cannot do it for you."

Urban It isn't by any means clear, though, that the universities should at all times decline defense-related contracts. In the Second World War it was regarded as an honorable duty for scientists to contribute to the fall of Nazism with any kind of knowledge they and the universities could muster. Defense-related programs were eagerly seized on and promoted, and the results were telling. It was the unpopularity of the Vietnam war that made defense-related research sinful in the eyes of the young generation. This underlines (whatever we may think of the rights and wrongs of the Vietnam war) the high motivation of the student protesters, but it also shows up the somewhat unprincipled grounds on which the universities now reject all defense-related work.

Johnson This raises a difficult and perhaps unanswerable question, and the university has to realize that at a time of budgetary stringency the loss of an unsavory contract may cost it a good deal more than the face value, for contracts of this kind have always produced a sizable overspill into basic research and other areas of indirect subsidization. Vice-President Hubert Humphrey once said, when this issue was being discussed heatedly in America, that if the universities didn't want defense-related work, then the government would have to turn elsewhere and set up its own enterprises to do it. "Is that what you, university people, want us to do?" he asked. "You want government grants to use them as a base for building research generally and even to improve and broaden your teaching at the undergraduate level; well, if you want the ends you must also want the means, and that means taking on the work the government wants you to do," or words to that effect.

This was quite a challenge to American higher education. It forced everyone to think seriously whether we really did want the government to look elsewhere for the satisfaction of its research needs, of which, incidentally, the defense-related work was only a small part. For the implication was clearly that, if the government were to be forced out of the universities as far as military research was concerned, then eventually the universities would find themselves gradually phased out of the nonmilitary work too, which would be a near disaster for them. The problem has not been totally resolved, but, as I have just said, the vast majority of American universities will now not engage in contract work that has publication restrictions.

Urban Whether, with the abatement of the excitement over Vietnam, this policy will undergo another change remains to be seen. I should think a "just" cause could as easily reactivate the clamor for war-related work to be resumed at the university as the "unjust" war in Vietnam generated protest against it.

However this may be, doesn't the fact that the comprehensive American universities are being tapped for a great variety of practical services create tensions inside the faculty between academic purists and academic pragmatists? In other words, is there a conflict between the concept of the university as a place of high learning and the public-service utilization of the products of learning?

ohnson There is a clash. The conventional academic would prefer to stay in his ivory tower, not soiling his hands with the practical problems of society. It is in the nature of academic work that professors want to be concerned with theory and pure learning, and if they do concern themselves with application, they want to do so on their own terms, not those of the hurly-burly world. How do we cope with the conflict? I'm not sure that we do cope very well. There is a dynamic tension between the two sides, with the resulting search for what is useful but uncontaminated. But in the majority of cases we do manage to persuade the scholar—or he persuades himself over a period of time—that his own professional interests are best served if he can see what he is doing in terms of the social needs his work helps to satisfy. And most scholars like to get some reading on the effectiveness of what they are doing. They can then observe for themselves that teaching, research, and the outreach function belong together as a self-replenishing cycle which has better feedback and correction when the public-service aspect is present than without it. And this realization permits them to engage in public service willingly, not grudgingly. I would have to say, though, that there is a proportion of the faculty which never gets directly involved in rendering service to the outside public or offering courses off campus.

Urban The problem has surely arisen whether the public-service function mightn't be better performed if public-service personnel were separated from teachers and researchers, and if my own experience is anything to go by, a separation of personnel on those lines would at once raise the thorny questions of prestige and pay and all their attendant evils.

ohnson There is a problem in that the power to accord prestige and control pay resides in the faculty. They are the ones who determine whether their colleagues in the public-service field are going to be promoted or not, and the common impression among those looking after the public-service work of the universities is that they are at a disadvantage, that they are second-class citizens.

But this is a distortion. It is true that some faculty member become public-service personnel and draw a supplementa income (fees or outside contracts), but in most America universities extension work is in the hands of separate unit which make public service their full-time responsibility. The members are on the payroll just like other academic staff an make their careers there.

Urban Taking your own university as an example, what sort o resources and personnel go into your public-service work

Johnson At the University of Illinois $26 million was spent o organized public-service functions in 1972-73—one-tenth o the university's operating budget. This is in addition to service rendered by individual faculty members outside the control o the university. The College of Agriculture alone, which now reaches into Chicago as well as the rural areas, has twelve hundred employees, and the general extension units emplo two hundred more. Almost six hundred of these are profes sional employees with academic standing.

Who is served? We teach home economics to rural yout through the land-grant institutions; we serve city, state, and federal officers with technical and professional assistance; w run courses, seminars, and conferences for industrial manag ers, designers, and workers; we organize policy research and face-to-face instructional work for individuals; and, generall speaking, we undertake applied research of a problem-solvin character wherever there is a need. We also concentrate o certain foci of current concern. We have a center for urban problems, one on public affairs and governmental relations and an institute on trade union and industrial relations. We have health-related units which not only carry continuing ed ucational responsibilities for doctors, pharmacists, dentists and nurses, but also operate health delivery clinics and com munity health centers. As vice-president for public service, have the responsibility of trying to coordinate what goes on in all these activities on behalf of the president of the university and our board of trustees, which governs our three campuse in and outside Chicago.

From this university model you will see that, if the comprehensive American university is not without walls, its walls are certainly very low, with plenty of access routes to the surrounding bustle of life. This is a good thing and a challenge to the university, for academia and society have undoubtedly different centers of gravity. The service functions provide external signals which the inward-looking universities need. In a world as dynamic as the present one, what the university teaches and what it seeks to discover must be closely geared to the needs of the nonuniversity world.

Urban "Closely geared" puts me on my guard again. If the university insists on a direct nexus between academia and society, am I not, after all, justified in my suspicion that, overtly or covertly, the public—and that ultimately means the government—has a decisive influence in determining what should be taught and what should be researched at the university? Can you be fully autonomous academically or politically while so many of your interests are outward-directed and so much of your support comes from outside sources? I am going over this point again because if the European universities gradually assume public-service commitments similar to the American— and this is undoubtedly what we have to expect—then maintaining the university's autonomy vis-à-vis public bodies will be at the center of our debates much more than it is already. I am not now thinking of the influence of defense-related contracts and the like, but rather of the extent to which the principles of *Lehrfreiheit* (freedom to teach) and *Lernfreiheit* (freedom to learn) might themselves be jeopardized by a subtle and perhaps unconscious self-censorship by the faculty itself.

Johnson We have to recognize that the university exists in a specific social and governmental environment and it has, to some extent, to make its peace with the regime in power or else it will cease to exist. We have already discussed the considerations that go into striking an acceptable balance. However, taking the American model as our example, there is nothing in our experience to suggest that either the government or the public bodies with which we cooperate would want to interfere with the academic freedom of the universities. This is not to deny that from time to time some public figure will vigorously contend that the university is unresponsive to public needs, does not produce the desired and timely results, or protects individuals with "unreliable" views. But the autonomy of the university is generally respected. Members of the faculty determine who is admitted—limited only by the bounds of equality of opportunity—what will be taught, by whom it will be taught, and the standards applied to the selection. Under no circumstances is there any intrusion by political screening to find out whether a man is politically or philosophically "reliable." Once in a while we do have a case where an individual's academic freedom has been ignored or even violated, but the very fact that a case like that is always widely publicized and often brought to the courts shows its exceptional character.

Urban Would it be possible at your university for a Communist to hold a chair, in philosophy, for instance?

Johnson It is not only possible—it is a fact.

Urban Forgive my skepticism, but in the last turbulent years of university history there must surely have been pressures brought to bear on you by the government to conform on various issues of curriculum, discipline, and personnel policy.

Johnson Let me bring in a personal note here. I was for almost seven years president of the State University of New Hampshire. Some time before the spectacular demonstrations started against the Vietnam war, that is, well before 1968-69, we had a small march of a dozen or so students on the New Hampshire campus. They were opposed to nuclear war and had deliberately violated the law as a political gesture. It was really a demonstration for pacifism, fed by such highly classical American sources as Thoreau's essay "Civil Disobedience," which defends the private conscience against majority expediency. Their defiance of the law had very little to do with the draft, with Marcuse, or with the "military-industrial complex."

It was a typical American cry for freedom, dissent, and individuality, which used the war issue to dramatize its point.

The governor of the state of New Hampshire did not see things in that light. He sent me a wire in which he told me summarily to dismiss every one of the demonstrators. They had, he said, violated the law; they had planned the violation in advance and made a spectacular show of it. Therefore they had forfeited their right to continue in the academic community. I refused to dismiss the students. This created a crisis that was publicized nationally, but I persisted and the trustees of the university gave support on the ground that this was not a simple case of breaking the law but a matter of conscience and political protest, and if we penalized the students for making a political point, we would be penalizing them for democratic dissent. So the university successfully resisted heavy political pressure.

Urban   Did you suffer any repercussions?

Johnson   There were threats, of course; the governor said he would take retaliatory action in cutting our budget, but he could not follow through, realizing the public outcry such a punitive step would create.

In a free and democratic society, the independence of the university is ultimately respected, because it is the necessary condition for impartial service to that society.

Richard Löwenthal

Turmoil and Reform
at the German Universities

Richard Löwenthal is Professor of International Relations at the
Free University of Berlin and a former Fellow of All Souls College, Oxford (1972-73). Richard Löwenthal's earlier appointments include Research Associate at the Russian Research Center, Harvard University, and Senior Fellow at the Research Institute on Communist Affairs, Columbia University. He has published *World Communism: The Disintegration of a Secular Faith; Der romantische Rückfall; Hochschule für die Demokratie, Grundlinie für eine sinnvolle Hochschulreform; Sozialismus und aktive Demokratie;* and is joint editor of *Die Zweite Republik, 25 Jahre Bundesrepublik Deutschland—eine Bilanz.*

Urban The German variety of the crisis of the Western university seems to be more profound, more persistent, and more consistently ideological than any we have witnessed in other countries. Unlike the American and French universities, th German universities are still in a state of turmoil, legislatio alternating with pleas for counterlegislation, resolutions b rectors' conferences with "nonnegotiable" demands by stu dent assemblies; the debate continues with considerable acr mony both within the universities and outside. Is there an thing in the chemistry of the German situation that makes less responsive to treatment by rational reform than othe systems of higher education?

Löwenthal I believe there are three main answers to you question. The first is that in no country has the student revo been mainly a result of the internal problems of the university This is proved by the fact that the timing and forms of i outbreak have been similar in the United States and in cont nental Western Europe, despite the radically different nature c the American, French, Italian, and West German universit systems. In every case, the revolt has been mainly an outbur of general alienation from existing political and social cond tions—a protest against the war in Vietnam; against froze Cold War attitudes in general; in the German case against th official fictions of Bonn's former policy on the German que tion; but also against the increasing bureaucratic remotenes of the forms of Western representative democracy; an beyond that against the emptiness—the lack of meaning, an of common tasks—of life in a competitive consumer society To that extent, it was not primarily a revolt against the state c the university, but a revolt of the young against existing soc ety. The protest was merely centered in the university, with th incidental result of making the various internal weaknesses c the university more visible and focusing attention on them Hence it could not be overcome by "rational reform" of th system of higher education.

My second answer is that there are indeed special cultur factors in the German situation. The tradition of giving ever grievance an ideological form, to direct it against the "system and indeed to turn it into a countersystem, is far stronge here—as also in France and Italy—than in Britain and th United States. Thus, from the beginning, the language of th student revolt in continental Western Europe was far more Marxist than in the United States. As for Germany in particular, the radical break with all national traditions, and also with traditional authority, which resulted from Hitler's tyranny and its collapse, has strengthened the need of Germany's second postwar generation for an ideological faith—a secular religion to show them what to live for. This may be the deeper underlying cause why the youth revolt in the Federal Republic of Germany has not only been more ideological, but also more lasting, than similar revolts in other Western countries.

My third answer is on a more pragmatic and day-to-day level. As far as the real internal problems and weaknesses of the German university system are concerned, the crisis has not responded to "rational reform" because there has been no rational reform. There has been, first, a prolonged period of neglect of problems long recognized by everyone, and then, under the impact of the student revolt, a sudden rush to pass ill-conceived laws, based on the assumption that all the university's ills could be cured by merely giving the students and the junior teaching assistants, who often led the revolt, a majority vote in university government. The idea was that this would both appease the radical students and ensure reform of the universities. The actual result was that rational reform was prevented by the total politicization and ideologization of the universities. The would-be revolutionary student leaders, far from being appeased, were enabled to entrench themselves, at public expense, in key positions in the universities and thus acquire a vested interest in carrying on their work of destruction.

Urban You are saying that, apart from the political and social causes of the student revolt, there were indeed important specific defects of the German universities which were crying out for action but had not been tackled by the reform laws. What were these defects?

Löwenthal To begin with, the German universities were adapted neither to the mass influx of students since the war nor to the demands for professional training as distinct from the nineteenth-century German conception of the university as a seat of scholarship.

This is, of course, a problem that universities all over the world have had to face. The Americans, for instance, have coped with it much better, and so, in their different way, have the British. Most continental universities were frozen in their traditional forms of organization. While the German universities were admittedly not as rigid as the French and Italian, with their Napoleonic uniformity and centralization, the German system was far from being as elastic and modern as the American and British.

The German malaise took a number of forms. For instance, in the humanities and social sciences we have the specifically German concept of academic freedom—*Lernfreiheit*. This means that the student is free to study, or not to study, anything he likes—he is entirely in control of his curriculum and has to pass no intermediary examinations. After a period of time, determined again entirely by himself—it can be four years or eight—he presents himself for final examinations. If he fails, he can sit for his finals again at almost any time he feels he is ready.

Urban   This was, incidentally, the system all over East-Central Europe until well after the war.

Löwenthal   Quite, but in a modern state, in the 1970s, this is a fantastically old-fashioned way of doing things, whatever intellectually respectable roots it may have had in the past. *Lernfreiheit*, would, of course, be quite impossible in the exact sciences and medicine, and it is inconceivable in any modern country outside Germany, whatever the field of study. But in Germany the old system largely survives in the humanities and social sciences and has made for a huge waste of time, energy, and money.

Urban   Ralf Dahrendorf says in *Bildung ist Bürgerrecht* that, notwithstanding its great economic achievements, Germany is still a traditional society which badly needs modernizing, and he does not expect that German education can be emancipated from the past unless the whole mental climate and lifestyle of Germany are first brought up to date.

Löwenthal I see the German university's failure to expand and modernize in more practical terms. Whereas in England, for example, there has been a steady growth in the number of universities over the past twenty years, in Germany there has been very little until quite recently. The explanation is simple enough. In the climate of postwar recovery from destruction, misery, and homelessness, the German electorate would not give the *Länder* parliaments authority to spend large sums of money on such apparent luxuries as the expansion and improvement of higher education. One has also to remember that in the 1950s the students were quiescent and the universities attracted no public attention.

The consequences of this stinginess were not long in coming. Soon there was a growing shortage of university professors as, in the old universities, there were not enough chairs. As the number of students grew, a good deal of the teaching had to be done by so-called teaching assistants who were, in reality, taking over an increasingly important role without being given a corresponding status. This meant a growing stratum of well-trained but highly dissatisfied young people doing responsible work and being treated as though they were the personal servants of the professors. This has been a great cause of discontent in Germany.

A third issue was academic self-government—traditionally a very clumsy affair in Germany. For example, all professors active in the field of a particular faculty were under an ex officio obligation to attend meetings with long agendas with which only a few of them were concerned. Endless time was wasted at these meetings. Then there was the problem of the university rectors. These were usually elected for one year only; by the time they had learned the ropes, they had to go. So there was a considerable need for more efficient forms of teaching and administration, irrespective of the student troubles.

Urban Was, then, the German students' protest primarily a response to these defects of the university?

Löwenthal The irony of the situation is that it was not. The discussion about the shortcomings of the traditional university system and the need for modernization had been going on for years. When the political student revolt broke out as an international phenomenon, a number of people in the press and politics jumped to the conclusion that the student rebellion was a direct consequence of the defects of the German universities. But this was a misjudgment of the situation. The shortcomings of the universities had been there—happily or unhappily—for a long time without producing revolts. Conversely, revolts did occur in a number of famous American universities which did not suffer from German types of defects.

When reform was finally begun, its purpose was not simply to provide a modern system of higher education but to get the young people off the streets and to stop the unrest. So reform was legislated in a great hurry in a number of *Länder* in the expectation that by one act the universities would be modernized and the radicals appeased.

This turned out to be a disastrous miscalculation because the radicals in the student movement could not be pacified by rational reform. At the same time, however, they were willing, and indeed eager, to exploit the openings provided and get their hands on the levers of power to advance their ideological program. The argument was that, in order to modernize the universities, they—the students—must be given a major share in the running of the universities. The slogan was: "Democratize the universities!"—let the students and teaching assistants each have a one-third share in the decision-making bodies, with the remaining third left to the professors. Later it was suggested that this tripartite arrangement might be scaled down a little and a share be given to nonacademic personnel. And, in fact, in one *Land* after another, laws were passed along these lines.

Urban Did the spirit of *Mitbestimmung* (codetermination) in labor-management relations influence the legislators?

Löwenthal Only in the sense of generating a false analogy: the university conceived as consisting of "interest groups."

What persuaded a number of well-meaning politicians with very little experience of the universities (some of them had never seen a university from the inside) was not only the general idea that democracy was a good thing and therefore democracy in the universities must also be a good thing, but that reforms had not taken place for a long time. Why had they not taken place? Because the old, tenured professors, the holders of chairs, were opposed to them—they were in power, and they were against change. So, it was argued, let's give a majority weighting to people with an interest in reform—the students and teaching assistants.

This argument contained a number of errors. First, it is by no means obvious that the idea of democracy can be transferred lock, stock, and barrel from society to the university, implying equal rights for those who are qualified to teach and those who are supposed to learn. Second, by no means had all professors set their faces against reform. It is true that reform did not come about from the inside and that legislation was necessary, but giving students and teaching assistants a majority vote at a time when there was a highly ideological, semi-Communist, semi-anarchist student movement at the universities was not a good idea. It meant that, instead of achieving the objectives the legislators had set themselves, that is to say, modernizing the university, what came out was an ideologization of the university. In universities like Berlin, Bremen, and Marburg a large number of unsophisticated, uncritical courses in Marxism-Leninism were started. The kind of teaching and orientation that had to be forced down the throats of students in Eastern Europe was eagerly demanded by students in Western Europe.

Urban Was the revolutionary bias restricted to the teaching of Marxism-Leninism or did other subjects also have to be presented in a Marxist-Leninist framework?

Löwenthal Oh yes, the teaching of economics, philosophy, history, even of modern languages and literatures, was, in a number of universities, taken over in part by student tutors, fresh from courses in Marxism-Leninism and with very little general knowledge. The students were pressing to be allowed to take their examinations without ever having listened to a so-called bourgeois professor and to choose their own examiners from among the ideological family. And in some universities these pressures were successful.

Urban What truth is there in the report that once they have found a footing inside the university, these Marxist and anarchist teachers surround themselves with like-minded colleagues by an exercise of ideological nepotism, so that the teaching bias becomes self-perpetuating?

Löwenthal The report is true, and its impact has been three-fold. It has affected the curricula, examination standards, and the selection of personnel. Standards went down and the climate was ideologized. Of course, there has been scholarly resistance, but the resisters were duly denounced as black reactionaries, and in a number of universities where the rebels did not finally win, a kind of trench warfare developed between the radical students and their supporters on the one side and their opponents on the other, paralyzing the work of the universities. This has been the situation in Heidelberg, where the ideological element finally failed to capture the commanding heights of the university, but was, until recently, strong enough to paralyze the university by unceasing internal warfare. Also, where the radicals do not have clear majorities, there has been a great deal of intimidation by radical student groups, and professors have been put under severe pressure. There has been intimidation also to stop teachers from saying things the radicals did not want to hear. Lectures on certain topics have been prevented and whole courses have had to be scrapped. And where the heads of the universities have been elected by radical majorities, there has been no authority to enforce discipline against the radicals. All this has resulted in great damage to the German university.

However, starting in 1970, public opinion has gradually become aware of what has been happening, and consequently there has been growing pressure to reform the reforms—to change some of the new laws. The subject is now hotly debated amidst a great deal of bitterness and acrimony.

Coming back to your initial question—why is the turmoil so persistent in Germany?—I would say this is due to one principal reason: At the height of the student disturbances, most of the German *Länder* (in Germany, as you know, education is the responsibility of the *Land* governments) passed reform laws, giving, as I have indicated, considerable power to students and teaching assistants. As a result, many radical groups have ensconced themselves in important positions in the universities, and it is very much worth their while to hang on to them. Parallel with the new laws there has been a sudden expansion of university budgets. The *Länder* parliaments, with guilty consciences for having neglected the universities for so long, appropriated a lot of money that fell, in a number of cases, into the hands of the enemies of democracy. New positions were created—many of them tenured—and given to left-wing extremists, so that by now we have, in the German universities, established anti-establishment strongholds. These strongholds do not, of course, automatically disappear when the ideological wave recedes, as it now appears to be doing.

Urban Are these strongholds evenly spread over the faculties and disciplines?

Löwenthal There is hardly any faculty free of them. They are deeply entrenched in the humanities and some of the social sciences. The accepted view is that sociologists started the rot—and it is true that some of them use the word "sociology" as a pseudonym for Marxism—but it is not confined to them. The rebellion was very strong among philosophers and theologians too. But the ripest fruit to fall into the radicals' lap were the future teachers, and especially the students of modern languages and German literature, whose ideologization and radicalization started earlier than those of any other group. This was partly owing to the circumstance that teacher training in Germany was particularly in need of reform. The whole system was antiquated: The students enjoyed *Lernfreiheit* with all the debilitating consequences I have already mentioned. Now, in the context of the pressure for reform, a number of teacher-training departments decided to do away with *Lernfreiheit* and to have strict, structured curricula with controls, intermediary examinations, and the rest.

At this stage a surprising thing happened—surprising, that is, if you are not familiar with the psychology of radicalism. The reforms set in train were entirely in line with the demands of earlier, progressive, but nonrevolutionary, student leaders (those of the early sixties) who had been genuinely interested in educational improvement. But now the ideological students, led by the Communists, took up a very different position: They bitterly opposed the structuring of teacher training. They said that this kind of reform was preparing cannon fodder for the capitalist system, and they used student opposition to the structuring as a weapon with which to drum up general rebellion, especially in the education departments of universities and teachers' colleges.

I might add that there was little response to all this in the natural sciences, and not very much in medicine, although many medical students went along with the argument that the proper role of medicine was social medicine.

Urban You said at the beginning of this discussion that the educational problem was not decisive in unleashing the student crisis, yet you have already put your finger on several sore spots in the traditional German system. This makes me wonder whether the German variety of student unrest wasn't more concretely based on the defects in higher education than the American protest, for example. In the United States, student dissent started, and continued, as a thinly veiled protest against the condition of the modern world—Vietnam, the consumer society, racial discrimination, and so on. The German students seem to have had something closer to the bone to have grievances about.

Löwenthal I would not say that. The two started in exactly the same way—the educational issue was picked up much later. The German student movement became a mass movement when a student was killed in Berlin during a demonstration against the visit of the Shah of Iran. This happened outside the university and had nothing whatever to do with university problems. Vietnam, too, was extremely important in Germany, as it was throughout Western Europe. So were "alienation" and several other nonuniversity factors. The general protest issued into a protest against the state of education precisely at the point where education was already in the process of being reformed. It was at this stage that the political student movement, which had opposed the Shah and capitalism and Vietnam, became a movement *against* real reform. The radicals began to oppose attempts to rationalize the university, to limit the time of study, and so on, paralyzing, or attempting to paralyze, what their nonideologized colleagues had been rightly demanding for many years.

Urban   I was surprised to hear you say that students of theology were in the vanguard of radicalism. Has this something to do with the strong reform movement in German Protestant theology?

Löwenthal   It has to do with the fact that we have a lot of pastors who no longer believe in God. They are spiritually adrift, looking for a cause they can wholeheartedly serve. What is left of their faith is a real desire to do good in a miserable world, but as their sense of the misery of the world is no longer compensated by confidence in the beyond and salvation, nor is it as a rule guided by much solid knowledge of the real problems of society, they are putting all their energies into a search for some secular form of salvation. There are quite a number of church bodies in Germany that believe it is their Christian duty to support guerrilla movements in various parts of the world. A very strange phenomenon.

Urban   You said a minute ago that there were moves afoot to reform the reforms—to change, through fresh legislation, some of the misconceived measures you have described.

Löwenthal   Yes; for instance, the West Berlin Senate, which was one of the first to pass a law on democratization, has been concerned with the unintended results of its legislation, and is now trying to revise it so as to strengthen the element of public control of the university, reassert order, stop intimidation, and change some of the majorities in the various bodies of the university.

But now there is a more general problem coming up for public discussion. A number of university professors, representing different *Länder* of the Federal Republic, have brought actions against some of the so-called democratization laws. They have filed complaints with the constitutional court in Karlsruhe asking it to consider whether the new university legislation of the various *Land* parliaments was not violating the principle of the freedom of scholarship as guaranteed by the Constitution. In May 1973 the first verdict was pronounced in one of these submissions.

The court stated that the idea of organizing a university on the principle of group representation (*Mitbestimmung*) by professors, teaching assistants, and students might not be a very sensible idea but it was lawful. However, there were certain safeguards that must be implemented.

The first requirement was that in matters directly concerning research and new academic appointments the university teachers must have a clear majority over all other sectional interests.

Urban   This, I take it, is to exclude the possibility of co-opting members of the ideological fraternity.

Löwenthal   Yes, if they are unqualified. There is no objection in principle to appointing university teachers with different ideologies, including radical ideologies, if the university is assured that they will maintain scholarly standards. In other words, the court squashed the idea that student majorities may appoint teachers simply because they have the right ideology.

The second ruling of the court was that in questions concerning the curriculum, teaching methods, and examination standards, the university teachers must have at least half the vote so that they cannot be overruled by a nonteaching majority.

Together, these decisions amount to a mandate to change a

number of laws. Of course, the court's interpretations will be protested. Even before its findings were made public, the planned revision of the West Berlin laws had already sparked off student strikes and demonstrations, and I can foresee a lot more trouble of that kind. In that sense the situation at the German universities may get worse before it gets better. This is a crisis the authorities will have to expect and stand up to. On the whole, responsible politicians seem now to be aware of that need and are prepared to face it, thanks to the changed climate of public opinion. The Bavarian minister of education has already pushed through a law ensuring a clear majority to tenured professors in all decision-making bodies, despite large and noisy student protests, and things calmed down very quickly. Even more important, the federal government, with a Social Democratic minister of education, has prepared a *portmanteau* law to ensure a minimum of structural unity for the universities in different states, and that law will also incorporate the requirements laid down by the court. In short, there are indications now that the tide has turned at last, though it may take a long time before the worst-hit universities or departments recover their previous scholarly standards.

Urban Do the findings of the constitutional court go far enough? Won't the power which the students as a group enjoy on the university's decision-making bodies go on being considerable?

Löwenthal First, one should not underestimate the importance of the general principles laid down by the court. It has made it clear that the constitutionally guaranteed freedoms of teaching and scholarship are violated not only if some anti-liberal government foists its doctrine on the university, but also if a perfectly well-meaning government imposes reforms of which it has failed to foresee the damaging consequences. And it has laid down that the state is not only constitutionally bound to respect the freedoms of the individual teacher and researcher, but is positively responsible for protecting him and his freedoms against dogmatist and terrorist groups within the university. These are the court's interpretations of the basic law of the Federal Republic and, as I say, they will have far-reaching effects.

Second, do the court's findings go far enough? Will the student groups not retain too much power?

I would say: not necessarily. The strength of student representation is, at most, one-third, and, on an average, not more than one-fourth. In any case, after the court's decision, in matters of research and appointments, student representation will be only marginal. Also, the court does not set a ceiling on the representation of university teachers—it sets lower limits only, so that beyond that there is considerable margin for maneuver. It prescribes no fixed proportions; it leaves it to the legislative bodies to work them out within the limits indicated.

Urban Let me go back to the basics of group representation—is *Mitbestimmung* appropriate to the functions and ethos of the university? Earlier in this series of discussions Professor Paul Seabury said that any analogy between *Mitbestimmung* and the university is misconceived, because the university is not a factory and students are not workers.

Löwenthal I would agree with that. In a production unit there is usually a conflict of interest between labor and management, and one must have a mechanism for dealing with it. That is why, on the factory floor, it makes perfectly good sense to have shop stewards, unions, and codetermination. But students are not an interest group in that sense, and they do not make a productive contribution. That is why students' strikes are nonsensical, for the strikers do not damage anybody except themselves. The issues that have to be decided in a university are largely not issues of group interest; hence the university is not a place for the settlement of conflicts of interest.

The issues that affect the life of a university are partly internal issues of scholarship—and these have to be judged in the light of expertise, ability, and proved achievement—and partly genuinely political issues in the sense that someone has to decide on social priorities. Is the social need for archeologists greater at any time than the need for industrial administrators?

Do you want to spend more on philology than on biochemistry? And so on. These are basically political questions which involve value judgments. Clearly, they are not to be decided by people who happen to be students at the university at any particular time; they have to be decided by society as a whole, through the accepted democratic mechanisms of decision making. On the other hand, the technical questions involved in implementing these political decisions are for the experts, for they alone are qualified to answer them. So what remains for student participation are issues of teaching techniques and student welfare. On problems of this kind, student representation is proper and reasonable, but this is a limited range of issues, and to organize the whole life of a university around it does not make sense. One of the great difficulties with the present attempt to reform the reforms is that we are unlikely to get away from the misconception that codetermination is a basically valid concept for the government of the university as a whole, because, as we have seen, the concept of codetermination as applied to the university is not in conflict with the Constitution—only with common sense.

Urban Why is it that so many German university students are committed to radical ideologies—Maoism, Castroism, Stalinism, Trotskyism, anarchism—at a time when the German Communist Party is minuscule as far as membership is concerned and virtually nonexistent as a force to be reckoned with at the *Bundestag* elections?

Löwenthal When the German student movement became a real force in the middle sixties, its intellectual leaders were often men of considerable originality and independence. They were critical of Stalinism and the East European regimes and at the same time passionately opposed to capitalism and imperialism. The models they followed varied from those of Trotsky and Rosa Luxemburg, on the one side, to Mao Tse-tung and Castro, on the other. However, in the course of time the hard-line Stalinists made a great deal of progress at the expense of these disparate groups, so that by now the National Union of Students (VDS), for instance, is openly controlled by the so-called Spartacus group which is Stalinist. So is the SHB (*Sozialistischer Hochschulbund*), which was earlier known as a social democratic union but is no longer allowed to call itself "social democratic."

Urban Why have the Stalinists gained so much at the expense of the others?

Löwenthal Largely because they were better adapted to making rational use of the opportunities created by the new legislation. The other groups possessed no cohesive long-term strategy and no experience in exploiting political situations. Some were given to the cult of spontaneity, some were anarchists, some believed in violence as an end in itself, some had illusions about instant revolution and the improvement of the world at one fell swoop—think of the mood in Paris in May 1968. The frustration of all these expectations was followed by a bad hangover. The illusions about immediate power vanished with the intoxication; all that remained was a hatred of existing society, and it was the Stalinist party liners who proved most adept at getting hold of people in this mood of dejection and refocusing them for their own, long-term ends. For example, they were using the positions which were now available to them to impose their teaching programs on the universities.

Urban The "long march through the institutions"?

Löwenthal Yes, this was originally Dutschke's phrase, but the Stalinists were much better equipped to organize the long march than the kind of groups Dutschke was leading. All these factors add up to one reason why the Stalinists gained at the expense of the others.

But there is also another and fundamental question. Why should the most active section of the student population of a country which is enjoying free, democratic institutions, which is prosperous and secure, not involved in anything like the Vietnam war, but is, on the contrary, rapidly improving its relations with the East, and in which the Communist Party polled a mere 0.3 percent of the vote at the last general elections—why should such a country have a student population so strongly disaffected?

Urban Isn't it, though, the case that, in practice, the German protest is not predominantly ideological—that the majority of German students are conspicuously absent when doctrinal issues are debated and put to the vote, and indifferent to the whole student-society *Problematik*?

Löwenthal Yes, but even if you take that into account, the fact remains that a large number of the politically interested and active students are supporting antidemocratic, Communist, semi-Communist, or anarchist causes; and this in a country where there are no strong traditions of that kind.

I believe the problem has to do with the peculiar loss of tradition and crisis of authority in the postwar years which was more profound here than in other Western countries. And that in turn was ultimately a consequence of the Third Reich and its collapse. One of the outcomes of the nationalist paroxysm of Hitler was a repudiation of all traditions and a rejection of national identity. The reaction of the generation of people who had been drafted into Hitler's army as young men and women—of the people who had gone through the war and then the shock of defeat and the shock of disclosures about the crimes of the Nazi regime—has been to want to be anything but Germans: Europeans, decent human beings, yes, but, please, not Germans. So these people, although they were, of course, aware that they were Germans and knew something about German history, wanted to repress what they knew.

Today's students are the children of that generation. The past does not weigh on them, they have nothing to repress; but many of them have genuinely lost the consciousness of their national identity and are thus trying to replace the roots they have lost with an artificial, ideological collective identity. They want to see themselves as members of the international revolutionary proletariat, of the liberation movement of the underdeveloped nations, and so forth. This loss of a sense of identity is a very German phenomenon. A French Communist would not dream of denying that he is a Frenchman as well as a Communist, or a Dutch European Federalist that he is a *Dutch* Federalist, but in Germany it is a fairly widespread assumption that one cancels out the other: If you have an ideological identity, your German roots can be forgotten.

Urban Hasn't the traditional authority of the German family and German institutions acted as a brake? The sense of authority was always strong in Germany, and I should have thought that even today it is stronger than in most other West European countries.

Löwenthal I doubt whether that is so at present. True, there was more of this traditional authority in German politics and society than almost anywhere in the West. Even after the war, traditional family ties and bureaucratic structures held their own quite remarkably. It was only in the sixties that these ties came to be questioned in the context of a belated radical enlightenment. Some of the changes that were now being pressed for were undoubtedly long overdue, because (and here Dahrendorf is right) Germany's social authoritarianism just did not fit in with the modern world any more. But while respect for traditional authority was thrown out, nothing has taken its place. Young people in Germany have simply not been brought up to respect democratic authority. Thus, there ensued a manifest movement against *all* authority—producing as its necessary consequence a subconscious and often desperate longing for *absolute* authority.

This phenomenon is not restricted to Germany. The desire for a substitute faith is one of the shared characteristics of this age of secularization. Naturally, where the destruction of traditional authority has been particularly sudden and radical, as in Germany, the longing for a secular faith is especially strong. The immediate postwar generation reacted to the collapse of the Nazi pseudoreligion with healthy skepticism, and that generation was in many ways the most liberal and pragmatic Germany has ever known. But in the generation that is going to university at the present time we can see a revival of this longing for a secular faith. What is available to satisfy the hunger is not very solid. Underneath the pretensions of faith there is despair. This is a generation with a large number of suicides, neuroses, and depressive illnesses. It does not *really* believe, but it desperately wants to believe.

Urban Personally I was not surprised to see young Germans take the course they did. I would have been surprised to see a similar development in England, but anyone who has looked at the intellectual history of Germany over the last hundred years could predict with fair certainty that, once the war damage was undone, the young Germans would be among the first to feel ill at ease among the aridities and aimlessness of the consumer society. The idealistic commitment in German philosophy and the romantic commitment in German letters and *Volk* culture alone would have been enough to make Germany an uncertain recipient of purely utilitarian social values.

Löwenthal The barrenness and drabness of the consumer society are, of course, the big issues of the radical movement, and there is something healthy in the fact that these problems are being given an airing. Clearly, if you work only for yourself and for marginal increases in consumer satisfaction, your life is empty. Our desire to feel that we are partaking of a task transcending our daily needs is a very basic human require-ment which some advocates of our economic system overlook at our peril. But I can foresee improvements in this field in the Federal Republic—not as a result of radical agitation, but rather because the Social Democrats have put these problems on their program: They are trying to define common tasks and community values, and to restore a sense of the individual's involvement in the social good. This ethos is being increasingly accepted, and not only in Germany.

Urban You said the longing for a secular religion is wide-spread among German youth. How far is this true of the adult population?

Löwenthal As the German elections show, it does not apply to them generally. One of the oddities of the German situation is the students' high degree of isolation, which they are desperately trying to overcome.

Another hopeful sign is that the radical student movement has spawned an ideological left wing within the "young" organization of the Social Democratic Party. The people who make up that wing are not Communists, they are not even crypto-Communists, although there are always a few crypto-Communists among them who are usually given short shrift. These people genuinely believe in democracy, but their social program is much more radical than the official policy of the SPD, and in many cases it is utopian. This left wing exerts considerable pressure within the Social Democratic Party. Here we have a much healthier phenomenon than the millenarian and Stalinist sects we discussed earlier, because this left wing of the SPD is composed of people who have got away from the cult of violence and the worship of dictatorship, and are trying to pursue their utopian aims within a democratic framework. And once they are on that road, it is possible to reintegrate them gradually into democratic society.

This is a highly indirect and, so to speak, unintended product of the student movement, for many of the young people who joined the extreme left of the SPD first saw their move as one station on the long march through the institutions. But German democratic institutions have proved healthy enough to absorb the utopians and to initiate a learning process among them—to decolonize the colonizers. The radicals came in trying to change the democratic processes of society, but it looks as though the democratic processes of society are beginning to change them.

Urban How did the East Germans react to the student rebellion in the Federal Republic?

Löwenthal At first, when the rebellion was strongly anti-Stalinist as well as anticapitalist, the East Germans were extremely worried about it. They were also very critical—and from their point of view rightly critical—when, at one stage, the student movement took on the form of a neo-Bakuninist cult of violence. Now, of course, they are delighted at the progress the Stalinist party liners have been able to make at the expense of other dissenting groups. While it would be quite wrong to claim that the East Germans had clandestinely started the whole thing (they had no influence whatever at the beginning), they are now well placed to exploit the student crisis because their people are in key positions. They control (as I've said) the National Union of Students and they run courses in Marxism-Leninism at a number of universities. A lot of grist for their mill.

Alain Touraine

An Academic's View
from the French Barricades

A former Professor of Sociology at Nanterre and now at the School of Higher Studies (Maison de Science de l'Homme, Paris), Alain Touraine played a leading part in the May 1968 events. He is the author of *Le communisme utopique* and *Université et société aux Etats-Unis*.

Urban   The Paris upheavals of May 1968 found a critical observer in your colleague, Professor François Bourricaud, some of whose comments were aimed at your own role in these events. You were teaching sociology at the time in Nanterre, where the Paris troubles had started, and I understand that you negotiated with the university on behalf of the student movement on the night of May 10-11, 1968. Bourricaud's charge against you was that you believed that the post-industrial society could be achieved by student rebellion. He said the students wanted two things that were mutually incompatible: social responsibility, interdependence, and rational solutions on the one hand; and romanticism, free play of the passions, mysticism, and spontaneity on the other. The two were to be fused under some slogan such as self-government or autonomy. But this, said François Bourricaud, is a utopian idea—you cannot run a future society on a mixture of creativity *and* control, spontaneity *and* rational organization.*

Touraine Nobody could seriously believe that political movements are governed by "ideas." To explain human behavior one has first to look at the social milieu in which that behavior has taken shape. The problem on May 11, 1968, was not a problem of ideas but one of barricades, and you were either on one side of the barricades or on the other. To define the problem in abstract terms—organization versus spontaneity and such like—is entirely misleading. It is the manner of a retired professor looking at history.

The problem was entirely different. First, it is very wrong to think that the student "movement" was a coherent organization—that it resembled a political party in any sense, that students had any way of making systematic decisions and following them up with action. No, revolutionary upheavals are not programmed; they happen in complex and usually chaotic situations, without a master plan or a mastermind.

The complexity of the 1968 crisis was made up of two elements. First, a growing number of students realized that they were not going to spend their working lives in the academic or professional world but that they were much more likely to end up as employees of large organizations. We hadn't, in 1968, reached the state of the American and Japanese students' awareness, who had sound evidence before them that the universities—far from being communities devoted to disinterested scholarship—were, directly or indirectly, aiding the war in Vietnam. But we could see that we were to be more

*Cf. François Bourricaud, "The Preconceptions of University Protest in France," in *Can We Survive Our Future?* G. R. Urban, ed. London, 1972.

and more incorporated into a power system, and that the social sciences were to be used as tools for social control. That is why social science students were the spearhead of the movement opposing the technocratic power of large organizations.

Second, this new orientation was appearing in an antiquated academic setting. The French university system constituted a liberal, abstract, professional universe which was preparing students first and foremost for the academic succession. Quite clearly, there was not, there could not be, enough academic employment for all the students who were being trained to be academics. Hence a great many students felt that the French university was crumbling, that they were living in a ghost town, and that they had nowhere to look for hope and support.

In other words, you had a conflict and a crisis, and the two were hopelessly intermingled. Some people tried to subsume the two under some trendy slogan such as a new "lifestyle" or "cultural revolution," but, at least as far as Paris and Nanterre were concerned, these labels were very wide of the mark. The Nanterre students were not much concerned with cultural problems. They were interested in the social conflict that was emerging, and in the *language*, that is to say the methods, of social conflicts in general. But the center of the stage for them was occupied by the labor movement. The only thing they really wanted to do was to go out to the factories, communicate with the workers, and get them on their side—and this they did not succeed in doing. They tried very hard; they visited working-class areas, but they could not persuade the workers to give them a hand with the street fighting or to support their demands for university reform. However, the attempt was made, and therefore it is wrong to say that the students indulged in a puristic and socially naive movement of their own. They did have their eyes on the main chance.

Urban You were on the spot as one of the actors, not an observer.

Touraine Yes, I was on the spot from the first day to the last and I had decisions to make. I said at the time, and I have maintained since, that the only intelligent attitude was to try to accept the dual orientation of the student movement—that is to say, to encourage the social conflict aspect of it and limit the consequences of the institutional crisis to the university. When the movement was picking up momentum in May, 1968, and a concrete conflict developed with the Ministry of Education (where, incidentally, François Bourricaud was the main counsel of the minister and was responsible for advising him to close down the university and the French Radio's offices), one had to take sides. The police were out in the streets, the conflict aspect of the situation was very clearly visible and my personal attitude was, first, to be physically present, and second, to be not exactly in favor of confrontation, but to be sure that the conflict was made to bear fruit in the given situation. I did not negotiate with the authorities; I was physically on the barricades, and that is something different.

After the end of May, the movement began to disintegrate rapidly, and during the next academic year—political and industrial support having completely disappeared—those of us who remained at the university were a small and shattered rearguard. The "university crisis" aspect of the situation was absolutely predominant not only in the eyes of students but also in those of the assistant professors, all of whom found themselves in a precarious position. It was in that situation that I began to perceive that the crisis of the university had to be overcome and to do whatever was in my power to limit the damage. And that is still my personal policy.

Urban What does that mean in practice?

Touraine For example, I refuse to have any truck with "spontaneity," if it means compromising the exigencies of intellectual work. I refuse to accept any laxity in the teaching practices of assistant professors. Disorganization has nothing to do with university reform.

The movement *is* disorganized. In March and April, 1972, when secondary school children mounted a demonstration of their own, participation by university students was almost nil. Nobody from Nanterre, nobody from Vincennes, nobody from Paris 7ᵉ showed up.

Urban Are you saying the movement is moribund?

Touraine I am not saying that. The movement is in a crisis and disorganized. When you have an army in retreat, there will always be stragglers laying their hands on whatever they can; yet it would be silly to say that the stealing has anything to do with national defense. Or, to take another example, unemployment on the scale of the 1930s produces extremist social behavior, but this cannot be equated with the labor movement's positive attitude to social conflict. Yet the protest is part and parcel of the overall situation: unemployment or the fear of it. There is always a dialectic between the two. By the same token I am prepared to say that the crisis aspect of 1968 and what has followed it are perfectly respectable and have a certain value so long as they can be turned into starting points for positive action, such as providing an impetus for a countermodel of education, a countermodel of society, and so on. The problem is to understand the dialectics between crisis and conflict.

Urban You are then—if I may summarize your opinions—making two points: First, the French university was antiquated, rigid, and unable to provide training for those who would not fit into the academic succession; second (and this flows from your first point), it was inculcating in students certain expectations about the type of work they would be called upon to do, but these expectations were false because the jobs the students would be actually offered were of the humdrum, alienating kind. Their preparation and their diplomas were wasted on them.

Touraine The students were linking these two aspects. They were, in fact, saying to us: "You professors—with your polished language, magisterial lectures, and liberal minds—are cheating us, because you are not telling us that in real life we will not be able to use any of your ideas. We are going to sell goods and services, working for IBM, not Plato."

There is great resentment against the French university on this count, yet the students' attitude is highly ambiguous. On the one hand they reject the university for its irrelevance, but on the other they are trying to stay at the university as long as they can because they hate and fear the outside world still more. They suspect that we academics are camouflaged agents of General Motors, but at the same time they feel that we are not irredeemably lost. They accuse the university of giving them a fake culture, a fake independence, a fake freedom, but they are nevertheless clinging to the university. But with all that, the conflict between students and teachers was, on the whole, very limited in 1968 because nobody really cared about the university.

Urban Did the students work out a countermodel to the university they were rejecting?

Touraine Yes and no. During the May crisis definitely no, but after the failure of May, the counterculture began to make some headway. May, 1968, was, by today's standards, a rather old-fashioned affair: no drugs (but lots of red wine), no great sexual freedom (rather the contrary), and intellectually able and highly motivated students. May was not a cultural up-heaval at all; it was a straightforward political rebellion. We were interested in attacking the power system; the themes of cultural change were incorporated in the political arguments.

After May, 1968, the political countermodels one could see emerging were all put up outside the university by Maoists, Trotskyites, and other radical groups. Inside the university there was less talk of alternative models. The radical students' general political orientation was toward the traditional French Left. The rebels were looking to the Communist Party for guidance.

Urban Were the Communists prepared to return the interest? They had an opportunity to move during the May revolution which they did not use—they sat tight, not realizing perhaps that the educational system had great possibilities as a source of social and political leverage, and that the decline of the heavy industrial labor force made it the more urgent to capture the bastions of the intellectual proletariat. Other, and less generous, explanations for Communist inactivity have also been put forward.

Touraine I don't think it is accurate to say that the Communist Party sat tight. The Party was positively against the whole student movement. A book subsequently put out by the French Communist leaders made that crystal clear. Soon after the May upheavals I participated in a public discussion with leaders of the French Communist Party. The audience were Communist workers from the basic industries. Well, there was no doubt left in my mind that both the rank and file and their leaders were hostile to everything the students stood for.

Urban Has the Party now realized that it missed out on a good thing?

Touraine Yes, after a period of antagonism the Party decided to make room for the energies of the student militants and incorporate them in the Party organization; and this has been done with a good deal of success.

Of course, most of the student militants were, as I have just said, keenly interested in the Party in the first place, and a number of those who had been active in the May events joined the Communist Party after the collapse of the May revolution in order to turn their energies to better account.

Urban If the failure of the May rebellion was due to the noncooperation and hostility of the Communist Party, did these young activists have no qualms about joining it?

Touraine The young radicals had always accepted the central role of the working class. Perhaps their activities in May did not bear this out, but that was their ideology. Also, the Communist Party is by far the youngest party in France. The clothes, hair styles, and other gear of the young French Communists are indistinguishable from the rest of the young. That image too was a point of attraction. Above all, the student leaders believed that in the light of the organizational debacle of May, 1968, they ought to join a body that was efficient and of the working class, and the Communist Party was both these things. And those who did not join the Communist Party often opted for one of the Trotskyite groups—such as the Communist League, which is a rival Leninist organization. But the Communist Party has come a long way since its summary rejection of the student movement in 1968. In the spring of 1973 it came to terms with the Communist League and supported the secondary school children's demonstrations.

Urban But why exactly was the French Communist Party so dead set against cooperation with the students in 1968?

Touraine Why was the Catholic Church against Protestantism? Why does any church or party give up its monopoly with so much reluctance? This was one simple, but fundamental reason. The second reason has to do with the fact that the Communist Party in France is profoundly representative of working-class culture—of working-class values, attitudes, tastes, orientation—of a working class that is growing up.

Urban A working class jealous of the gains it has made in its advance to petit bourgeois status.

Touraine I don't know what "petit bourgeois" means. Goldthorpe has shown that even in England, where the working class has been much more established than the working class is in France, bourgeois attitudes did not take root, not even among the relatively rich strata of the working-class population. This is *a fortiori* true of France. The French Communist Party is not part of bourgeois society—it belongs to French industrial culture, and that is something very different.

The truth of the matter is that the big battalions of the Communist Party—people employed in the large, partly state-owned manufacturing industries—believed on rather nineteenth-century lines that work equals physical effort, and those who didn't get their hands dirty—administrators, intellectuals and the like—belonged to the superstructure and were petit bourgeois. From this traditionalist working-class point of view the students belonged to the bourgeoisie, and there was class opposition to them both at the grass roots and from the Communist Party as a whole. That too shaped the Party's opposition to the student movement in May 1968. But the most concrete reason for the Party's hostility was political realism: de Gaulle had been losing ground since 1962, and since 1965 there has been a reasonable possibility for the first time in twenty years that the Communist Party might come to power through the ballot box as a partner in a left-wing coalition. The Communist leaders did not want to throw that chance away by showing themselves to be a nonparliamentary opposition hitching its wagon to student anarchism.

Urban In one of your books you advocate "creative protest" as a weapon against "dependent participation," and M. Edgar Faure has taken issue with this distinction. What do you mean by these two phrases?

Touraine By dependent participation I mean to convey a very simple idea: Our society is alienated not because it imposes restrictive police control or abject poverty, but because it confines us to a state of dependence while giving us the outward trappings of independence. For example, a certain policy is devised for you and you are asked to participate in carrying it out, but you are not allowed to participate in creating the rules of the game. The Gaullist concept of participation, for example, is just another word for incorporating people in a social order, good or bad. But this social order has not come into being as a result of *your* decisions. You are being manipulated.

Urban M. Edgar Faure, in his 1968 *Loi d'orientation,* puts great stress on participation. His law provides for a joint participatory committee for university government, but it also lays down as a general principle that "the participation of each individual at every moment and in every way in shaping his own future constitutes the basic article of a new social contract." The only areas it exempts from participation are assessing the students' performance, the recruitment of staff, and the planning of teaching and research. Are you accepting these reforms as effective steps in the right direction, or do you feel that the participation envisaged by M. Faure is also "dependent participation," that is, a fraud?

Touraine It is true that you find all these stipulations in the law, and it is true that the minister has talked vaguely about participation on many occasions. The 1968 law was unanimously passed by the National Assembly, although I doubt whether all the deputies who voted for it were really for it. If they passed it nevertheless, it was simply because the French government could not (as it never can) come up with genuinely new ideas, and grabbed the opportunity to rid the system of an awkward problem: Let the professors and students fight it out in their participatory bodies—this was the latent idea. I am not disputing the sincerity of M. Faure's intentions; he tried to give some content to a model of education. But we all know that M. Faure had no political importance at the time; he was the government's trouble-shooter. Nevertheless, a certain process was being set in motion; but to explain that, I must briefly review the nature of the French university—a university that never was.

France has never had a real university, only isolated and mutually jealous schools and faculties. Up to 1968, no universities as such existed in this country. Take my own example. I am a normal product of French higher education. I spent three years at Nanterre, for reasons to which I'll come in a moment, but the rest of my professional life as a sociologist has been spent outside universities. Why should this have been so?

French higher education has never been organized around universities. To speak of the Napoleonic "system" shows at best a great misunderstanding. There was a law school and a medical school, and practically nothing else. These schools were monopolies and behaved accordingly by resisting new knowledge. Every time a change in the field of learning occurred, we French hastily created a counteruniversity. When the Renaissance appeared—when mathematics, Greek, and Hebrew became important—we created the College of France, which is a university in all but name. When biology began to matter in the eighteenth century, we created the Museum for

Natural History. When, in the nineteenth century, the Germans developed philology and experimental science, we established the Practical School for Higher Studies. When physics, chemistry, and "big science" arrived in our own time, we responded by creating a National Center for Scientific Research. All of these are totally independent bodies, not universities in the ordinary sense of the word.

Urban Surely you must have been through a university as a student?

Touraine I never went to a university, and I used to despise university students as intellectually second-rate. I was a student at one of the *Grandes Écoles*, and my only contact with the university was the formality of sitting for a university examination and taking a university degree. After graduation I entered the Center for Scientific Research and then I joined the School for Higher Studies, where I am now.

Urban You owe us an explanation why you went to Nanterre.

Touraine I went to Nanterre, as did a lot of other people, in the expectation that Nanterre might become an anti-Sorbonne, the antiuniversity university, and it did; the spirit of Nanterre was completely opposed to the spirit of the Sorbonne. We wanted to make sure that the great currents stirring the world did not stop at the gates of the university.

The French are, ironically, buying a university system probably at the time of its final decay. The university is ceasing to fulfill its task—the culture it offers is not open to new ideas and knowledge. Its teaching models are antiquated, there is a rigid faculty framework, and the university suffers from inhuman dimensions. We are groping for new institutions to take over the functions of the university.

So, in 1968, "universities" were created, and the main problem they are having to face is not any question of participation or self-government, but how to learn to speak up for themselves and exact decisions at the national level. One of the great misunderstandings about the French university system has been to say—as almost everyone did say—that it was weak because it was overcentralized.

Urban This is certainly what M. Faure was saying, and he was urging self-government as a remedy.

Touraine Yes, but reality was unkind to M. Faure's analysis and predictions; paradoxically, since the *Loi d'orientation* of 1968, centralization has increased, and that, to my mind, is a sign of progress if you consider that before 1968 the problems of the university went by default because they were not being thought of at all. University education was supposed to be the preserve of academics in the same way as points of dogma are left to theologians to settle. Any public discussion of the organization and future of the university was taboo; the government made itself conspicuous by observing a deafening silence. So the French university system was not even centralized—it was just nonexistent.

If you compare it with the American system over the past twenty to twenty-five years, you will notice that the Americans have been moving to a higher degree of standardization. You can now speak of an American national system of higher education, which was not the case fifty years ago. And in America decisions *are* being made. In France there was a kind of gentlemen's agreement among bureaucrats, local worthies, and the university professors to lay on, from time to time, a little shadow-boxing for the edification of the public, but in fact to do precisely nothing. No decisions were taken. There was a silent agreement to respect traditions, spheres of established interest, petty rules, civilities and privileges, and to leave reforms for another day.

However, little by little the country has now come to accept the idea that decisions have to be made, and this, as I say, is progress. The fact that one man can speak for an entire university is new and very important. Typically for France, the law has created a number of institutions, none of which functions. One institution that does work—the Conference of University Presidents—was not foreseen by the law. This is a body of forty or fifty men, and when they tell the minister that they have adopted policy A or B, the minister has no choice but to bow and accept it. The Higher Council for Education and Research, with rights of participation, is of no consequence. It is playing at parliamentarianism. But university autonomy as symbolized by the Conference of Presidents has already made some impact in that it has shown the capacity of the system to make decisions. It is a slow process, and I don't know how far it will go and whether it will achieve real results. But a political machinery has been created which may, from time to time, bring forth a little mouse. So there is no contradiction in saying that the universities have achieved a certain personality (autonomy is perhaps too strong a word) and that they are at the same time more centralized than they were before.

Urban   Am I right in thinking that, since 1968, the French university is more inclined to heed the fact that the rapid advances of knowledge make it virtually impossible for the same man to be creative at his research and also to be an effective teacher?

Touraine   The tension is not so much between teaching and research as between knowledge and the social uses of knowledge.

The traditional image of the university—still very much alive in our day—is that of an institution which transmits certain values, which has a certain spirit and resembles in some respects a priesthood, with student novices sitting at the feet of professor-initiates. It is the image of a culture-dispensing, ideological type of institution. But in France the university has been performing this function with rapidly decreasing conviction and efficiency. Students come to the university to acquire qualifications for jobs, and the university has to equip them with these qualifications. The assimilation of cultural values is incidental to the vocational training.

Another factor that has to be taken into account is the university's propensity to create more and more and transmit less and less knowledge. Knowledge is a productive force which, like any other productive effort, creates its own momentum of power and policy. The university ought to have a double function here: First, it ought to reconcile the supply of new knowledge with the students' demands for skills and degrees; second, it ought to make knowledge socially useful and responsible. The relationship between science and politics has been, and rightly, I think, the central theme of the student movement throughout the world's universities. It is preposterous to suggest that science and scholarship operate in a social vacuum, or that they create their own social ethos. They work and are made use of in the context of a given society with its specific interests and priorities. You can accept or reject these interests, but what you cannot do is to claim that science is immune from their influence. Knowledge is like fuel—it can drive the motor of a democratic or dictatorial, of a warlike or peaceful, type of society, but it is seldom left unutilized.

Urban In another discussion ("A Hippocratic Oath for the Academic Profession")* we found that about a generation ago it was true that the university would teach students how to make bombs and how to build cathedrals, but it would not teach them which of the two objects they ought to make. But we also found that this moral neutrality of the university is no longer acceptable and that it is, in fact, no longer practiced.

Touraine The university has never been as neutral as that. It was, especially a generation or two ago, in fact conspicuous for its hidden ideological commitment. For example, the American system of higher education, as it was until quite recently, is explained by a deliberate policy to create a national elite, as far at least as the leading universities were concerned. Some of the protagonists of the system were Darwinists—they put their campuses outside the big cities because (they didn't, of course, say this) the cities were full of Italians and Slavs. Their intention was to create a highly integrated class of young white Anglo-Saxon Protestants and to equip them with a near monopoly of knowledge. Knowledge was the cement of the American ruling class, and there were no doubts in the minds of this ruling class how to put it to use.

*See pp. 273–296 below.

I am profoundly opposed to this abuse of knowledge. Our purpose must be to create a critical ideology in order to separate (as the Greek word *kritein* implies) knowledge from the social uses of knowledge. This idea has already had a very positive response, especially in the United States, where both students and teachers have been made conscious of the need to speak, for example, not so much of medicine as of health care, not only of the technology of road construction but of mastering the process of urban concentration, and so forth. "Knowledge for what?" is the vital question the student movement is posing for the entire academic community. And of course the question is often resented. Many academics find the ivory tower a safe place to live in. It guarantees the freedom of purely "curiosity-oriented" research, obviating any necessity to get involved with the practical consequences of scholarship. To have jolted the academic community out of this unconcern with the world is one of the signal achievements of the student movement. There are no neutral subjects in scholarship.

Urban I'm sure you realize that you are uttering a very controversial opinion. There is a strongly entrenched view—best represented in this series of dialogues by Professor Max Beloff—which holds that "it is not the business of the universities to discuss possible implications of the truth. The business of the universities is to find the truth and to teach it." Beloff concludes that the degree of relevance of what the scholar is doing is something for society to decide.*

Touraine I am by no means opposed to that, but if we accept Professor Beloff's philosophy, we must face the consequences, for it means writing off the university—no less. If the discovery of truth is an end in itself, then we must be prepared for the fact that teachers and research workers will want to spend all their time in libraries and laboratories. They will want to keep abreast of the latest developments in their fields of learning and be left alone by society and politics.

*See pp. 153–177 below.

An Academic's View from the French Barricades 143

But the university is not a laboratory. The act of teaching is not a scientific activity, and those who say that it is are guilty of a gross misrepresentation. When—for instance in a Soviet university—you decide that ten percent of entrants should read chemistry, five percent medicine, and three percent archeology, you are making political choices as a university teacher. You are paid to make those choices and you are highly conscious of the fact that you are part of the real world. The research work you are doing as a scholar may well be highly respectable, but that does not exhaust your functions as a university teacher. You are where you are as a scholar, responsible for your decisions to scholarship and society, and ideally you should share those decisions with students and other members of staff. The university consists of creators, mediators, administrators, and consumers of knowledge. They all have a right to codetermination. What is important is that control of the university should be vested in a participatory political body. Suppose the government or some regional organization came to you with a forecast that in the next five or ten years they would need so many sociologists to tackle racial problems, so many teachers for their schools, so many engineers to deal with water conservation, etc. It would then be up to the governing body of the university to consult various professors: Have you the knowledge, the personnel, and resources to satisfy these requests? A decision would then be made on the basis of codetermination, in the light of the professors' expert advice. The professors would supply the knowledge but they would not control the decision making. At the same time their functions as creators of knowledge would be fully respected and their openness to the world's practical problems encouraged. The ideal type of scholar for this role is the one who is intellectually rigorous and conservative but politically pliable.

Urban Aren't you saying that you favor technologists ready to serve any political system, and especially a leftist system, as that is the one you advocate?

Touraine The process of codetermination would see to it that socially irresponsible initiatives didn't pass muster.

Urban Do you think the kind of reforms you have sketched out have any chance of being realized in France under the Faure legislation?

Touraine It does not seem very likely. Germany has made some real attempts to build participation into the university system but I wonder whether the reforms go far enough and whether they will be lasting.

In the past, all major initiatives came from America, and although it is true that the participatory type of reforms has not caught on in United States universities, I still expect the American universities to be the pioneers and pacesetters. They are less burdened by tradition than we are and more willing to experiment.

*   *   *   *

Urban We have now looked at the university's function as a producer and supplier of knowledge, suffused with a certain left-wing social purpose, and if I were to sum up your idea of the university I would call it a "knowledge industry under social control." It is clear from your strictures on elitist education that you hold no brief for any concept of the university as a conservator and transmitter of cultural values of a "reactionary" kind. The question is: Do you think it is the university's business to transmit a general education and certain permanent values we associate with it? When you urge scholars to take account of the social uses of scholarship, you, too, are assuming that they are heirs to a certain social and cultural tradition—a left-radical tradition. But the traditions I like to think the university hands down from generation to generation are of a broader kind.

Touraine I don't know whether there are such things as permanent values. Nor do I know what sort of traditions the university is expected to pass on. There are no permanent landmarks in human thinking and history. I am a historian by training, so I am by no means uninterested in the past, but I know well enough that every age, every culture, has an extremely selective interpretation of the past. We are all conditioned—not necessarily in any crude sense—by the assumptions and social exigencies of our age, so that when we look at the "permanent" landmarks, we are in fact looking at ourselves. You do not speak of Plato as an unchanging milestone in philosophy, but of the reasons why the Italian Renaissance or nineteenth-century Oxford perceived Plato in the way they did. The knowledge of the past is always the result of hermeneutics—interpretation—

Urban —All history being sociology and social psychology?

Touraine —That is part of my meaning, but I'll come to that in a moment. Let me make myself brutally clear: I think we must, for once and for all, squash any idea that we are legatees of a Judeo-Graeco-Christian culture. One of the most reactionary documents to be published in modern educational history was the Harvard "Red Book" of 1945 (*General Education in a Free Society*), for it makes us all gratuitous heirs to a so-called Christian civilization and Western culture. I am conscious that my milieu contains survivals of that culture and civilization, but I can see no reason why I should regard myself as being in any sense tied or indebted to a Christian civilization that is, in my time, nonexistent as a formative influence.

Urban May I remind you that in 1945 the "Red Book" was very far from having a reactionary intent or effect. As Professor A. D. C. Peterson pointed out, at the end of the Second World War and in the first days of peace people were much concerned with the success of totalitarian regimes in securing commitment among their younger generation, and it was feared that the Western democracies might collapse in a crisis of self-confidence. Therefore the general education which the "Red Book" recommended envisaged special courses intended to be taken by all students in common and to introduce them to the heritage of Western civilization. The idea was to foster an understanding of and commitment to a free democratic society of the Western type. And in those particular circumstances, when Hitler and Stalin ruled the historical landscape, the commitment encouraged was positively progressive.

Touraine General education was a reactionary idea *ab initio*, whatever the intent of the Harvard report. It was reactionary at birth in the late nineteenth century, when it was invented by the ruling class to counteract the first attempts to give the public a mass elementary and, later, technological education. Established and wealthy but without the legitimacy conferred on its predecessors by a long historical background, the ruling class of the last century bought itself cultural ancestors the way it also bought old castles. That's what general education was and is about if you skim off the surface and look at the social reality.

Urban The principal trend in these discussions, represented by Lord James, Professor Beloff, and Lord Ashby, has been to emphasize the overriding importance of a general education, not at all in the sense that it might impart a narrowly Christian ethic, but on the broad assumption that general education alone is likely to encourage (in the words of Lord James) "fundamental beliefs in the individual as a free object of care and tolerance, of kindness . . . of decency."*

Touraine The phrase general education covers a lot of sins. "Indoctrination" would be a more fitting word for it. I am not against general education—I am for it provided that it is a general education without content.

Urban Without content?

Touraine Yes, I believe the whole process of transmitting content and values is fraudulent because it is (as I have just said) class conditioned. We have to abandon the notion that there are so many "great" books which everyone ought to read, or that we ought to put young people through certain courses of study so that they may imbibe what this or that

*See pp.1−17 above. The quotation is found on page 17.

committee believes to be the great traditions of human values or the great revelations of the human spirit.

We need an entirely different concept of general education: a training of the critical mind so that it can look behind the phenomena and arrive at the truth. Content, for this approach, is not only unnecessary but positively inhibiting. Mathematics is a good example of acquiring a searching, critical faculty without content. Sociology is another, in the sense that it imparts a technique for uncovering the true connections of things behind language, ideology, social relations, and so on. These are the proper "languages" of a general education precisely because they do not burden you with the retention of information but concentrate exclusively on the one ultimate goal of education: the capacity to create freedom and oppose power. And that is *par excellence* the role of the university in our time.

Urban You realize that this rather eviscerated concept of a general education hasn't many followers. The idea that mathematics and sociology should become the *linguae francae* of the critical mind strikes me as extremely open to criticism. It was Lord James, again, who described mathematics as an "ancillary skill." "You must have some mathematics," he said, "if you are a chemist or an economist, but that is not part of education—it is a skill like riding a bicycle."* Coming from an eminent scientist, these words carry a good deal of authority.

Touraine Not with me. What I am saying is that, once we have disposed of the business of vocational training, we should understand the characteristics of the mind as it operates in those two main areas that concern us, science and politics. The grid for understanding the first is provided by the mathematical type of analysis; the grid for politics is provided by the methods of sociology. The first equips us with the tools for understanding how scientists reason and arrive at their conclusions; the second provides a tool for understanding the structure of society.

*See p. 13 above.

Urban   Your two intellectual skeletons would still have to be filled in with something concrete. Whether you call it content or give it some other name does not strike me as being too important.

Touraine   But it is. Content is the creation of social conditions and power relationships. Knowledge is not, and it is vital that the two should not be confused.

Urban   I suspect you object to the kind of broad commitment to the heritage of the past which Lord James talks about simply because you are opposed to liberal values. You do not want to take anything from the past unless it has been sieved and analyzed by the special tools of sociology.

Touraine   Yes and no. The problem is that in a liberal type of general education we are asked to take facts and laws and documents on trust, whereas we know perfectly well that a "fact" may be a case of special pleading, "documents" may be deceptive, and so on. It isn't a question of Right or Left. It is a question of right or wrong. If you accept the picture of a society as it is given to you in general education, you are most probably buying a bias, and if you are conscious of buying that bias because you are a conservative or a liberal, that is O.K.— you have made a political decision in favor of a conservative or liberal society. What I cannot tolerate is the naive acceptance of the social order as natural, as given, because it impedes analysis. The "spirit" of an age and other vague descriptions of that kind are totally meaningless.

Urban   Well, whether we regard general education as reactionary propaganda or the acquisition of tools for a critical understanding of science and society, it is certainly true that a university education, as it is conducted in most countries outside the United States, is itself creating social divisions in the sense that it creams off the best brains and is a stepping stone to a meritocracy. No one seems to quarrel with the idea that the university fosters an intellectual elite and that scholastic achievement at the secondary school should alone qualify for university admission. But the reverse side of this state of affairs is that the vast majority of the population, who haven't the opportunity, because they haven't the brainpower, to go to university, are now permanently branded as inferior and are confined to looking after all those soul-destroying, repetitive, and dirty jobs without which society would cease to function. What I am saying is that by tying social ascent to intellectual merit alone we are creating a proletariat of the intellectually second-rate from which there is no escape. Michael Young discusses this possibility with great wit in his satire *The Rise of the Meritocracy*. He warns that we must not ignore the casualties of progress: "The danger that has settled in upon us . . . is that the clamoring throng who find the gates of higher education barred against them may turn against the social order by which they feel themselves condemned." And although Young, writing in 1958, was projecting himself to the year 2034, it is already true that the vast majority of our population is marked second-rate or stupid. They are condemned to the assembly line because they did not measure up to some arbitrary test of ability at the age of sixteen or eleven—an indignity every bit as serious as racial discrimination, which in a sense it is.

Touraine I cannot see this as being a major problem at the moment, although it may become one in time. What is generally wrong with the present system is that a small, highly educated section of society is privileged, whereas the large mass is underprivileged. If unskilled men doing tedious jobs had the same pay structure as physicists, the problem would not arise.

When the student movement tried to make common cause with the workers in 1968, their intention was to fight for the emancipation of people at the lower ends of the pay scale and social status. But they did not think this could be achieved by sending everyone to university. Nor is Michael Young right in predicting that those debarred from a university education may turn against the social order. They may, but not because they find the gates of higher education barred against them. This is an intellectual delusion. They would want more money, recognition, and social justice.

Urban But surely it is, or soon will be, true to say that the *felt* social differences between those at the top and those at the bottom are greater today than they were a hundred years ago. In the nineteenth century, educational injustice enabled people at the bottom to harbor the illusion that they were, in reality, as good as or better than those placed above them. "Inequality of opportunity," Young says, "fostered the myth of human equality." Today a man in a humble job knows that he is there because he is of low caliber. He knows (I'm still summarizing Young) that he has been tested again and again and labeled second-rate. He realizes that he has an inferior status not because, as in the past, he has been denied opportunity, but because he *is* inferior. And so he will lose all self-respect and vitality and present contemporary psychology with a very grave problem.

Touraine I would not quarrel with this analysis if I were persuaded that the way to power—and that is always what we are ultimately talking about—led through intelligence, education, and competence. It is true that bright people have, generally speaking, a better chance to be high flyers than dull ones, but there is no evidence that they are more likely to become our rulers than people possessing a different set of qualities such as political ambition and the ability to rule. Supposedly egalitarian Russia has talent scouts and even special schools for the most gifted, yet that is not the way in which members of the Politburo are recruited. Nor is it the way in which establishments are made in the Western countries.

As to dull and dirty work: In Western Europe the urgency of this problem is alleviated by the fact that a very large number of these unpleasant jobs are being held down by labor imported from Southern Europe.

Far be it for me to offer this as an excuse for our social system or as approval of the social policies of the Southern European countries, but foreign labor is an important fact which will go on influencing our situation and will probably prevent the hypothetical problem you have sketched out from becoming a reality for a very long time—assuming, that is, that full employment continues and our social system does not undergo major change. If it does undergo radical change, my hope is that in a truly reformed society the dirty, boring, and inhuman types of work will be allocated to different sections of society on a just, rota basis. After all, most of us have spent a year or two in the armed forces doing jobs we intensely disliked. As long as one knows that the sentence is not for life, the chores are bearable.

Where I differ from you fundamentally is in your apparent conception of meritocracy as a mere intellectual elite. The sociological meaning of meritocracy goes far beyond the recruitment of competent people for sophisticated jobs. Meritocracy is about power and authority. In political terms it is about the power of large, anonymous organizations to manipulate you. It is about monopolistic power which has to be understood and fought.

Max Beloff

Can the University
Be Conceived
as a Model of Democracy?

Max Beloff was, when this dialogue was recorded, Gladstone
Professor of Government and Public Administration at the
University of Oxford and a Fellow of All Souls College. He is
now Principal of a new British independent institute of higher
education, the University College at Buckingham. His many
publications include *The Foreign Policy of Soviet Russia: 1929-
1941; Soviet Policy in the Far East, 1944-51; The Age of Abso-
lutism, 1660-1815; The United States and the Unity of Europe;
Imperial Sunset* (volume I); and *The Intellectual in Politics*.

Urban A recent report sponsored by the Carnegie Foundation says that the modern university ought to be fulfilling four
functions. Two of these are the traditional ones of teaching and

research, the third is public-service work, and the fourth is to present a model of an ideal democratic community. Do you see the third and fourth of these functions as something the university could be reasonably expected to perform?

Beloff There was a justification at an earlier stage for universities to take upon themselves public-service functions, because universities were the preserve of a fairly narrow section of society preparing the sons and daughters of this rather privileged class for a limited number of future occupations, and if there was to be a broadening of educational horizons at the adult stage beyond the walls of the university, it had to come, at least in great part, from the university. This is now a less and less tenable function of the university, because extension work appears to be drawing into its scope virtually the whole of the population; therefore the demands made upon the universities are increasingly distant from, and are in fact alien to, the kind of subject matters and the kind of approaches which it is suitable for the university to pursue. The teaching of new skills, refresher courses in the use of improved fertilizers, etc., may be necessary activities, but to undertake them within the walls of the university would mean changing the form of the universities as we know them. In a limited way functions of this kind assist universities. For example, it is quite useful for a young university teacher occasionally to be confronted with an audience or seminar other than a group around the age of twenty, to be talking to trade unionists or soldiers or whatever. But limits are set to the value of this by the nature and the number of extramural courses a university can undertake without diluting its character as a place of disinterested inquiry, and without playing havoc with the staff-student ratio. My view would be that the future ought to see the scope of university work diminishing, not expanding, and that the extramural functions ought to be entrusted to other institutions such as the Open University in Britain,* which is quite different from the traditional university in the sense that it has neither

*A new form of British higher education, conducted mainly by correspondence combined with special radio and television programs. See pp. 5-6 above.

face-to-face teaching nor research functions. It is the poly-
technics and other colleges of higher education that should
cater for extension work as, in fact, in very many cases they
already do.

On your fourth point—the university conceived as a model
of a democratic community—I feel that the Carnegie Report
got hold of completely the wrong end of the stick. Whatever
one's views about the democratic organization of society (and
we are not discussing our social or political views), and even
supposing that one fervently believes in democracy somehow
defined as furnishing the ideal institutional framework for a
just polity, it would still be totally inappropriate to the university. The university is a community which is necessarily hierarchical because the functions which it performs are performed
at different levels according to different ranges of qualification
and experience; and although it may have democratic elements in it—in this country the universities of Oxford and
Cambridge are ultimately governed by an assembly, at least
notionally, of the entire permanent teaching staff—there can
be basically no similarity between the responsibilities of a
professor, a junior teacher, a graduate student, an undergraduate, a laboratory assistant, and so on. The correct analogy is
not with society but with other hierarchically organized communities—an ocean liner, for example, in which no one suggests that any decision should be made by an assembly of all
those aboard; in which, indeed, the captain is given very
specific responsibilities which few people on land have. The
same thing applies to an aircraft—no one suggests that the
passengers take part in flying it. And the same would apply in a
hospital—no one would suggest that a democracy of the wards
is feasible if people are to be cured. The university conceived
as a model of democracy is outright rubbish.

Urban Whether or not we agree with the fourth point of the
Carnegie Report, it is nevertheless a fact that the report would
not have incorporated it had there not been wide agreement in
the United States that putting up a democratic model is precisely what the universities ought to do. I am not disputing the
rights and wrongs of the proposition; I'm only stressing the

popularity, and therefore the sociological significance, of the fact that it has been put forward by an influential money-dispensing organization.

Beloff The fact that a large number of people believe something which is not true, is not evidence for its truth. Most people before Galileo believed that the sun went around the earth; it didn't. A lot of people in America made entirely the wrong diagnosis from the university troubles of 1968-70. The American universities have undergone an enormous expansion in the last decade which brought with it an intake of large numbers of young people who were unfitted for university study. It was discovered that this made them unhappy and discontented, but instead of saying that we must either devise institutions in which they will find their intellectual needs better met, or admit that we have overexpanded and that the universities cannot exist on this scale, the American universities are now imposing upon themselves duties which they can only perform at the price of sacrificing their original functions. And the result of treating universities as democratic assemblies, or models for some future utopian society, is the steady lowering of the standards of university teaching and research. This will not show itself immediately, but already there are voices from America and from the continent of Europe that say: Well, probably the university is finished; we cannot recover it and we will have to build research institutions and specialized schools or the next generation will have no one capable of solving the problems of health, the environment, etc. One cannot combine research, scholarship, disciplined learning with the kind of machinery and attitude which are appropriate in quite different fields of human activity. I am quite unimpressed by the fact that American educational experts believe that the university ought to provide society with a democratic paradigm. They are, in any case, very prone to go along with whatever is the fashionable theory at the moment.

At one time they were all in favor of the Dewey method in education, and nobody was allowed to acquire formalized learning. They are now repenting that and putting grammar and formal mathematics back into the schools. The fashions are volatile. The trouble with democracies like the United States is that, through the mass media, foolish ideas get circulated extremely rapidly.

Urban   There is nevertheless a very noticeable trend in Western Europe to emulate the public-service activities of the American university. There is a feeling that the university as a recipient of large public funds ought to validate its existence in ways that are and can be seen to be relevant to the daily concerns of the community. There are moves afoot to coordinate the public-service activities of the EEC universities, and there are already isolated cases of knowledge being taken from the universities directly to the shop floors—admittedly with left-wing political motivation—as, for example, at some Italian universities.

Beloff   If it is merely a matter of a label—if there is a building down the road from the university which calls itself part of the university and goes in for these activities, many of which are obviously useful and ought to be done by someone—this does not matter. But if it means that scholars are going to spend even more time than they do at present in organizational activities, in public appearances at the expense of their pupils and subjects, then I continue to maintain that this is wholly bad. After all, no one suggested thirty or fifty years ago that university professors or university students—the good ones—had a great deal of surplus time on their hands; it was usually considered that students had to work very hard in order to attain the qualifications for their future careers, and that professors had to spend a lot of time teaching them and doing their research in order to keep up to the frontiers of their subject. As it is, we spend more and more of our time, in all universities in all countries, on purely administrative matters which do not contribute to learning or teaching. It is reckoned in a recent book that the average British vice-chancellor*—and Britain is not as bureaucratized as some countries—spends at

*In Britain, the vice-chancellor is the actual head of the university.

least a third of his time in contact with government departments, with outside bodies, sitting on committees, or flying to Brussels or Strasbourg. All this is at the expense of his primary function. And the reason that students are discontented is that their teachers are not with them, or if they are with them in the flesh, they are not with them in the spirit, because they are busy consulting the timetable for the next plane to Brussels. The model for restoring learning to universities is a ban on air travel.

Urban You were saying that, in view of what happened at the mass universities in America, we should devise institutions for those who are intellectually unfitted to benefit from a university education, but whose aspirations would nevertheless have to be met. Now this is, formally at least, a step toward the democratization of higher education, for it would mean giving a lot of secondary school graduates a chance to attain an educational standard which would otherwise be outside their reach. Could these "junior college" years be turned into an education in democracy in the substance too, seeing that these new institutions would not be inheriting the hierarchical traditions of the university?

Beloff No. In fact the younger the students, the less broad their horizons and the less capable they are of making any useful decisions about the activities in which they are engaged. Education is hierarchical, however you look at it, but, of course, you would expect more and more decisions to be made by individuals as they grow in maturity. The kindergarten child must be watched all the time because otherwise he may set the place on fire or flood it by turning on a tap. By the primary school stage you expect a certain amount of self-discipline and allow the child some autonomy; you allow more of this at the secondary stage and still more at the undergraduate level. You would expect a student reading for his doctorate to be very much master of his own time, but even he can contribute only marginally as far as the appropriate organization of studies, the appropriate kind of teaching appointments, or the further development of a particular branch of research are concerned. The people who argue for the democratization of education simply ignore what they would demand in any other circumstances. They would (as I've already remarked) not expect it in a hospital and say "Whether my appendix is to come out or not is to be decided by an assembly of everyone, including the hospital porters."

Urban Nevertheless the expectation that democratization has to come and will come is real. The hierarchical structures of an ocean liner or a hospital may well be valid analogies, but I cannot see that any amount of rational exposition will make the demand for democratic participation go away.

Beloff But our experience is that it is not a genuine demand. We can learn here from the history of labor-management relations. Industrial strikes usually revolve round a set of demands that the workers make in a particular situation. One may or may not be able to meet them, but it is a common experience that the demands the workers make are not always related to the genuine cause of their discontent—they may be simply a way of rationalizing it: "If we had one pound more a week we should be happy," whereas what they really want may be a different attitude on the part of management, a different organization of the working day, or the like. Good firms realize this and, by getting at the real problems, they appear to be producing greater satisfaction.

By the same token I believe that student discontent is genuine enough, and until the causes are found and remedied it will probably continue. However, the demand for participation seems to me to be a rationalization, because when in fact you grant it, as we have to a large extent granted it in my own former university (in Oxford there are student representatives at almost every level), the students are not interested in participation and do not attend the various committees to which they have been admitted, or if they come they are bored by three-quarters of the business and behave accordingly. It is clear in retrospect that participation was a slogan. The students wanted to establish a right, and having established it they are not interested in making use of it. So we have to find the real causes of the malaise and remedy those.

In any case, the good students—the people on whom one relies for one's future scientists or doctors or administrators, the people, that is, who form the essential cadres of an advanced society—do not take part in any of this. First-rate students, unless psychologically disturbed, are never involved in student politics. I would make that as an absolute assertion on the basis of having been a university teacher for almost forty years.

Urban The view I have heard most frequently expressed by university teachers was that the brightest students were the ones leading the rebellion.

Beloff It depends how you define bright. If you mean that they show up well on some IQ test, I'm prepared to believe it. But a good student for me is someone who has the discipline to settle down in a library and read a difficult text in Latin or Greek, or follow a difficult argument in mathematical logic or in biology, or whatever his field of work may be. He must have real motivation for study and above all a capacity for self-discipline. You will find that a student of that sort will not take part in student politics.

Urban You said a little while ago that student demands were rationalizations of the real causes of discontent, but you did not say what those causes were, apart from the one you had mentioned earlier: the physical or spiritual absence of the teaching staff, which may well be the heart of the trouble.

Beloff Students coming to the university—as most of them do—at the vulnerable age of eighteen or nineteen expect a fair degree of recognition as personalities, a fair degree of intimate contact with the people who are responsible for them and with whom they are supposed to work. When the universities expanded, not much thought was given to this problem, and this has brought about a situation in which eighteen-year-olds find themselves in the hands of large, impersonal forces with which they are psychologically unsuited to cope. I have had this put to me over and over again, and I believe the complaint is legitimate—the universities are at fault. I have to come back to the point I made earlier because it is important and does bear repeating: University teachers spend too much time on external activities and too little with their students. If teachers were more accessible, if one could walk into a teacher's room at any time of the day (I have always made this a principle myself), I think you would not get discontent. It is being treated as cogs in a machine they do not understand that is worrying the students.

The only time I have been treated like that was as a private soldier in the army—and I began to feel rebellious. But at least I knew what I was doing in the army: We were fighting Hitler's Germany. The students are not only being treated impersonally, but a great many of them do not know what they are doing at the university—how being at the university fits into their lives. I roughly knew how the army fitted into mine.

Urban You are saying that student discontent is an educational matter, yet there is a good deal of evidence to suggest that it goes beyond the inaccessibility of teachers, the depersonalization of the individual, and so on. Students are said to be protesting against the state of modern society: against its aimlessness, its brutality, its vulgarity, and all the other vices they tend to associate with the lifestyle of the bourgeoisie. Now these two protests may well go together, the challenge to the university being only the tip of the iceberg. You may well be rising against your condition as a cog in the university-machine because you know that in real life you would be a cog in something even much larger and much more difficult to protest against.

Beloff This may be true in the United States; I think it is less true in Western Europe, and I do not believe it to be substantially true in Britain. In some cases student leaders like to identify themselves with what they believe are the grievances of other sections of society. But this is artificial and is usually regarded as artificial by the supposed beneficiaries of the identification. There is very little evidence—and this is, by now, familiar ground—that workers in the mass-production factories, who have their own grounds for feeling alienated, regard the students' intervention in their affairs as in the least logical. They see no connection; they regard the identification as wholly artificial.

Urban Whether one thinks of Berlin, Paris, or New York, the workers' reaction was uniformly negative.

Beloff Now let us take a period when there was, perfectly rightly, a very considerable concern at the universities with society at large. When I was a student, forty years ago, there was mass unemployment and there was a good deal of feeling about that. A certain amount of political and social action was undertaken but none of the students who took part in it thought that their various activities had anything to do with universities. In the universities they did their work, they read their books, and in their spare time they might organize kitchens for the hunger-marchers on London, but they didn't in the least think that they could relieve their social conscience by challenging the university. Nor did their teachers. A man like Tawney, who was a great exponent of egalitarianism and social justice, would never have expected his students to pull down the London School of Economics because they disliked the state of society and wanted to do something about it.

Urban But doesn't the recent student pressure on the universities pay a backhanded compliment to Cardinal Newman's liberal idea of the university in the sense that the student rebels see in the university a means for setting the intellectual and moral tone of society, for cultivating the public mind, etc.? For if you think you can do these things through the university, you are in fact assuming that the university has come through the trials and corruptions of society relatively unscathed; you are saying that, with all its faults, the university is capable of rescuing society from some of its vices by pitting itself as a model against society. Therefore, when you attack it for its shortcomings, you are really investing in it morally and intellectually.

Beloff The university has a responsibility to society to be as good as it can. So has industry, so has commerce, so—in an unfortunate world—have the armed forces. One expects each human grouping to do what it can. At different times, different sectors of society come under particular strains, and you have a breakdown or a near breakdown. You cannot provide employment or housing, or you have malnutrition—you have problem after problem. But the idea that society is totally corrupt is preposterous. There have always been thinkers on the margins of society who believed this, and probably it is desirable that there should always be thinkers who have that view in order to prevent people from getting complacent. But very few people would want a world which was run on the principles of a Rousseau, least of all those young men and women who claim to follow his views on the corruption of society. For Rousseau is prescribing one of the most totalitarian societies anyone has imagined, including the death penalty as a sanction against wrong beliefs. The trouble is that students used to read Rousseau—now they merely repeat slogans derived from something they think Rousseau said. This, incidentally, is the difference between a good and a bad student.

Urban   We have now taken a brief look at the pros and cons of entrusting the European university with extramural functions similar to those performed by the large state universities in the United States. You expressed the view that the university should, if anything, diminish rather than expand the scope of its activities. Unless, you said, expansion could be inhibited, the university would stand to lose its character and would fail to perform its proper functions.

I am now assuming that, under public pressure, the European university will, nevertheless, increasingly cater for "recurrent" education or "permanent" education. The question then arises: What disciplines and what kind of people should and are most likely to benefit?

Beloff   Some disciplines change more rapidly than others. What may be appropriate for some branches of medicine may be unnecessary for some branches of law, and vice versa. You have to judge the need of going back to the university in terms of the knowledge and techniques which are now available in your subject but were not available when you left the university.

Can the University Be Conceived as a Model of Democracy?   163

Urban Isn't there also a rather recently recognized need for men who have spent a large number of years in the same job to be sent on refresher courses so that they can recharge their batteries and broaden their horizons?

Beloff This is very desirable if only because twenty or thirty years of routine tend to make people run down on their intellectual and moral equipment. People gain enormously by having a year (if it can be afforded away from their occupations) spent on something perhaps tangential to their main interests. In Britain the Foreign Office, the home civil service, and the armed forces send people off for a year now on sabbatical leave to universities. Their work there is not expected to make them better diplomats or administrators in any practical sense, but it is thought to jolt them out of routine, acquaint them with fresh points of view, and generally rejuvenate their thinking. For this kind of continuing education the university is, of course, the appropriate place, because the men and women who are given a sabbatical year want to be in touch with people who teach at the frontiers of knowledge, and they are in the universities.

The danger seems to be that if you had too many of these mature students, you might increase the size of the universities, with the resulting disadvantages we have already discussed. Personally I would be prepared to cut down the number of "initial" students to provide places for those returning, rather than concede something that would make the universities bigger than they are already.

Urban Wouldn't this rather drastically change the age composition, and with it the character, of the university?

Beloff It would, and I think to everyone's advantage; for apart from the mature student benefiting from the experience, the university would also reap important psychological benefits. A mixture of more mature students would prevent the conglomeration of what the Americans call peer groups, that is, of very large numbers of people almost exactly the same age, and no one else. This is an artificial human situation that does not exist except in higher education—people otherwise live in families where there is a spread of age groups. I am sure we would have a healthier community at the universities as a result of mixing older students with young ones.

Urban You would not want this infusion of older blood merely to make the universities less rebellion-prone than they have been lately?

Beloff I think it might have this effect; but it is not my primary reason.

Urban One of the most keenly discussed educational problems in Western Europe is what the Germans call *der zweite Bildungsweg*—giving a second option to those who were either not seeking admission or were for some reason denied admission to the university at the "normal" age of entry, that is, between eighteen and twenty. It is widely felt that a late developer, or anyone who has had second thoughts at the age of thirty or forty, should be given a chance to acquire a university type of education—qualifications and knowledge that give him satisfaction and make him more useful to society. How would these people fit into the structure of higher education, or shall I say, more cautiously, post-secondary education?

Beloff It would depend on the circumstances. If we are talking of people without any initial formal training in a particular discipline coming along later in life because they have been excited by the possibility of acquiring knowledge, then you want a separate institution for them like the Open University, which has no formal requirements for admission. But if it is the case of someone who left school for one reason or another, has gone into employment, feels that he would have a more satisfactory life if he had further qualifications which would entitle him to a more interesting and more specialized form of employment, and if this implies university study, then obviously he ought to have a claim on a university place. What one would then have to find out were the obstacles, if any, to his being able to make full use of a university's facilities because of his lack of preparation, of prior schooling, of the basic skills which are required. Perhaps one would therefore need some preliminary training to get him to the level at which the university would be profitable for him. There is certainly nothing divinely ordained that would require that university students should arrive between the ages of eighteen and twenty. On the contrary, I think, as I have just said, this is one of the weaknesses of our system.

Urban The Robbins Report* makes the point that over the previous ten years more than a million adults had qualified for university entry but were refused admission. One answer to the frustrations building up in society as a result would be to make university entry possible at any age. This has been suggested by educational writers but it is very difficult to see how it might be put into practice. The present tendency is still to concentrate attention on expanding fulltime post-secondary education end-on to school. Also, with earlier retirement and more leisure, there is bound to arise a demand for higher education by age groups older than any we have yet seen. Perhaps Ralf Dahrendorf is right in claiming that education is a "civil right"—perhaps study, even though it may be just therapeutic study, ought to be made available to senior citizens as well as young ones.

Beloff There are two problems here, one practical, one intellectual. The financial provision which the state makes is hardly geared to people of that kind; it is almost entirely intended for and geared to the needs of secondary school graduates. If you take a man of forty-five—he has a family, he has responsibilities. One would have to see how these could be met. The provision of higher education for middle-aged people would certainly be a serious problem which has not been tackled on any large scale.

The brunt of the intellectual problem is that a mature man may have inadequate preparation for embarking on a univer-

*Controversial British report on higher education published in 1963.

sity course. However, that seems to me to be an institutional question, and I am certain an answer could be devised if one had the money and the facilities for doing so. The problem is analogous to the situation where certain groups within the population are underprivileged because of race or social background. Experiments are being made in various countries to help these people to catch up by giving them a specialized preuniversity education. There is no reason in principle why older age groups in our own society should not be given similar facilities.

The real danger comes from a different direction. You do not want people at universities who are unhappy on another count, for some of the older students may well find that they cannot keep up with the younger ones, and therefore instead of becoming a refreshing experience, university study may become a further blow to their self-esteem. But, by and large, all these questions are soluble. They boil down to one: How do you allocate your resources?

Urban Continuing education, recurrent education, refresher courses leave me with an uneasy feeling that the university is on the verge of becoming a factory, with *neophiliacs* occupying all the commanding heights in the hierarchy. I accept the view that technological change and change in the state of knowledge are now so rapid that, to keep up with them, one's professional identity may have to be altered every fifteen years or so. I can quite see that the recurrent type of education is very relevant to the needs of the knowledge-based professions—medicine, the law, etc. Nevertheless, one also likes to think of the university as a seat of high culture with a body of knowledge that spreads around it certain moral values that are peculiar to the university: respect for study, self-knowledge, humility, and so on. This aspect of the university would emphasize the permanent features of human achievement, the steady beat of the human pulse rather than its arrests and palpitations. There is a sense in which the university is not only the creator but also the conservator of knowledge, and the more rapid the pace of activity on the frontiers of knowledge, the more important it would seem to me to underline the role of the university as a storehouse of wisdom. If the university is (as it is) responsible for the acceleration of change, and if it has landed us all in a state of "future shock," should it not also make us more shock-resistant than we are?

Beloff   There must always be a mixture; the intelligent reading of the great writers of the past—creative and speculative—must always be a central function of university education. However, with the spread of studies, even these are undergoing often fundamental change. Classical studies, for instance, which were the staple of higher education for centuries, and seemed to be well set for a long time, have been revolutionalized by new developments in archeology. The whole method of approach to Roman history is different from what it was sixty or seventy years ago. Prehistory is also being revolutionized, partly by the application of new techniques that make the dating of deposits and archeological artifacts much more precise than we could make them with the knowledge that was available twenty or thirty years ago. It may be that in purely speculative philosophy and in literature this is not so, but even in literary criticism scholars shift their ground as they become aware of new facts in the mental or physical horizons of their writers. So I don't think we can speak of inherently static and inherently dynamic subjects. All subjects are dynamic but some are better pursued over a lifetime, while others can be pursued intermittently, in the course of practice.

Urban   What then are the real reasons for the view—widespread and I think justified—that the university has a quality of permanent excellence about it, not only in the sense that it is old as an institution and that it speaks to us with authority from a platform we respect, but also in the sense that it possesses some overriding virtue which other institutions in modern society do not possess? I am trying to put my finger on the charisma of the university, on the justification or otherwise of the academic's boast: "*Extra universitatem non est salus*"—that outside the university there may be intellectually good works, but no real salvation. Perhaps it is a subtle hangover from the ancient superstition that raised medicine men and rainmakers to the status of priests and kings.

Beloff Different people would define this factor in different ways. Most people would say that this quality exists and ought to exist, otherwise the university would not be a university but a mere combination of technological institutes. My own view is that when you try to define this quality you come up against some really simple notions—simple in theory, difficult in practice—and the first of them comes back to the earlier part of our discussion.

The basic obligation on someone in a university is to follow argument where it leads, to accept evidence for what it is worth, and to be utterly indifferent to fashion, to popularity, to what at the moment the market holds dear. Not accepting the view that truth is decided by the counting of heads—that is the aristocratic element in a university. However unattainable it may be, truth is something you follow by pursuing certain techniques and disciplines, and when you think you have found it, you say it.

In the past, in the world of learning both outside and inside the universities, the great disputes occurred when such discoveries ran up against accepted teaching. In the seventeenth century, for instance, the physical sciences came up against the church's interpretation of classical astronomy; in the nineteenth century the biological sciences ran up against the doctrine of instant creation, there was the great debate over evolution, and so forth. In the twentieth century I don't think we have much to fear from entrenched ecclesiastical dogmas. What we have to guard against are popular dogmas like egalitarianism—some notions of society that deny the differences between human beings, that forbid people to investigate genetics, which is held to be a dangerous subject because it may prove that some people, or some groups of people, are more intelligent than others. This is something that, if you discover it, it is improper to reveal. No one would terribly mind if you proved that in the animal kingdom some animal groups run faster than others—that antelopes are more agile than hippopotami—but if you say that you ought at least to be able to try to discover whether some groups of human beings may be more intelligent, more musical, more artistic, or whatever, than other groups, then this is considered dangerous because it has possible implications. It is not the business of universities to discuss possible implications of the truth. The business of the universities is to find the truth and to teach it.

Urban I'm reminded of the Oxford high-table toast: "To higher mathematics, may it never be of any use to anyone!"

Beloff It is not quite that, because a great deal of what universities teach is useful either directly, as in the case of medicine, or indirectly, as in the study of the classics, which on the whole makes people more intelligent in dealing with human situations, or arguably so. There is very little in university education that is not relevant to some aspect or other of human activity. What I am concerned with is that the scholar should not get mixed up with deciding the degree of relevance of what he is doing. The degree of relevance, the likely effect of research, are appropriate decisions for society to take (society may say, "We will not spend any money on this or that type of research"), but it is not the business of a scholar, having discovered something, to suppress it. And it is very dangerous for society to demand that he should.

Urban This independence and integrity of the scholar which you advocate is mocked by Communist ideologists as, at best, a bourgeois delusion. Perhaps we might take a brief look at the university structure in Eastern Europe to see whether the delusions are all on one side; and this will lead us on to the more general question whether the East European/Soviet model of university education is coming closer to or still diverging from the West European model. One feature that is, superficially at least, common to both is state control.

Beloff There is, if anything, a very slow convergence in some areas of study. The Soviet scene is particularly difficult to compare, as one has found in such limited contacts as Soviet scholars have been allowed. The basic element in interuniversity contacts is in the research field, and this has been made difficult by the fact that most Soviet research is done at the academies, whereas the universities are much more teaching institutions, concentrating on the production of graduates. The ambition of a Soviet man of learning is not to be at the university at all but to be in an academy. (This has roots even in prerevolutionary Russia, where the eighteenth-century tradition of the academy persisted rather longer than in the West.)

Eastern Europe, of course, is another matter. Prague has one of the oldest universities in Europe and is one of the seminal sources of our whole university tradition. In the nineteenth century other East European centers were influenced by German and French models. I don't think it is the degree of state control that differentiates the East European universities from the ones in Western Europe—universities all over the world (with the partial exception of the United States) are state controlled, if only in the sense that they are state financed.

The difference in Eastern Europe is that universities are servants of a particular ideology, a particular set of social and political beliefs that affect different fields of study in different ways. The ideological influence is not very important in the exact sciences, but it is pretty disastrous in certain fields of social science and in the humanities. As long as this is the case, dialogue is difficult. One notes this at international congresses—an international physicists' conference with Russian participation can lead to a meaningful dialogue, but when one meets Soviet historians or philosophers, the limitation on their ability to follow an argument, because it must not lead in certain directions, is so great as to make one wonder whether the whole enterprise is worthwhile.

My impression is that in the last few years there has certainly been a greater degree of freedom to make personal contacts and that there are coming to be a number of areas in which scholarship on a fairly good level is possible in these countries. Of course, they tend to be areas a little remote from anything that has an immediate application or even a tacit relevance to present political and social conditions.

Urban What sort of conditions would you like to see fulfilled for the dialogue to become meaningful in the whole area of interuniversity contacts?

Beloff As long as there are any limitations on the freedom of scholarship and scholars in Eastern Europe, the East European universities and academies are not full members of the world-wide academic community. The essential feature about universities—and this goes back to medieval tradition, when it was facilitated by a common language, Latin—is the mobility of the scholar. Any limitation on his freedom to move where he likes and when he likes, and ultimately any limitation on the mobility of the student, is a limitation on the idea of the university. It must be one of the hopes of the academic community to bring these East European and Soviet universities back into the general circuit of learning. It should be as simple a matter for a Prague scholar to spend a year studying in Oxford as it is for an Oxford scholar to go and spend a year in Paris or at Harvard.

Urban Governments hold the purse strings of university education both in the East and in the West. Governments also prescribe planning targets which embrace the intake of students, the subjects taught, and even curricula. In the Soviet Union and in Eastern Europe, it has long been accepted that universities and various specialized institutes satisfy the state's manpower requirements, and the government, in turn, holds out a prospect of secure jobs waiting for students at the end of their study. In Western Europe, brainpower planning through the universities is a relatively new phenomenon, and it is far from being universally accepted. Clearly, some of the needs of the community for qualified manpower must be, and have always been, taken into account and met, for example, in medicine and law. But is it, I wonder, consonant with the idea of the university that the university as a whole should become, as it were, a service industry, cooperating with government planners on a customer-contractor basis? For example, would it not be the case that gearing the university to the policy objectives of government would make for prescribed forms of "problem-solving" research to the detriment of "curiosity-oriented" research? Supposing the university goes along with the manpower-planning policies of government, can the planners' estimates of manpower requirements be accurate enough to prevent shortages and waste?

Beloff One would like manpower planning to be accurate, not for the sake of government, but for the sake of individuals, because of course it is very frustrating to come out of a university with a perfectly good degree and then to be told that this qualification is of no use, since there are no jobs available in the specialty and there are not going to be for a long time. The difficulty is that in Western Europe, and certainly in Britain, manpower-planning forecasts have invariably been wrong; that is to say, the planners haven't the ability to forecast either changes in technology or changes in social demand. There are notorious examples of this in all fields. For instance, an estimate of Britain's needs of medical manpower made just after the war only forecast half the number of medical personnel that the country currently requires. As a result, we have managed to maintain the numbers only by the importation of doctors from other countries. We simply underestimated the extent to which a more urbanized, more industrialized, more affluent society would make further and further demands on the medical profession. Some manpower guidance is probably inevitable, if only to make sure that we do not hurt the individual more than we need; but accurate planning is terribly difficult.

Another difficulty is that there may be differences between what students want to study and what the government tries to make them study on its assumption of where they are most likely to be profitably employed. This means that there would be qualified secondary school graduates who would either not be getting a higher education at all because their ability would not fit in with the state's manpower requirements, or would be educated in a field that does not coincide with their natural potential. This again is something to be deplored.

You may have other kinds of policy controls, too. Governments may decide that some kinds of training are more expensive than others, and if their major objective is to have as many young people as possible in universities, then higher education must be in what might be called the cheaper subjects.

I do not think there is a final answer. Universities have, to some extent, always been vocational. In the Middle Ages they turned out priests and lawyers, because these were the only two professions for which society had any demand.

Urban How do you see the general-education component in the balance of university studies?

Beloff There is a very important argument for a fairly broad undergraduate degree. You have to give students enough knowledge of general educational value in the course of their studies for a first degree so that, even if the subject which has principally occupied them turns out not to be the basis of their future career, they will have something of value that will remain with them. It seems to me much worse to be someone who has spent years studying dentistry and then finds that there are no more teeth left to fill, than to be someone who has spent years studying Shakespeare and then finds that there is no room for a drama critic. Shakespeare will be with him whatever he does, whereas if you cannot practice dentistry your studies have been utterly wasted. It is very important to give the student something he can hold on to, something he can derive satisfaction from, irrespective of his actual vocation.

The difficulty is that there are certain professional subjects, like medicine, where you have to make an early and pretty unalterable decision whether or not you want to invest your energies, owing to the length of time required to qualify before you can practice. There are other subjects of equal educational value and giving equal satisfaction which can be studied in much less time. It is for society to decide what it can afford and what sort of studies it wants to further, not only in terms of facilities and actual expenditure on education, but also in terms of how much of people's lives a particular society thinks can be reasonably devoted to self-improvement rather than production. Because the East European governments have the kind of economic planning they have, and because they have greater powers of coercion at hand than any Western government, they can decide on certain manpower targets and require the universities to fulfill them. Not only that, but they will also know how to employ qualified manpower, even if unprofitably—even if much more could be got out of the population by redeploying it. But this is one of the penalties of having a planned economy. In Western societies, which on the whole preserve a certain flexibility in their economic growth and social pattern so that they can respond to changes in technology, the miscalculations are likely to be smaller.

Urban You said the general-education component in the first degree course should equip the student with educational values and inner resources for the rest of his life. I wonder how much this kind of education really helps him to come to terms with himself and society. My experience in America has certainly been that it is leading to frustrations, that it leaves the graduate hanging in the air both because his training is not vocationally directed and because he has increased cultural expectations which he cannot easily satisfy.

Beloff America is most unlike Europe in this respect. You have a different attitude toward culture in America, a different attitude toward the achievements of the past, a different social atmosphere which makes people feel that if they cannot professionally use their university training, then it is useless and even burdensome. This has not been the view in Europe. There have always been classes in Europe who have known perfectly well that the knowledge they were acquiring would not be of any direct consequence to them. It was simply something they knew they had to acquire for the benefit of the innermost recesses of their being, as a source of strength. There is a different cultural pattern in Europe which is consistent with Europe's being a long-settled civilization, while America is still affected by a moving frontier. This is one of the examples of the immense gulf which, despite external similarities, still exists between America and Europe.

Urban I'm not sure whether the frustrations of a general education *are* limited to America. Sir Alan Bullock (Vice-Chancellor of Oxford University) said at a recent educational seminar, "One essential of liberal education . . . is that it should raise in the students' minds questions to which no final answers exist." This is a very different conception from the general education you have referred to—it would perturb rather than satisfy, frustrate rather than provide a source of strength for all except the intellectually toughest or most cynical.

Beloff I would not have put it that way. I would have said a liberal education helps one to distinguish between those questions to which answers can be given and those to which (in the nature of man) they cannot, and to explain how people have arrived at the answers to those things to which answers can be given. The study of literature or music or philosophy may provide consolation for the answers that cannot be given, or make it possible to live with the lack of an answer. But it would be a very curious young man whose principal concerns were in questions that could not be answered.

Urban Is consolation, then, one of the aims of learning? Shortly before his death I asked György Lukács (at whose feet I once sat in Hungary) a similar question.* "The secret of life," he said, "is a . . . rational existence. . . . I need no consolation."

Beloff Lukács was speaking for himself. Learning can, and does, and should, offer consolation among other things. Life is imperfect, the world is imperfect. People need consoling in a broad sense. And those who have had the fortune to be at a university may derive consolation, as well as pleasure and satisfaction, from things which those who have not had this good fortune may derive from becoming excited about motor racing or football or whatever else it is that consoles them. In any but a perfect society consolation is surely part of what everyone needs. We need something that takes us out of the immediate problems and concerns of the material world. And the people who get most happiness are the people who, at some stage, have been brought up against the greatest of human achievements. This is what I was taught myself when I was young. I still believe it.

*Cf. "A Conversation with Lukács," *Encounter*, October 1971.

Jeanne Hersch

Jaspers, University Youth
and the Human Condition

Jeanne Hersch is Professor of Philosophy at the University of Geneva and a former Visiting Professor at Hunter College, New York, and Pennsylvania State University. Between 1966 and 1968 Professor Hersch was Head of the Division of Philosophy of UNESCO and between 1970 and 1972 Swiss Representative on the Council of UNESCO. She has been politically active in the European Federalist Movement. Her many publications include *L'Illusion philosophique; Une philosophie de l'existence: Karl Jaspers; L'Être et la forme; Idéologies et réalité.* She has translated several works of Karl Jaspers and of Czeslaw Milosz.

Urban I should like to start this discussion by inviting you to comment on some of Karl Jaspers's ideas about the contemporary university, and I am doing this for two reasons: first, because Jaspers's book *The Idea of the University* has become a formative influence in our time, and second because we are fortunate in having in you not only a former student and disciple of Jaspers, but also a Swiss philosopher of international distinction who takes a professional interest in the crisis of the university.

Can and should technology be assimilated as one of the main faculties of the university? This question is less naive than it sounds, for the West European university is still dominated by the study of the three "upper faculties": theology, jurisprudence, and medicine—all of which address themselves (as Jaspers remarked) to those areas of human life which have remained largely unchanged for many hundreds of years. Clearly, these upper faculties cannot cover the whole of modern existence.

Jaspers makes two points in this connection. He urges the universities to incorporate technology as an equal partner, for "it is technology that has now taken over the job of molding man's natural environment, of transforming human life even as it transforms nature," and he disapproves of the mushroom growth of institutes of higher education outside the universities, such as, for example, technological and agricultural colleges, because these, he suspects, can only lead to more specialization and to a loss of contact with the unifying and civilizing influence of the university. Indeed, he asks whether the establishment of these independent institutes does not violate the idea of the university; and he answers, albeit tentatively, that there may be some connection between the growing vacuity of modern life and the spread of these specialized schools.

Hersch Jaspers did not believe that any organizational reform could rescue man from the aimlessness and emptiness of modern life. The problem goes far beyond the question whether you have your institutes of technology inside or outside the university. Technology is a crucial field of our activity, and because it is so important we must find ways of relating it to the study of man's activities in their totality. It is too easy to assume that technology is merely a means that you have a right to despise, while wishing it at the same time to increase, without being able to understand what it is. Jaspers believed that everything that exists in the human condition deserves to be understood and is therefore a proper concern of the university. He thought it was false to live in a highly technologized society and to avoid studying the human consequences of creating and having a complex technology. I'm reminded of the differences between the puritan and humane conceptions of the human body—the first relegating the body to the brute and sinful forces of nature, the latter, however, taking body and mind as an integral whole and treating the body with the appropriate respect. On that analogy one might say technology is the "body" of modern society, which must be related to and understood as part and parcel of the human condition. What I would stress is not the question of teaching or not teaching technology at our universities—of course it has to be taught—but the importance of integrating technology and its multifarious influences on man and society into the mainstream activities of the university.

But one need not go outside the traditional concerns of the university to find cracks in the unity of the university. Even jurisprudence, theology, and medicine have lost their university character to the extent that they are now studied in and for themselves—away from the principal purpose of university study, which is the pursuit of truth. Jaspers points to the independent pursuit of these upper faculties as an act of not keeping faith with the university.

Urban It is not only that the pursuit of these, and other, traditional fields of learning has become more and more unrelated to the unifying ethos of the university, but also that the methodologies involved have become technologized. Often people who look to the humanities as a means of escaping from technology are forced to the conclusion that they have nowhere to go, because even the study of Greek has become computerized.

Hersch Ah, but this is admitting defeat before you have fought the battle. Many people are, as you say, fighting technology in order to rescue their humanity. That was not at all the attitude of Jaspers, nor is it mine. You must bend technology to serve human needs. You must not allow yourself to be overwhelmed by the insistent availability of technology. You must retain your identity and your sense of purpose as a human being.

So long as technology is used as a means for collecting more facts, more information with greater precision, you are using technology in its proper place, and it would be quite wrong and dishonest of us not to use it. You cannot refuse facts simply because you do not like the machinery by which they have been obtained. Technology becomes perverse and dangerous only if you ask it questions which it cannot and should not be able to answer, that is if you want it to decide the meaning and purpose of what you are doing. The momentum of technology does not, in itself, carry it in the direction of truth. Technology goes the way you, as a free agent, want it to go.

Urban When you promote technology to the rank of jurisprudence and medicine in the hierarchy of university study, aren't you promoting a type of scholarship that has shown itself to be much more self-seeking and much greedier in its demands on time, money, and equipment than any we have yet seen at the university? It is easy enough to say that technology has to be assimilated into the ethos of the university, but when it is actually brought in, you will find—as I found on some American campuses—that untold millions are spent on technological equipment and the palaces that house them, while classics departments are tucked away in some corrugated iron hut or disused garage. Size, prestige, and influence, then, all militate against the kind of assimilation you have in mind.

Hersch The danger exists and has to be faced, but the alternative to integrating technology is that of taking no notice, or taking insufficient notice, of *the* major force of our time. If the university were to do that, it would simply debar itself from dealing with one crucial aspect of reality and therefore it would fall short of its proclaimed goal, which is the disinterested pursuit of truth. But let me stress, at the risk of repeating myself, that the business of the university is not the study of technology per se; it has rather to concern itself with the moral, social, and biological impact of technology on the individual and society.

Genetic manipulation, certain psychiatric treatments that make it possible for a patient to live quietly in society because his personality has been changed by chemical means—these are the kind of points where technology as an activity of man is drawn into the core of the university's interests. Take the rather vulgar example of the so-called thinking machines. A lot of people who ought to know better actually believe that there are machines that can think. The human brain—it is then assumed—is like a thinking machine, only a little more complicated. If the universities would tell us the truth about these so-called thinking machines, it would soon become clear that machines can do no thinking, and we would all have a better understanding of technology on the one hand and thinking on the other.

Urban My impression is that Jaspers himself was awed and perhaps puzzled by technology. Let me quote him once again: "Today we feel," he says, "that this colossal phenomenon [of technology] must stem from metaphysical sources. . . . Something until now has remained silent behind the great mass of ingenious technological devices, something dimly perceived by a few individuals like Goethe and Burckhardt, who reacted to it with a mixture of horror and distaste. Perhaps the best interests of intellectual life as well as of technology are served by making the university their mutual meeting place. Perhaps then technology and the confusion which has resulted from it would be infused with meaning and purpose."

Hersch I would stress the last of Jaspers's remarks—the need to infuse technology with meaning and purpose, and this is what the university can do *par excellence*. Technology has attracted a lot of superstition of the kind I have just referred to. Many people believe that technological devices can transcend technology, that technology has a life, a mind, a will of its own. All this can be repudiated if we understand technology as something designed by man out of his free will and as something that continues to be a tool in the hands of its creator. The pathetic fallacy can be much more dangerous when applied to technology than in any other field, for its consequences are more awesome. If you attribute soul to a daffodil you are indulging a poetic fancy which will harm no one and may make the world appear more beautiful to many. But when you believe that some marvel of technology has outmaneuvered its maker by generating a superior intelligence and a will of its own, then you are believing dangerous nonsense.

Urban So by drawing the study of technology into its orbit, the university would reduce it to size and clear away the superstitions?

Hersch Yes, it would, or in any case it could and should.

Urban In the United States the technological faculties have always been closely integrated into the life of the university. Nevertheless, America offers the most flagrant examples of the tail wagging the dog: "big science" setting the pace and dictating the ethos at a great many universities. The intellectual unity of the university is conspicuous by its absence.

Hersch Quite so. When you set up specialized schools to teach vocational skills and professional expertise inside the walls of a university, you are not teaching technology and not making a university—you may be destroying it. Forestry or business administration or television production cannot be considered as faculties of equal status with technology. Jaspers himself is very clear about that. These are auxiliaries which do not merit incorporation. That the American universities cater for all these things is explained by the history of American universities and the utilitarianism of American educational thinking.

The place for learning techniques is outside the university, the place for studying technology is inside the university. For example, the teaching of the skills required for making a television serial on, say, suicide is something for a technical school; the study of the issues raised by exposing millions of people to so many television broadcasts on a sensitive topic like suicide is the responsibility of the university. The task of the university is to unify—to create a sum total of the awareness of our age, and this requires the integration of the technological faculty.

Urban Could it be that some of the reluctance to fuse technology into the mainstream of university study is owing to an aristocratic conception of what university study is about? Jaspers himself wondered whether the university was called upon to elevate to a higher level each and every branch of knowledge and technique. Does the university contain, he asked, "an esoteric element, forever intelligible only to a minority?"

Hersch Jaspers was certainly opposed to tying university admission to any class or race, and he would certainly not agree that any "aristocracy"—whether of the upper classes or the working classes—has a more reliable compass for seeking out the truth than any other. But that isn't the brunt of your question. It is certainly true that the disinterested pursuit of truth, the pursuit of facts that may have no practical application, is not a common aspiration of man. In that sense the university has to select and reject. Anyone who claims that he can run a university without selection is guilty of a dishonest statement. The only question is: What are your criteria for selection—IQ, judgment, sensitivity, some combination of these, or criteria that go deeper still? Democracy certainly does not mean the abandonment of selection. On the contrary, if you open the gates of the university to all, you have to select quite rigorously. Otherwise you are creating a mass university with elite pretensions, and that is a sure prescription for social trouble. This is what has happened in some American universities, which have really ceased to be universities, and it is also happening in some European countries.

The American experience is rich in lessons for us all. We can see in America that the leading universities maintain a very high standard; we can also see that in a wealthy society more and more young people are conscious of their ability to benefit from a form of higher education that need not be as demanding in time and intellectual discipline as the university. Furthermore there is a growing number of people who want to go back to school many years after they have finished their formal education. In Europe people of this kind either have nowhere to go, or their opportunities are restricted. In short, I believe we need a tertiary level of education, rather on the pattern of the junior colleges in the United States, to bridge the gap between the middle schools (grammar schools, *gymnasia,* high schools) and the universities. These tertiary schools would perform the functions of the first two years of the university and they would admit much larger numbers than the university, thus satisfying the educational ambitions of able and sensitive people who are not necessarily university material. They would also cater for recurrent education.

Urban Would this not make for a new layer of second-class citizens? Class divisions created by educational background are a daunting feature of the history of European education. Public school, *Abitur,* and *baccalauréat* have all been used in the past to create social divisions and to reinforce old ones.

Hersch There would be a certain leveling, but for the majority of students tertiary education would be a leveling up, not a leveling down, for without this fresh opportunity they would be denied access to any form of higher education. I would envisage the hard core of university study beginning after a period of "fraternization" with scholarship at the tertiary level, relieving the university of the pressure of numbers. In American terms, the university proper would start with graduate school.

Urban In many universities this is already the case now, although the existence of two universities within the walls of one is not openly admitted. In the United States the recognition of the need for separation was identified a long time ago—in the 1930s—by Abraham Flexner.

An elite of the intellectually gifted is, in fact, a form of "aristocracy," and I believe Jaspers was referring to the intellectual performance he expected from this elite when he said: "The university must maintain its aristocratic principles if it is not to fall prey to a universal lowering of standards." But I wonder whether Jaspers didn't have in mind something broader than intellectual performance alone. You stressed a minute ago that the dedicated pursuit of truth has always been a minority activity, and I would add to that that it has also been a bit of a priestly activity, or so it has been considered by civilizations throughout history. When Jesus is called "rabbi" in the New Testament, we are given to understand that there was, in the eyes of his disciples, no hard and fast division between teacher and seer.

Hersch This is true, but we have to make very careful distinctions. Who is to decide, and by what criteria, whether a person belongs to this body of seekers and seers? Are they all to be found at the university?

Urban Do the Italian "barons"—as the self-perpetuating class of Italian university professors are mockingly but rightly called by their critics—belong to it?

Hersch I very much doubt it. There are people outside the university whose life and work put them in this caregory; and there are many inside the university whose life and work exclude them from it. I would find it hard to think of any group of university professors as having a quality of priestliness about them. It is indeed very seldom that any individual can live up to the demands of his profession in this elevated but very proper sense of the word, for the demands are formidable.

I remember once saying to Jaspers before a lecture: "Isn't it terrible that I can never face my students without feeling that I am insufficiently qualified to give a lecture—without being deeply worried whether I shall be able to lecture at all?" Do you know what Jaspers answered? "I have exactly the same experience." He felt that the university was a trustee of the whole heritage of our civilization, a repository of truth and humane values, and he was acutely conscious of the responsibility of speaking in the name of the university.

Urban You obviously share this view.

Hersch Yes, I do, but I would qualify Jaspers's opinion. It is my *hope* that the university is all these things, but I don't *know* whether it really is. A great many developments, especially since 1968, have seen the university lose its sense of purpose and dignity. The university is (or ought to be) a place where people come together to learn how to look for knowledge—it must not become a forum for propaganda. One of the disastrous consequences of the 1968 turmoil is precisely that the university is now being used for propaganda, and this is undermining its raison d'être.

The attack on the university is led by the assertion that objective truth does not exist, or if it does, we are forever incapable of finding it because every teaching and every method of study is conditioned by class consciousness and is therefore *ab ovo* biased. The assertion does, of course, contain some truth, but this cannot be allowed to mean that we give up trying to achieve objectivity, that we cease trying to understand every point of view with as open a mind as we can. If you assume that everything, including the questions you ask of reality, is distorted and relative, and that it is, therefore, impossible for you to delve under the surface of the phenomena, you do not belong in the university.

Urban But isn't it part of the rationale of the university that it should make room for every kind of persuasion and accommodate even those intolerant of the freedom of the university? Jaspers's view was that the university should admit "people who have made what is called the *sacrificio intelletto* ("the sacrifice of the intellect")—even those who would be intolerant if they could. The university feels confident that it can afford to do so." Is this view still valid after our experiences in 1968-69?

Hersch The university can and must be able to afford to accommodate a man of intellectual achievement and integrity even though his scholarship may serve interests we do not approve of. This may be Marxist or some religious type of scholarship—so long as it is not made into propaganda, we should give it the same rights every other point of view enjoys. But people who are not ready to give others the rights they are claiming for themselves have no right to demand those rights. I am more emphatic on the need to restrict certain freedoms if they are abused than Jaspers was, because the last ten years have changed the whole intellectual and social climate in which universities operate. Supposing we were faced with the question of rescuing the university from those who would wreck it, wouldn't we then be justified in being restrictive and not giving free play to extremists and propagandists? I realize that restriction is a fallback position which we don't want to use until all other means of self-defense have been exhausted, but it is a position we cannot give up.

We have seen in France and Germany that, out of a spirit of tolerance, little by little, teaching posts have been given to people who have made the intellectual sacrifice. These teachers, in turn, never appoint anyone except their own kind, so that all dissenting views, and in fact all views other than their own, are gagged. If you open your mouth to speak away from the prevailing dogmatism, you are shouted down, and worse. This is intolerable and need not be tolerated. So my view is, admit everyone as far as possible, but do not commit suicide.

Urban These political appointments make me wonder whether scholars of integrity might soon be forced to the conclusion that the university no longer offers an appropriate environment for the disinterested pursuit of knowledge, and opt out of the university system as it exists at the present.

Hersch Under the pressure of events, the thought has often occurred to me that if I were prevented from teaching what seems to me right and true, I would leave the university. I would certainly not cave in and teach what I think is false and should not be taught. I would go away, and other people finding themselves in a similar situation might do the same. Eventually some of these self-exiled university teachers might band together and go on working in the framework of some academy. But this would mean the destruction of the modern university. A modern university needs financial support on a scale which only the state can provide. University autonomy has been much fought about. I strongly feel that the state is the natural protector of that autonomy. But when the state becomes an adversary of the university's independence—repudiating its responsibility for the maintenance of scholarship and intellectual excellence—or even just fails to protect it by omission or because it lacks political courage, then the university is in deep trouble. This is, of course, the case in totalitarian countries where the universities are not only unprotected from sectional interests but have been put under direct state control. But I cannot see why we should allow anything of the sort to happen in our part of the world.

Urban Your academy would be a "counteruniversity" to the one that has fallen foul of its proper purpose, and you would thus hope to lead the university back to its original mandate. Didn't the Paris students also think that the university was corrupt and in need of a corrective, and didn't they, too, propose to put up a counteruniversity, even though one very different from the university you have in mind?

Hersch I really cannot agree that the two are in any way comparable. I was in Paris in 1968 and I made it my business to be at the Sorbonne and the *Theatre de l'Odeon* during those crucial May days. Two things impressed me most: first, the lack of novelty and sophistication in anything that was being said and demanded; second, the extraordinary loss by the older generation of any critical sense. There were parents and even professors saying that in two short weeks the students had found the key to a new civilization. I could not detect a single new idea, a single new program in the Paris turmoil—everything had been argued over, chewed over, pawed over for more than twenty years in leftist journals. Yet, to their disgrace, the older people stood there with their mouths open.

I happen to believe this uncritical admiration by the adults, together with the sight of the university and the state reaching breaking point under the impact of the student rebellion, had a traumatic effect on the younger generation. It saddled them with a feeling of insecurity from which we are still suffering. The students were pushing for participation. They wanted to rule the university, to be looked upon as adults and independent, to be able to sack the teaching staff, and so on. This is what they were saying they wanted, but what they really needed was something quite different. I'm not implying that the students were telling lies—they simply did not diagnose their real problem. The needs they were expressing were not their real needs.

Urban How did this come about?

Hersch They had built up a false consciousness about their identity and the questions that were exercising them. Their needs were not adulthood and independence but more care and mothering by experienced adults. I can tell you from pesonal experience that students have never sought out adults and teachers more than they have since 1968. It is now difficult to go home from the university; the students surround you with their problems, asking you this or that, holding you by the arm—they simply feel abandoned and very much in need of a father and a mother. At the time Pierre Emmanuel wrote a perceptive article about this phenomenon in *Le Monde*, "The Revolt of the Orphans"—

Urban —Paralleled in Germany by Alexander Mitscherlich's "Fatherless Generation."

Hersch Yes. Here is another example: I am correcting examination papers at the moment. Well, you run into an entirely new kind of handwriting—small, broken, and sick. We never saw this kind of handwriting before—now it is common. The students have become fragile and their handwriting mirrors this fragility.

Urban Is this fragility reflected at the examinations?

Hersch Oh yes, my constant worry at the examinations is that students will have nervous breakdowns, or that they will collapse mentally even before the examinations. They used to be made of tougher stuff.

Urban My experience in California was similar. We had suicide threatened when a harmless bit of plagiarism was discovered in a thesis; we had students pleading with examination boards that their poor performance was due to incest, drug addiction, and so on.

Hersch That is why I never take the substance of anything the students theorize about very seriously. Of course, I take their *unhappiness* extremely seriously, for they are really miserable. That they are tearing themselves apart with frustration, fear, a sense of not belonging, and aimlessness is a sociological fact of our time.

Urban Which of these would you put down as the crucial factors?

Hersch The central psychological reasons are, on the personal plane, fatherlessness, and on the intellectual and spiritual level, a loss of any sense that the world has meaning. Everything is being questioned but no answers are given. The students want radical change but they have only the faintest notion what change might be for. But the most serious malaise is this, so to speak, metaphysical void in which the young people now find themselves. There are no signposts left, civilization isn't going in any particular direction, no aims are worthier of pursuit than others, no loyalties are binding, every statement and every fact has a question mark put against it. This is anarchy, and we know from history that people do not settle for anarchy for any length of time.

The sad thing is that the parents are just as clueless as their children. I have trembling parents coming to me all the time, asking, how should I behave toward my son or daughter? What should I tell them? If they would only take a firm line on anything—even if it were the wrong line—they would be doing their children a greater service than indulging their own uncertainties and fears. The dithering is quite terrible.

There is a distinguished clinical psychiatrist here at the University of Geneva—a man of independent views but with a certain left-wing orientation. We were talking about these problems the other day. "If you were to ask me" he said, "to identify the ideal mother in our present situation, I should say she is a Mediterranean mother, surrounded by a crowd of children—a mother quite prepared to smack them if necessary without being the slightest bit upset about it."

Urban Weak parents shift the smacking to other people. I remember parents in California universities approaching commanders of the campus police: Would the police please not spare their sons and daughters at the next confrontation.

Hersch A terrible example of cluelessness and cowardice.

Urban Can I take you back to the spiritual void you mentioned just now? Why is it so much in evidence? When I was a student after the war, we had six years of slaughter and destruction behind us, and one would have thought that if there was a time to fear that civilization was going under, that human values had lost their meaning, that was the time. Yet the 1950s were a period of calm and conformity. Perhaps it was the urge to reconstruct after the destruction that crowded out the more militant passions. Perhaps the 1950s were just an example of the proverbial time of stillness—*after* the storm.

Hersch This is an intriguing problem. The eruption of metaphysical uncertainty has many causes. The most conspicuous among them is the one I have already mentioned, and it has to be put at the doorstep of the social scientists: the devaluation of values—the definition of values as mere projections of social or biological determinants. Students refuse to admit that there are valid, objective criteria for determining the truth of a fact or the worth of an idea. That road leads to nihilism and chaos. If you accept the idea that any given society has such-and-such values only because its social structure demands those values to be upheld for its protection, then you can no longer assume that somewhere, "out there," there is a society with a value system which an independent observer could respect. By "unmasking" everything, you have left yourself without worthy objects of inquiry. The world is *entlarvt* ("unmasked"), and you are left without bearings.

Urban Aren't you contradicting yourself? Can you be against relativization *and* uphold your (and Jaspers's) claim that the university's job is to seek truth irrespective of where the search may lead us? What if the search leads someone to conclude that values *are* socially determined? Aren't you in fact saying that certain types of truth are harmful and ought not to be admitted?

Hersch No, I would never say that.

Urban But you are clearly implying it.

Hersch It is a good question, so let me try to answer it. I think "unmasking" facts, going behind the phenomena, is an important activity within legitimate limits. For instance, you can say that a given set of ethical concepts is linked with the structure of society, but you are never justified in saying that these values are the mere products of social structures. You have never the right to say that values are a curtain hiding the social facts from us. I don't think science can invalidate values. You cannot destroy them by "unmasking" them.

Urban Would you say, then, that every kind of truth should be sought and made accessible to the public?

Hersch This is a footnote, though a highly interesting one: There is a superstition growing up around us that information is a cure-all. If we haven't the answer to some problem we say we will provide more information. If there is a block of apartments where people can no longer live together, we claim it is because people lack information. So we give them more, hoping, quite wrongly, that this will help them. But the cult of information, like the cult of sincerity, is a lie. Biological facts about human reproduction are taught at school, and the expectation is that sex education will rescue us from frustrations and suffering. But this is a manifestly idiotic expectation—not because I think one should not give sexual information, but because it is nonsensical to imagine that biological information about sex has anything to do with the subjective sexual experiences of individual men and women. A doctor in the act of sexual intercourse is a subjective human being in the first place, and his objective knowledge of what is happening at the physiological level does not interfere with his experience.

Coming back to the university, I would say that information should be given about everything, everything objectively true, but we must not pretend that information equals understanding. On the contrary, we must learn to appreciate the profound difference between objective "knowledge" and subjective "existence."

As to the causes of the metaphysical emptiness of the younger generation, there is also another factor that reinforces this feeling of being in a no man's land. I hesitate to name it, for it has sentimental connotations in popular usage—it is lack of love. Young people do not want to be loved by their parents, or at least they are not being loved in the way in which they would like to be, so they feel that they are not being loved at all. And with the emancipation of sexual life, even that superbly important anchorage which a profound love relationship can provide has been dissipated. All the resting places have been removed; and that is tragic.

Urban   Doesn't the philosophy of the love of mankind offer a substitute? It cannot offer a *proper* substitute, but the students are doing their best to emotionalize "mankind."

Hersch   Yes, there is this love philosophy about the Third World, about the whole of hungry mankind, and so on. A student of mine came up to me the other day saying he could not bear to live with the fact that two-thirds of mankind were going hungry. I said to him, "You are quite right—it is very difficult to bear the idea, but if you really cannot put up with the thought, you should not be studying philosophy—you should switch to agronomy and do something about starvation."

Do you know what he answered? "But I like violence." "What," I asked, "are you telling me in one and the same breath that you cannot live with the idea that so many people go hungry, and that you like violence?" "Yes," he said, "because through violence I feel I can reach reality." So here we have it: Violence is real, the love of humanity is unreal, and agronomy is uninteresting.

Urban   I am reminded of a discussion (in the March 1973 issue of *Encounter*) between the American writer Arnold Beichmann and the Columbia SDS leader Dotson Rader. Rader makes the point that it is futile to suppose that the revolutionary Left is willing or able to base its actions and thinking on rational argument. He says: "The thrust of the Left is against reason. It's antirational . . . it's anarchistic and nihilistic. . . . [The motivation] comes emotionally. It comes out of the gut. And that is why attacking the Left for this and attacking the Left for that is a very rational argument, but it doesn't work." And the prelude to this statement is Rader's contention that a revolutionary has to be able to depersonalize his enemy and be prepared to shoot his own mother.

Hersch   This is, once again, the conception of violence as a shortcut to reality. When your values, if you have any, possess no meaning, you deal with reality in the simplest and most brutal way: by taking it by the scruff of the neck.

It may well be true that the flight from rationality satisfies a genuinely felt frustration with rationality. Rationality is an empty notion unless it is carried by something outside itself. You have to want to reach something that rationality can *help* you to reach. If you look at the classical philosophers—Descartes, Spinoza, Malebranche—you will find that for them rationality and clear thinking are supreme activities because they are, as it were, God's ways of thinking, and the classical philosophers were in love with rational thought for that reason. Rationality may also serve as a means of discovering the beauty of the world, as Oppenheimer thought. But when nothing has any value left in it, then rationality itself loses meaning.

There is also another factor here. It is one of the characteristics of human nature that nothing that is not at risk of being lost is fully valued. We are, in our civilization, obsessed with the idea that all things are, or should be, exchangeable. We like nothing to be unique, for if we agree that there are things that are unique, their loss would cause insupportable suffering, and we don't want to suffer. If we suffer, we take tranquilizers or antidepressants to put us out of our pain. Well, if everything can be translated into the coinage of something else, you cannot undergo great loss. That means that nothing of any great value is ever lost to us and hence nothing of any great value is worth pursuing. So here again rationality has forfeited its carrier—the ambition to achieve certain ends worth pursuing. With the disintegration of the ends, rationality itself becomes dust in our hands.

Urban You were quoting your Geneva psychiatrist as saying that the young generation needs the firm grip of a Mediterranean mother. Let me expand this analogy and put it to you that the irrationality and nihilism which threaten to engulf us may produce a backlash every bit as serious as the permissiveness which has caused it. Society may want to express its abhorrence of the lack of ground rules by opting for an alternative that promises to impress values on it with an iron hand. It may find such a system preferable to chaos.

Hersch I am afraid you may be right. I would certainly not rule out the possibility that our situation may be inviting fascist repercussions of that nature. But that some people can at all say—thirty years after Hitler and the Second World War—that such a system may be preferable to the one we have, is a shattering admission of defeat. It shows more clearly than anything how far we are gone; and I, for one, would draw the conclusion that mankind is simply unable to bear the human condition at the present time. We are in the grip of some yearning to escape human limitations; we are aspiring to the state of angels or brute beasts, and sometimes to a combination of the two.

The human condition is a condition of rationality and law. We have discredited both. We are trying to jump off that narrow band where you can be free but not enjoy complete freedom, where you are precariously placed between happiness and misery, where the joy of creativity is constantly threatened by death, where you are forever seeking truth without being able to hold it.

But the answer is surely not fascism, which gives you neither freedom nor, for that very reason, truth. I know a schoolboy of seventeen who happens not to share a lot of the left-extremist views of his classmates. I'm told he has to watch his words very carefully, for a dissenting view would at once mark him off as a "fascist" and lose him all his friends. He is under relentless pressure of a kind one can, paradoxically, only describe as "fascist." This is surely pernicious. When I was at school there was no question of my expressing views other than those I truly believed in. The fear instilled in this young boy has had the typical effect of making him feel that he needs a "secret police" to guarantee the freedom of his opinions, and that again is an attitude dangerously close to fascism.

Urban Haven't the socialist countries in Eastern Europe, then, the edge on us in this matter? For whatever we may think of their philosophy, it is firmly held and relentlessly enforced.

Hersch I do not believe for a moment that that firm philosophy corresponds to the will of the people. The "socialist" countries counter fascism with fascism. Their solution is a nonsolution, for it—like the fascism of the Right—creates order over the dead bodies of freedom and truth. A cemetery is always an orderly place. The true torchbearers of the human condition are the Solzhenitsyns and Sakharovs and Sinyavskys of our time, for they are fighting to keep intact "the still point in the turning world"—the freedom, the rights, and the dignity of man, and in their voices lies my hope.

Alexander King

Multidisciplinarity and the Need for Diversification in Higher Education

Dr. Alexander King is a former Director-General for Scientific Affairs of the Organization for Economic Cooperation and Development (OECD) and a founding member of the Club of Rome.

Urban The modern university suffers from a split personality. As Lord Ashby has pointed out in *Technology and the Academics*, from the early Italian universities it has inherited the function of training doctors and lawyers; from Oxford and Cambridge the function of educating future statesmen and administrators; from Göttingen and Berlin the function of the university as a seat of scholarship and research; and from Zürich, Charlottenburg, and the Massachusetts Institute of

197

Technology the function of the university as a training center for technological specialists. With varying degrees of success the modern university has tried to do justice to all these functions.

However, in the last twenty years the numbers admitted to the university have grown so dramatically that the sheer bulk of the student population makes it seem doubtful whether the university can continue to reconcile all these functions in the same institution. To add to the university's difficulties, society expects it to assume responsibilities much more explicitly than it has done hitherto, and the extraordinary growth in knowledge makes for specialization which favors the independently established scientific institutes.

Is the centrifugal character of these factors responsible for the crisis of the university?

King It is the background to the crisis, but to understand the immediate causes we must first ask ourselves what accounts for the enormous increase in enrollments in the last twenty years. Partly, of course, a university education is being sought for conventional reasons—universities are foci of our culture. They are part of our mechanism of handing on knowledge from generation to generation, and knowledge increases self-respect in addition to being a passport to social mobility. These are, in themselves, perfectly respectable reasons for wanting to go to university.

Moreover, a university education has come within the reach of a large number of young men and women whose parents were debarred from any such opportunity. Going to university is the thing to do, because society, with its relative freedom from want, has taken up a number of social objectives which it can now afford—education being one of them. The social demand for higher education is strong, even where students and their parents have little appreciation of its intrinsic value, its burdens, or the real nature of the opportunities it creates. Finally, governments have—in some cases deliberately, in other cases rather by the way—looked upon higher education as a vehicle of social policy. They have been using it to give equality of opportunity to a wider section of the public and thus to lower disparities between classes. (I might add that although there is today undoubtedly much greater access to education irrespective of social origin, government social policies have not been generally successful for a number of rather complicated reasons. For example, there has been little change in the pattern of social distribution in higher education, and remarkably little at the postgraduate level.)

All these factors, combined with the fundamental splits in the functions of the universities which you have described, produced among them the crisis of the university. We have a crisis because we are not quite sure what universities are for.

Let me say at once that the existing university is, in my view, not appropriate for modern conditions. The nature of modern knowledge and the broad intake of the universities both demand that the university should provide teaching on a variety of levels and in a variety of orientations which it is not now providing. We need one type of institution of an essentially academic character working at a high level to provide the "seed corn" for the next generation—professors, research leaders, and the like. Parallel with that we need specialized schools training people in the higher professions—law, medicine, engineering. We then need vocational schools teaching at various levels of skill: technical schools, commercial schools, and teacher-training colleges. Among the present large numbers of entrants into the university, only a small number can be assumed to have academic pretensions. Others will have different qualities, often no less rich, and will require quite different approaches. All these different levels of teaching will be necessary if we are going to provide the scope demanded by students. To press them all into the academic mold would be against the interests of society and the students themselves, and would in the end produce large numbers of frustrated and bored individuals.

Urban   Would all these institutions be subsumed under "university," or would they be independent?

King   Yes and no. They should be both independent and interdependent. We need a diversity of linked institutions, linked methods, and linked objectives within the system of higher education, within which the traditional university is only one element, although an important one. I would not in the least mind if, to avoid stratification, they were all called universities, for otherwise one would be producing first-class, second-class, and third-class citizens, depending on their higher educational background.

Urban Nevertheless, the old university would not survive your reforms.

King It would, but other institutions would grow up around it. Too often, especially in Europe, the expansion of higher education is discussed as if the university were its unique locus that may perhaps have to be modified, slowly and marginally, but only in line with the assumption that the sole objective of higher education is to encourage scholarship. This is manifestly not so.

Urban Would you, in that case, look to the American university system for guidance?

King Yes, if we want to avoid stratification we might profit from the American example. The United States pattern offers a large range of quality and orientation. There is the Ivy League type of university, which is academically as advanced as any in the world, and more advanced than most, providing a quality which meets the "seed corn" need. But many other American universities are good, solid schools, training doctors, nurses, ice cream technologists, and so forth. These too are called universities, and there is remarkably little discrimination between the alumni of the first and second kinds. Of course, a certain snob value attaches to the Ivy League schools, but to call all American universities "universities" is, to my mind, right and socially desirable.

Urban I am probably not alone in fearing that in Europe a similarly catholic interpretation of what constitutes a university would debase the currency of university education. We are less egalitarian than the Americans and—rightly or wrongly—more given to upholding the mystique of alma mater.

King Broadening the concept of the European university would not take away from the cultural overtones it has acquired in our minds. Nor would it weaken the university as an institution. On the contrary, the university would be strengthened, for what are the alternatives? If the university refused to extend its scope to satisfy the increasingly diverse needs of modern society, then these needs would have to be met by independent institutions of high quality. The rival existence of these, side by side with the university, would dilute the prestige of the university to such an extent that it could no longer be what it has been in the past.

The concept of the university is well understood in Europe; diversifying its functions on broadly American lines should not affect the esteem in which it is held. I have no doubt that, although the European university has shown itself resistant to dramatic change in the past, it will gradually adjust to what is required of it under contemporary conditions. Moreover, looking to the existing system for reforms would not only be cheaper for the taxpayer, but from the university's point of view, too, it would be much more reassuring than starting an entirely new system of diversified higher education outside the walls and control of the universities.

Urban Soviet higher education offers another example of the abandonment of the notion that a university education produces scholarship. Is there anything in the Soviet model you would consider building into your diversified European university?

King The Soviet system offers a valid alternative in that, out of six hundred institutions of higher learning, only about forty are universities in our sense of the word. This is significant because many of the independent Soviet institutes—medical schools, engineering colleges, agricultural colleges, etc.—reach as high standards as the universities. The difference between these schools and the universities is not a matter of quality but of orientation. Soviet universities are general academic institutions of the classic type, turning out a proportion of graduates with a certain breadth and universality of knowledge. There is a good deal of mobility that enables Soviet scholars to move freely between the two systems. It is, as I say, a feasible alternative.

Urban Would you call a Soviet agronomist a university-educated man?

King Oh yes; I do not think the Russians would use the term education in quite the same way as we do, but for prestige and other practical purposes, a graduate from one of the specialized institutes would be on a par with a university man. The Soviet institutes provide a good professional education and not just a narrowly vocational training. Mind you, academic snobbery persists in the Soviet Union as it does in Western Europe. The Soviet Academy of Sciences, for example, is a highly elitist group, disliked by many for its cultural selfishness, and it no doubt regards itself as superior to all other sections of the Soviet world of learning. But this is not a view generally held either by society or the body politic.

Urban I am really rather reluctant to confront you with that hoary old chestnut, the antithesis (if that is what it is) between specialization and a liberal or general education; but let me do it all the same and ask you whether there isn't some truth in the opinion that a graduate from one of the specialized Soviet institutes would lack a certain breadth of vision, a habit of comprehending phenomena in their completeness and judging them accordingly? There are educational writers who tell us that any grounds for perpetuating the dualism between specialization and the *studium generale* vanished as surely as the nineteenth-century controversy between science and humanism. Yet in daily practice we *can* all tell the difference, in terms of the qualities I have just mentioned, between a graduate in dental mechanics and an anthropologist or a historian. Would this not *a fortiori* apply in the Soviet Union, where the polytechnical emphasis is stronger than it is in Western Europe?

The distinction is, to some extent, recognized inside the Soviet Union itself. In February 1972, for example, Academician M. Lavrentiev, a well-known mathematician, who is currently vice-president of the Soviet Academy of Sciences, made a scathing attack on the Soviet educational system. Writing in the trade-union paper *Trud*, he had much to say about standards. He complained that higher education had "gone into reverse," producing "a tremendous mass of indistinguishable individuals." He objected in particular to granting the title of engineer to thousands of graduates whose qualifications should have given them only the more modest title of technician.

King Yes, I would be perfectly willing to argue your case; but I might also argue in the opposite direction and say that many Western universities—especially with the dilution of teaching in the "soft" subjects—are so wishy-washy that one learns intellectually little more in them than one did at school. A university student is easily submerged in an artificial academic environment for which he is either not qualified or temperamentally unsuited. If, on the other hand, he fits in academically, the chances are that he will go so deep into specialization that he will become a one-sided person, in which case the university's traditional claim to be able to turn out whole men will be only fractionally achieved. I do not see that the human product of the universities need be better or worse than that of the institutes. Ultimately it is a matter of individual quality—the quality of individual teachers and scholars.

Urban The question then is, at what stage of diversification does a collection of specialized schools and departments cease to add up to a university? I am reminded of the case of the new Israeli university at Sdeh Boker, on the edge of the Negev desert, which has been expressly established to produce technological expertise for reclaiming the desert. According to an official report of 1967: "A new university city is being planned for ten thousand students and a corresponding number of university teachers. The university will equip young Israelis with scientific and technical knowledge for reclaiming the desert. Priority will be given to training technological manpower for future industries in the desert area." It was Jürgen Habermas who first criticized this narrow conception of the university to illustrate his point that the university forfeits its character the moment it becomes a mere school for training specialists for the economy. I share that view.

If Habermas had looked at Eastern Europe he would have found even more telling examples of universities that are nonuniversities. In Hungary, for instance, there is a school which calls itself "The Veszprém University for the Chemical Industries," and is exactly what its name says it is.

King The university at Sdeh Boker is a regional university of the normal type. Being a university on the edge of the desert it has naturally specialized in problems of desert life, desert biology, etc., to equip the population there with the knowledge they need. However, it is not true that it does nothing else—the university contributes to pure as well as applied science, although a great part of the knowledge it produces is directed toward application. You have to expect universities to have regional priorities to begin with. The development in the round comes later, depending on local conditions. In any case, a great deal of the work at the University of Sdeh Boker is now straight teaching and research, similar to that done by any other university. So I think this excrescence in favor of the desert enhances the university's value and functions rather than detracts from them.

Urban You show a certain sympathy in one of your writings with the views of Ivan Illich, that revolutionary critic of some of Western society's most cherished institutions, such as compulsory education and organized religion. Illich wants to "deschool" society, because he feels schooling has become a sacred cow which all must worship and submit to. Schools, he says, have failed our individual needs, supporting fallacious notions of progress and development that follow from the belief that production, consumption, and profit are proper yardsticks for measuring the quality of life. More specifically, he says that our universities have become recruiters of personnel for the consumer society, certifying citizens for service, while at the same time disposing of those thought unfit for the competitive race.

King   I have had conversations with Illich on "de-schooling" and I appreciate some of his views, exaggerated though they are. There is no doubt that schools and universities indoctrinate. The trouble is that our schools and universities instill the kind of ethic and values appropriate for a world that has gone. This has to be changed. I would certainly not be in favor of abolishing schools, but I would press for a de-scholasticization from within by changes in the curriculum and especially in teacher training.

The key to educational reform lies in the teacher-training colleges. Today these colleges are extremely pedestrian in most European countries—dull conservators of moth-eaten methods and rote learning, attracting second-rate students and staff. True, in France, the status of the lycée *professeur* is high, and transition to university teaching is not uncommon, but this is the exception, not the rule. The basic problem is that the inculcation of new knowledge operates with a time lag of twenty to fifty years. Far from being a vehicle of social change, education can thus degenerate into a prison of outworn ideas, and it is here that teacher education must play a vital role. We should be concerned with the educational product that will appear at the beginning of the next century. This is also incumbent upon us in face of the present need to nurture a European rather than a restrictively national view of the world, and it will require special measures if it is to be achieved.

I would strongly advocate that the European Community or some other supranational body set up a number of colleges of high quality and innovative intent.

Urban   What kind of teaching and curriculum would you envisage for these model colleges?

King   Well, such schools would have to be freed from the tyranny of the examination system. They would have to use the best teachers and draw in personnel from other university departments, industry, and public life. The curriculum would have to concern itself with teaching contemporary knowledge—an appreciation of social and economic history and many other fields—to enable the teachers, when they get out into the schools, to give their pupils an idea of the society in which they live and not of some idealized society which is long behind us or never was.

Urban Could you be more precise?

King It is difficult to discuss particulars, because I would base the whole of my desirable university and teaching system on the concept of recurrent education and would therefore, at every stage after the primary school at any rate, concentrate on providing three things: first, a broad knowledge of the contemporary environment; second, methods and intellectual tools to enable young people to extend their knowledge at various stages of their careers; and third—and I'll come back to this—some taste of scholarship and its possibilities.

Urban Let's look at the rationale of your desirable university and get the functions of teacher training and recurrent education in proper focus.

King My basic argument is that in the past people going to university have been of two types. There have been those with social privileges who under the pressure of society went to university because it was considered a good thing; but there were not too many of these. The second category—particularly since the First World War—has been people with a sense of vocation for particular professions: people who knew they wanted to be doctors, or physicists, or economists. The university as we know it—or as we knew it until recently—provided an extremely good training for them, and the university in this sense is the only institution where practice and advancement of learning are joined together. All this worked well enough so long as only two or three percent of the relevant age group went to university, but when you get five, ten, twenty, and even forty percent of the age group going into higher education, the picture changes. As the economic and social barriers to university entry melt away and the universities grow and multiply, the dilution of the university population by scholars without clear objectives becomes a great problem.

Those people who do know that they want to be doctors should certainly be given the opportunity, if they are of the requisite quality, to go through with it and become doctors as quickly as they can. But the great majority go to the university because they are seeking a ticket to a nonmanual job, or under social pressure, not knowing at all clearly what kind of job they want, or even what kind of field they want to be in; and their attachment to learning is from zero to something very small. I do not blame these apathetic undergraduates, because they are being forced into an academic institution while their real ambitions and abilities are not academic. It is wholly wrong to put them into the university.

Urban This means that we are keeping a very large proportion of the age group in a state of artificially extended adolescence—into their middle twenties—and surely that makes for trouble: social trouble, university unrest, frustration, lack of personal satisfaction, and, above all, terrible boredom?

King Of course it does. To get over this problem, university study must be diversified. I have already said that those with settled professional and vocational choices must be allowed to pursue their interests in specialized schools linked with the universities. But the majority are not of this kind, and for these I would design a two- or three-year course of more general, contemporary studies. This would give them a background of experience, information, and mental discipline to enable them to respond continuously to changing employment and social conditions. What is required is not some artificial insertion of lectures on literature in a science course, or vice versa, but a fundamental instruction in contemporary culture—with its different elements drawn from the humanities, social and natural sciences—appropriate to the needs of the men and women who will enter the work force and become mature citizens during the final decades of our century. My course would lift young adults out of the routine discipline of the secondary school. It would enable them to feel their way about, to have their enthusiasms, their love affairs, to go to the theater, to join political clubs—all this would help to mature them but at the same time aim for the future. Then I would want students to go out into real life knowing that they could come back to the university at subsequent stages in their careers whenever they felt they wanted to have new possibilities opened up or had a line they wanted to follow, either in relation to their jobs or in escaping from these jobs into something better. It is the combination of diversification and recurrent education that matters.

Urban I gather from the model you are depicting that a large part of all your higher education would be of a rather general character. While an education of this nature is by no means a new idea—we have dealt with it repeatedly in these discussions—other proponents of it tend to see a general course as preparatory to specialization and not as an end in itself. And in fact such general courses as exist at the moment are of this kind, coming usually in the first year of study.

King My dual approach of diversification and recurrent education would have revolutionary repercussions both in the universities and in the secondary schools. You are right in saying that in the universities my model would mean that a large proportion of teaching would have to be of a general character, but this could still be exciting. It would not contribute much to research, but—and this is the essential point—it would teach people to live a good deal better than they do now. But to make a university of this type a working proposition, the same kind of thinking would have to penetrate into the schools, and this takes us back to the point where we first encountered this problem: the modernization of the teacher-training colleges. Unless the teachers are themselves permeated with the spirit of contemporary knowledge, we cannot hope that those who leave school will be equipped for the kind of university study I have in mind for all but those fully dedicated to scholarship or professional study.

Urban You have said that any reformed curriculum would have to be forward-looking, because knowledge operates with a formidable time-lag. How would this requirement be translated into the subjects taught?

King I would not want my general course to be uniform—this is the first point to remember—because even within a general group of students, preferences, inclinations, and skills would soon appear, and one would have to give them appropriate chances to develop. Having said that, I would have a reasonable amount of history linked with geography; I would wish to teach at least one modern language other than the one the student speaks natively; I would want to teach some social and economic theory, and I would be inclined to advocate the teaching of at least one natural science, preferably biology. Biology would be particularly important, because it can be taught in such a way as to inculcate the scientific method as applied to multivariate systems and thus have a close bearing on the problems of society.

Urban Can you spell this out for the nonspecialist?

King One can no longer look at biology from a purely morphological point of view, or exclusively in terms of the idealized systems of chemistry and physics. It has also to be looked at from the ecological point of view. The concepts of heredity, genetics, the distribution of populations are variables that are relevant to daily life and have to be taken into account. Biology is a bridge between the humanities and science. The scientific method can be taught through it with beneficial influence on other subjects—that is its special virtue.

I would also do as much as I could to teach a good deal of mathematics and the basic concepts of statistics. I am not a statistician myself, and it is a subject I have always dreaded, but the more I look at human affairs in an international context, the more I feel that the concept of statistics is of great significance. Why? Because we all analyze facts and happenings on the basis of our individual experiences, which are limited. We take up matters in our minds which are striking to us, but their significance in relation to the totality of other facts is often so misconceived that they can lead to misjudgments, one-sidedness, and fanaticism.

Urban When you stress the importance of statistics I suspect you have at the back of your mind the intricate and interlocking nature of our ecological problems. You have yourself, as a founding member of the Club of Rome, stressed time and again that it is no longer possible to consider social policy, industrial policy, educational policy in isolation—they are all members of one body. So your interest in teaching statistics would have to do with your conviction as a member of the Club of Rome that the workings of the ecological cluster of problems are only dimly understood and that our only hope of understanding them better is by widening our approach, by thinking radically of the totality of our problems, and this means using statistical techniques.

King It is the other way around: I am not saying these things because I am a member of the Club of Rome—rather is it the case that I helped to found the Club of Rome because I realized that the problems facing us are intimately interactive, that is, that it is difficult to identify discrete problems and apply discrete solutions to them, except as palliatives which may suppress the symptoms but will have no impact on the roots.

Whatever the sequence, the interlocking, overlapping, multivariate character of the ecological syndrome has fundamental implications for education: If we are to be able to attack the cluster of problems that exercises ecologists—the instability of the world monetary system, inflation, the population explosion, the energy crisis, educational unrest, pollution, urban decay, the dehumanization of work, alienation, crime, and violence—we must have a multidisciplinary approach. The time is past when the politician alone, or the economist alone, or the engineer alone could hope to do justice to it.

Urban "Interdisciplinary approach" and "multidisciplinarity" are in-words in academia, but my impression is that very little has been done to put them into practice.

King Yes, much of the talk about multidisciplinarity is mere lip service. Existing university courses are still structured in the traditional static manner. Most of them are conducted in terms of the linear growth of individual sciences; that is to say, in terms of projecting in straight lines.

Since the middle of the last century, mainly as a result of the work of German physicists and chemists, we have classified science very carefully, putting it into boxes marked physics, chemistry, geology, and all the rest. For about a hundred years this worked well enough, but in contemporary conditions nearly all the important discoveries have been made in the interface between various disciplines. Subjects like biochemistry and geophysics arose, and we now have cybernetics with inputs from many different fields of learning.

For example, here at OECD, we have done work recently on a project we call "brain and behavior"—a very important departure, to my mind, for the future of humanity. To make progress in it we require chemists, molecular biologists, neurologists, neurophysiologists, psychiatrists, etc. It has proved very difficult to find these people and to get them to work together.

Urban You are in fact advocating a return to the ancient Greek idea of science conceived as the unity of knowledge.

King We are being driven in that direction by the facts facing us, not only in the natural sciences and technology, but between these and the economic and behavioral sciences and the humanities, too. The universities will have to draw the appropriate conclusions. The OECD project itself has given us clear proof that virtually everything within knowledge is connected with everything else. Some aspects of the study of brain and behavior—in molecular biology, for instance—have proved important growing points: temporary *foci* in the fabric of knowledge (rather than permanent disciplines) where a number of promising lines of inquiry converge. These temporary scientific fields, which may have a lifespan of no more than twenty years, will, in turn, extend by merger and cross-fertilization with other approaches from equally transient points of development to create still newer and equally temporary outposts at the frontiers of understanding. Modern science is a self-propelled kind of activity. It cannot advance within our present institutional and curricular structure. Any reform of the European universities must take this into account.

Urban Could universities at the undergraduate level keep up with such exacting requirements of multidisciplinarity? It takes a student many years of hard work to master a single discipline; to acquire proficiency in exploring interfaces would probably be the work of a lifetime.

King In our classic university approach this is terribly difficult, because people are subject-oriented rather than problem-oriented. Yet, as I say, the problems constitute single, interpenetrating, dynamic systems so that at least at advanced levels of instruction multidisciplinary approaches are essential. There is indeed a high probability that in the future science will be taught as one comprehensive, dynamic subject.

No such teaching is done at the moment. To take the social sciences as another example, sociologists, social anthropologists, social psychologists are looking at the same phenomena from different points of view, each separated from the others by virtually impenetrable walls of sectarianism. But if you recruit a team of scholars from diverse fields of learning and set them a common problem, they learn to talk to one another; each will contribute his skills and appreciate the skills of the others.

In the general education course I would cultivate the same kind of problem-oriented approach. I would, according to the nature of the problem, have groups of students attending workshops and seminars, looking at particular questions from a historical point of view, from the point of view of law and politics and engineering, etc. But a great change of attitude will have to come about in higher education before really effective work between the disciplines is possible. There is, especially in the United States, a good deal of experimentation, but not yet with proved success. In Europe we have hardly begun to seek such new approaches.

Hazards of Learning

Urban   Let me stick my neck out for a moment and rehearse to you the orthodox argument that a young man is best advised to acquire the skills of scholarship in one fairly narrow field because, once assimilated, these skills will stand him in good stead in other disciplines too. One of the justifications of the Ph.D. degree, too, is methodological. The habit of weighing evidence and testing the reliability of sources and imaginative insights equips the student with an ability to tell a valid argument from a bogus argument, a supportable hypothesis from a fanciful one, not only in the advancement of knowledge but in the whole domain of human affairs. It hardly seems to matter what his field of study is, so long as it helps him to learn intellectual discipline.

There are cases in Europe where single-subject courses have been replaced by so-called "contextuals" at the undergraduate stage—something rather on the lines you have put forward as desirable in general education. But student reactions that I have been able to assess were largely negative. Students complain that "contextual" or "interface" studies give them no firm footing in any one subject, that they leave the university with mishmash in their heads, and that they would feel intellectually safer if the university had given them one tool they could handle with complete confidence.

King   I think there is a great deal in this. I would not like to make university study exclusively problem-oriented. As I said before, students who have chosen a vocation and want to go in for long-term courses and hope to finish their studies in one packet, should certainly specialize. There is much to be said for learning a discipline thoroughly, and I agree with you that it does not matter too much what that discipline is.

My main concern is with the apathetic mass of unmotivated students who are unlikely to have academic flair, who are undecided about what to study, and who are unlikely to go in for research. These people would profit from the interdisciplinary approach. It would give them a breadth and balance of learning aimed at reconciling the various elements of contemporary culture, without which it is impossible to understand modern society. It is, in the case of these students, simply not true that specialization in a single discipline would inculcate in them a taste for scholarship; the typical European single-subject university course makes great demands on the memory but provides little intellectual challenge.

Your mention of the Ph.D. sticks a pin into me. I am personally very anti-Ph.D.—I feel that, particularly in subjects such as my own (chemistry), a lot of Ph.D. work is merely turning a handle, carrying out a number of observations, being manipulatively good at something. But, intellectually, Ph.D. work may or may not add to existing knowledge. I have been a Ph.D. examiner myself, and I know of a lot of cases where a candidate with very bright ideas, and having chosen a difficult subject, but not having got positive results, was given his Ph.D. degree with great difficulty or failed. At the same time, someone doing completely pedestrian work, which challenged his mind and the state of learning not at all, but got results and was able to publish, had no difficulty in obtaining his doctorate. There is a great deal of illusion about the Ph.D. degree; the possession of one is no guarantee of intellectual vigor or inventiveness.

Urban Nevertheless research work will, as you have indicated, remain one of the basic functions of your diversified university. The question is whether research activities will be compatible with the mass university of the future.

King The answer is a qualified yes. Despite the weaknesses of the universities and the mass of uninspired research—Ph.D. and other—which they undertake, they still provide the most propitious environment for fundamental research. Research is not only desirable for the intellectual product it yields, but also for its contribution to the vitality of the educational process. It is important in any higher education institution that has pretensions to be of quality, to have research going on on its premises. The research attitude, the excitement of probing the frontiers of knowledge, is easily communicated to students. It gives students the reassuring feeling that their teachers are in fact pioneering things and not merely handing on received information. It is also important that some of the best research professors should give courses to first-year students, so that the latter get some feel of the unfolding nature of knowledge, the throwing back of frontiers, the exhilaration of discovery, and realize that they are no longer at school, that they are in a place where knowledge is actually manufactured and the future made.

There is a further point to be made here. Scientific genius is like any other genius—discovery is intuitive. Discovery is rationalized afterward, but it is, in its origin, very much like writing poetry and music. Also, it is a young man's game. Unfortunately, in the natural sciences, a person has not usually accumulated enough information and experience to make exciting discoveries at the peak of his creativity. In the universities, with a well-known research professor being exposed to cohort after cohort of students asking awkward questions at the height of the inquiring stage of their lives, there is a fruitful cross-fertilization between creativity and experience. This allows the professor to go on being a first-class research worker until old age. The same could not be done outside the universities. An elderly research worker would go stale decades earlier in an independent institution or a government research laboratory. Therefore it is terribly important that the universities should maintain the research function and do it well. There is no reason why, in a mass university, teaching should be incompatible with research if financial provision is made for research and enough people have time to do a certain amount of it.

Urban Can we take a practical example to see how a multidisciplinary approach in research might help us to get the better of some of the difficult problems you have mentioned as being parts of the ecological *problematique*? In a lecture you gave in 1972 you said that government departments and universities were organized vertically, whereas our most urgent and intractable problems were horizontal. Could you spell this out for me? Would I be getting you right if for "vertical" I read "centralized" and for "horizontal" "decentralized"?

King Not quite. Our present structures of government were created for simpler times. They consist of a number of vertical ministries for sectors such as agriculture, industry, housing, transport, etc. Contemporary problem areas are more and more "horizontal" and therefore their attack by a series of vertical departments is too dispersed in influence in the absence of any integrating policy. Let us take a problem such as urban development. In some countries up to fourteen departments, ministries, and agencies are responsible for various elements of urban policy without any one of them being able to take a comprehensive approach: One department will look after public transport, another after road building, a third after public utilities, a fourth after general planning, and so forth. The orthodox solution, the interdepartmental committee, is of limited use—too often it proves to be a meeting place of departmental vested interests, where each tacitly agrees not to transgress on the other man's territory. Ministries of health, industry, housing, etc., are each empires in their own right, promoting policies which may, if successful, conflict with the policies of other sectoral ministries. There is therefore an urgent need—not for coordination, because coordination is too weak a term—but for integrated planning between all these departments and agencies; in other words, for multidisciplinarity. In the universities we have an analogous situation, the fragmentation of knowledge along closed disciplinary lines. Experiments are now being conducted to break down the barriers. The University of Manitoba—which, incidentally, appointed a few years ago a vice-president for multidisciplinary studies—has taken a lead here. It has set up a number of "paper institutes" to pioneer the multidisciplinary solution of practical problems. For example, it has an Institute for the Water Resources of Central Canada. The board of this institute, which consists of people drawn from the geology department, from agriculture, from economics, from chemistry, from sociology, and so forth, will develop a program for analyzing the totality of the problem of water resources. It will look into water pollution, supply and demand, geological prospecting, etc. This is an example of what I mean by horizontal working; it is the multidisciplinary approach by another name.

Urban I can see this working quite well in a relatively simple situation where your problems are homogeneous and you do not run up against the human element. But the really significant problems always have something to do with human choice, human reactions and traditions, and that, I suspect, is where your model may come unstuck. Our ability to forecast human responses is very limited; our ability to quantify them is nil.

King   This is not entirely true, although, mind you, we haven't enough experience to warrant a dogmatic yes or no. But take the urban problem again—the Manitoba method could easily be applied there. Of course, you may object that that again is a purely technological and homogeneous problem. But it isn't really, for urban planning involves a large number of social questions: public versus private transportation, schools, public amenities, noise control—the whole value system comes in. My contention is that if the universities developed an integrated, horizontal approach to this kind of problem, there would be a much greater understanding of the human values that come into play and it would be easier for these values to be taken into consideration by the physical planners. There would be conflicts, of course, but it is only through this kind of creative friction that we can make some headway.

Urban   It is still not quite clear to me how you would quantify human choices.

King   I am not saying that we know how to calculate them. All I am saying is that these questions can be, and should be, aired: questions of urban versus suburban life, the need or otherwise for satellite towns, high-rise sociology versus the suburban home. There are plus and minus effects here which ought to be considered by people like architects, town planners, transportation experts, medical officers, and all the rest, together. An integrated approach of this kind is much more likely to give us a tolerably informed idea of how human beings behave than an unintegrated, vertical approach.

Urban   This brings us right up against a cognate and very important problem which may well be unanswerable: Can the universities provide training for general decision making? Universities do provide training for making intellectual choices, but most of the really important decisions call for the judgment of human motivation, character, cultural climate, etc., and for these probably no training can be given at the universities. However, scholars will seldom admit that this is so—the representatives of the different disciplines are never loath to argue that it is precisely their subject that is uniquely equipped to inculcate the spirit of decision making. Historians believe that political history is *the* study in decision making, because history is politics with its face turned backward. Applied scientists believe that university education (as it is constructed at present) ignores the area of technology at its peril, for the practical spirit of technology carries within it the key to effective decision making. Literary scholars hold that an appreciation of high culture is the soundest preparation for decision making. Doctors believe that medical training is singularly conducive to sound decision making, because it begins on a broad scientific base, followed by specialized training.

King There is obviously something in all these claims, but none is valid exclusively. A general education can be so mushy that it never brings one to decision making at all. The scientific method, on the other hand, enables one to analyze facts and events and should help one a good deal in learning to make rational decisions. It gives one basic discipline—it makes one weigh and balance the various factors on which decisions have to be made. On the other hand, the excesses of specialization are such that the need to balance is easily lost sight of. I would not trust highly educated scientists and technologists in public affairs any more than I would historians and political economists. Each may have something to give, but I should think the technologist in particular is likely to be less useful than most, because he would keep his apparatus for judgment within such narrow limits that it would simply not be appropriate for application to public affairs. He would, if he were wise, refrain from applying it even in his personal life, because his expertise does not tell him how to balance the rational with the emotional—and this is what decisions are really about.

Urban In human affairs history is, I believe, the subject that teaches us most how to balance the rational and irrational, how to tell design from accident, accretions from nucleus, true evidence from fabrication, and so on, so that we can, against this broad background, make judicious decisions. One criticism of this theory, recently voiced by Sir Alan Bullock, is that decision making today frequently depends on techniques that did not exist in the past, and that consequently history as a training for decision making may be out of date.

King I do not believe it lacks relevance for that reason—history is excellent training, and I wish everyone knew a good deal more about it. It supplies breadth of vision and some of the other ingredients you have mentioned which should all help the decision maker. Yet history—by which I mean what historians write—is by no means always rational. Indeed, historians can seldom agree what history really is, much less how it can act as a guide to practical decisions. It seems to me, as a nonhistorian, that history tends to induce people to make the same mistakes—rather better and rather more elegantly—as science does, foreclosing new ideas, new possibilities and techniques.

Urban Isn't this a scientist's prejudice against what you would clearly consider to be a woolly and impressionistic subject?

King I don't think it is prejudice: I am tremendously interested in history, but I like it as a hobby—I do not think much of it as a discipline, and I think we should distinguish between the two.

But let me give you an example of the uses of the scientific method from my experience in operational research. During the war we were looking at the dive bombing of ships by German aircraft. The general panic impression at the receiving end was that the bombs tended to come on to the ship almost vertically, and the antiaircraft guns were trained at a correspondingly high angle. One day our operational scientists put a protractor on deck and by a very simple observation that anyone could do they determined the real angle of the bombs, which turned out to be somewhere around thirty degrees rather than ninety. The guns were adjusted and our defenses greatly improved. This is, of course, a very trivial example, but it does show you how experimental method and scientific analysis can be brought into everyday affairs.

This kind of scientific knowledge is only one of many factors the decision maker must consider in complex human situations—his scientific information must be balanced against emotional and often political and tactical considerations. However, unless the final decisions are left in the hands of men of general culture and broad educational background, the scientific information may be misused and faulty decisions reached. Even a sophisticated specialist in science or engineering would not normally have the breadth of judgment to balance his scientific information with the human factors—he would be likely to lack multidisciplinarity in a more important sense than a cultured man of good ability might.

Urban We are, I think, agreed that the imponderable and often irrational reactions of human beings cannot be measured with our present tools of knowledge. If we accept the proposition that the scientist is a mere supplier of knowledge to the decision maker who is himself not a scientist, what can the university do to maximize the decision maker's ability to digest his information and make reasonable, fruitful, and socially equitable decisions?

King We started this part of the discussion with more or less the same question, and the fact that we have been arguing in a circle is proof enough that there is no hard and fast answer to it. We are as vague about the sort of education that makes for reliable decision makers as we are about the question of how one acquires wisdom.

We'll have to be content with a partial answer: an informed guess is vastly preferable to a random guess. The decision maker's judgments are molded and colored by a number of unquantifiable factors as well as others that have been quantified and analyzed for him by the scientist. The scientist, on his part, has to realize that he is only providing analyzed data-inputs to make the decisions of the decision maker a little less unsure—so that the latter can act in the knowledge of facts rather than by hunch and ignorance. The difference between this and random decisions is very considerable.

Urban How can the communication gap between scientists and decision makers on the one hand, and the general public, on the other, be closed? That scientists can hardly talk to one another across the disciplinary barriers is serious enough. That they cannot easily talk to the public is a threat to democracy, for the public is increasingly under the impression that their lives are determined for them by faceless men whose ways of thinking, motivations, and language they do not share and cannot understand.

King The university has a duty to expose and publish what it is doing so that colleagues in other universities can learn from it and criticize it. This is being done. The same information is available to industry, government, and anyone else who knows how to make use of it. This, too, is being looked after satisfactorily. The real problem is, as you indicate, the communication of knowledge from the university to the general public. This can be done well and it can be done very badly. Let me start with the latter. University extension courses I happened to attend tended to be of two kinds. Either a professor of some subject which attracts public attention delivers a course of lectures in the town hall or some other public place, speaking over the heads of his audience with a specialization which is frightening and rather repulsive from the point of view of the generalist; or else he gives a rather patronizing explanation in very simple terms, which is almost as offensive.

University professors and decision makers should be willing to come out in public and explain what they are doing, what significance their work has either for the advancement of knowledge or for application in society. But this is best done in the framework of some collateral organization—a philosophical society, a club, anything of that sort—that has organized links with the work of the scholar or decision maker. The frequency of his appearance and the language he uses should depend on demand and on the existence of other bodies taking a comparable interest in general subjects, but the professors and decision makers should certainly be ready to step in when required. This practice is much more strongly established in the United States than it is in Europe, and I think we should follow the American example with the proviso I have made.

There is also a very important part to be played by scientific journalism in radio and television programs. My impression is that the impact of university extension work has decreased considerably since television has arrived on the scene as the main formative influence in our lives. The emergence of first-class scientific commentators in both radio and television has helped to narrow the communication gap. The expertise in these popularizing media can be formidably sophisticated and quite unpatronizing.

Urban I should have thought all these techniques might help, but they would not be getting at the roots of the problem. We are facing a world energy crisis, a doubling of the world's population in the next thirty years, and other problems of similar proportions. What channels of communication would you like to see between the world of learning and society to satisfy the informed citizen that he is not being manipulated by some conspiracy of scientists and bureaucrats?

King If we are to envisage a diversified system of higher education with many options from the strictly academic to the technical, the world within the ivory tower can no longer remain insulated from our institutions. There must be a two-way flow between the university and the community. This will require, in the senates and councils of academic institutions, not only student participation, but also representation of various social and economic interests from the outside world. Most important, a high proportion of individuals will have periods of formal education alternating with years not just of practical experience but of responsible work. Also, members of the faculty will enjoy much greater mobility between university and outside employment; there will be flows of qualified people between the professions and the university, much use made of industrialists and public figures as part-time professors, sabbatical years spent abroad, and an enhanced demand for university teachers as consultants in government and industry.

At the research level it may be necessary to build "research parks" in or near the university campuses, where research institutes of the university, industrial research laboratories, and government experimental stations will share common facilities such as workshops, libraries, expensive equipment, etc., encouraging cross-fertilization, assisting the university by giving special courses, and joining in multidisciplinary problem-oriented research of public concern.

Urban To sum up: You are arguing that the state of knowledge and the state of the world seen as a single system require a multidisciplinary approach to virtually everything human beings think and do, whether it is in the organization of government, the interrelationship of disciplines, the solution of ecological problems, or the society-university interface.

King That is so. I would add only one thing. In the absence of a multidisciplinary diagnosis of the malaise of society, we are attempting to solve individual problems because they are more amenable to our traditional techniques. But this is merely suppressing the symptoms of the disease. With the interworking of the system, the remedies we apply in one place can all too easily produce symptoms in another. These are not obviously seen to result from the "cure," and hence a unidisciplinary prescription may be enough to lead to the deterioration of man's social and physical existence as a whole.

Golo Mann

Do the Young Reject
the Past When They
Reject History?

A son of Thomas Mann, Golo Mann was for many years
Professor of History at Claremont College, California, Visiting
Professor at Münster University, and Professor of History at the
Stuttgart *Technische Hochschule*. He is the author of a biog-
raphy of Friedrich Gentz, entitled *Secretary of Europe*; *History
of Germany since 1789*; *Geschichte und Geschichten*; and his
most recent work is a long study of Wallenstein and the Thirty
Years' War: *Wallenstein: Sein Leben erzält von Golo Mann*.

Urban   One of the conspicuous features of the intellectual
climate of our time—clearly expressed in the student crisis of
1968-70—is the questioning of the value, and indeed the legitimacy, of history. "There is literally not one single institution,"

225

you wrote in a recent article, "not one single custom, that is not being continually investigated as to whether it was valid in the past, whether it is valid today, whether it will still be valid tomorrow. . . . Why should there still be professors, why parliaments, why churches . . . why teachers and pupils, why spelling. . . . Why study history?"

But while this attitude toward the past as a drag, as something irrelevant to our present concerns, is prevalent enough, it is, perhaps paradoxically, also true that the student rebels are looking for historical forebears. You noted this in 1968 when in "A Word to the Restless Berlin Students" you said: "Stop playing at Lenin." So while the young are retreating from history, they are also reenacting now this, now that aspect of a revolutionary past, but reenacting them in historically unanalogous contexts. What we have, therefore, is a case of "renaissances" in the pejorative sense in which Arnold Toynbee uses that word: contemporary guilt, satiety, cluelessness, and disaffection decked out in the gear of a romanticized but dead past. Raymond Aron, for instance, admitted that in 1968 he was himself playing at Tocqueville. Everyone involved, he said, imitated great ancestors and unearthed revolutionary models enshrined in the collective unconscious.

Thus, with one part of their split personalities, the young are saying, "Our situation is unique—the past has nothing to teach us," but with the other they are desperate to fulfill one of the deepest human desires: "to find [in the words of Sir Isaiah Berlin] a unitary pattern in which the whole experience, past, present, and future . . . is symmetrically ordered." Hence the links with the French Revolution, the Paris Commune, Lenin, Mao, and Che Guevara.

Mann To take the retreat from history first: It involves much more than a rejection of the study of history. It involves, as I tried to show in the passage you were kind enough to quote from one of my essays, a retreat from civilization itself. It involves the rejection of the classical and romantic literature of the eighteenth, nineteenth, and early twentieth centuries, of classical and romantic art, music, and architecture. At a modern art exhibition I visited recently in the city of Kassel, the artists had hung big posters all over the gallery: "Art is super-fluous." If, one might ask, art is unnecessary, why paint? Or is it—as I suspect it is—the case that while painters reject paint-ing, they want to live the life of painters?

It is one thing to say with John Dewey that "every thinker puts some portion of an apparently stable world in peril and no one can wholly predict what will emerge in its place," and quite another to say that *unless* a subject or a discipline or an inquiry takes us to definite destinations, we have no use for it. I see the retreat from history as an outcome of the philosophy that certain types of study have no useful destinations and are therefore to be rejected. It has its roots in American pragma-tism even though many who preach it in Europe believe, quite mistakenly, that it is Marxist. It challenges the value of all tradition, the sole principle of its criticism being: Will the alleged values of culture buy us the kind of traveler's check we can cash at a time and place of our own choosing? If the study of human affairs gives us no definite guidance—away with it. If classical literature—whether Shakespeare, Stendhal, or Goethe—does not equip us with yes or no answers to the human predicament, away with it. If Wagner is not convertible into psychodrama, away with him. So history, too, has become a contingent sort of study in a world in which all values and institutions are thought to be contingent.

Urban The hope that history or literature or art yields pre-scriptive values is a typically dilettante expectation. No critic of any reputation would allow for a moment that literature, for example, could or should offer guidance, except in the broad sense in which all expressions of the human will and imagina-tion are, in one way or another, didactic.

Mann It is, of course, a naive expectation. Great literature has never given guidance in the sense "do this; don't do that." There *are* works in the history of literature which set out consciously to propagate certain political and social ideas, but these are the exceptions, and the very best works do not do it. Does Tolstoy, with his great knowledge and wisdom, set up roadmarks for us? Was he, to use a fashionable German word, emancipatory in *Anna Karenina* or *War and Peace* any more than Homer was? The whole idea of mining art, literature, and history for some precious metal so that we may mint it into practical currency rests on a misconception of what great art and literature have been about in our old continent for, shall we say, the last two thousand years, to go back no further.

There is a didactic element in all art, but what makes art into great art is precisely the subtlety of the didactic ingredient. Extractable "lessons" are giveaway signs of the hack and the polemicist.

I have recently written a rather angry criticism of a new educational directive issued by the government of the *Land* of Hesse in Germany. The directive lays down how German language and literature must be taught at school. I should not really be using the word "taught," because one of the important points the directive makes is precisely to abolish teaching and to substitute for it something called "the handling of texts." The result is that there is nothing left of German literature except textual and social criticism, the great works of literature having been reduced to a common denominator with advertising copy and political sloganeering. The *Land*'s future teachers are given to understand that literary texts are there to be "unmasked," to be "seen through," so that deception is cleared away and "reality" is revealed unadorned.

In what sociocultural context was the poem written? Whose interests, consciously or unconsciously, did the poet represent when he spoke of the mountain stream, love, or perdition? Why was he trying to blind the people to their real interests?

These are the only sorts of questions asked of—and implicitly answered for—German literature. Soap powder, cigarettes, and Hölderlin are thus being analyzed with the same tools and the same unspoken—but often even openly admitted—bias. This is nonsensical and dangerous.

Urban Why do you say it is dangerous? I can see that it is nonsensical.

Mann I consider most of the reformers to be sincere people. They want to emancipate you and they want to free you from deception. These are fine objectives of which I approve, but by going about it the way they are, they end up doing precisely the opposite. They are building up a new type of missionary consciousness which exerts its own tyranny.

All great literature—whether conservative, revolutionary, socially critical, or completely apolitical—has always been a liberating influence. It has opened our eyes to fresh ideas, made us conscious of truths and problems we have not been aware of before, and, more generally, released untapped springs of the human mind in a thousand different ways. Those who would foist an exclusively critical approach on us as a surrogate for a rounded understanding and enjoyment of literature are depriving the young of this great and liberating experience. They are not giving them a new freedom, but taking freedom away from them. They are, perhaps unconsciously, indulging what they condemn most: the cheapest kind of commercialism.

An American manufacturer of jeans is currently running an advertising campaign in Germany and Switzerland. It shows the *David* of Michelangelo dressed up in blue jeans of the company's manufacture. I regard this as a shameless coupling together of the lowest and highest in a sense which would deserve a separate discussion. My point is (and I do not want to sound sanctimonious) that Michelangelo's *David* wearing blue jeans is only the most vulgar and publicly offensive manifestation of the spirit which informs the new educational policies of the *Land* of Hesse.

Urban A clothes shop in Chelsea displays an almost life-size crucifix, with the nails driven through the hands of Jesus serving as pegs for women's underwear.

Mann That makes my point even clearer. I find this debasement of the human spirit horrifying, and that is what those budding teachers in Hesse are expected to assimilate and spread in turn. The thrust of the Hesse educational policy (and of others like it) is to deprive people, during the most sensitive years of their lives, of all sense of right or wrong, of what is deserving of respect and what is not, of what is a worthy object

Do the Young Reject the Past When They Reject History? 229

of enjoyment and contemplation, and what is base, cruel, and meretricious. That policies of this sort can be put on the statute books passes understanding. I, for one, am fighting them.

Urban How would you respond to the students' contention that our situation is unique, that history has nothing to teach us, that we have, in fact, to construct for ourselves a contemporary consciousness almost from scratch?

Mann That our situation is in some ways unique is my opinion too, and I have said so many times. Whether the students are able to judge this uniqueness is doubtful, as their knowledge of the past is weak or nonexistent, so that any comparisons they make must be considered with great caution. As an older man and a historian, I can testify to the truth of Benedetto Croce's dictum: "All history is contemporary history," but I would add to that that all contemporary history is, or has its roots in, or feeds upon the heritage of, past history. The Peloponnesian Wars are by no means obsolete reading—they speak directly to us today.

Urban I suppose what the young have in mind when they reject history is the age-old complaint that their fathers have made a mess of the world and that they, the young, can do better. You clearly do not agree with that, for in "The History Lesson" you point to a certain type of awareness, *Zeitsinn*, which, you claim, only a knowledge of the past can give us. Could one describe the lessons of history with slightly greater precision? The "spirit of the age" is a rather vague notion.

Mann I never believed that history could be prescriptive any more than literature could. But I do believe that a historically informed politician will act more wisely than one who is historically ignorant—that a man like Churchill or de Gaulle was a wiser guide to his nation than President Johnson was to his. I cannot imagine a good politician unversed in history. History cannot give us precise instructions as to what to do in particular situations, but it does give us a time-sense—an understanding of the chain of events, of interrelationships, of transformations, innovations, the persistence of the old within the new.

Of course, it is as easy to overlearn the "lessons" of history as not to learn from them at all. Twenty years ago I wrote an article, "How Not to Learn from History," in which I tried to depict some of those fateful mistakes which had been inspired by the desire of politicians to avoid repeating the mistakes of the then recent past—the period between 1914 and 1933. My conclusion was that one can make fresh mistakes by applying analogies erroneously—the misapplication of information can be as dangerous as the nonpossession or nonassimilation of it.

Urban It was Tocqueville, I think, who said that one is apt to perish in politics from too much memory.

Mann Yes, and Tocqueville himself bore out the truth of that, because he was a very good historian but not a good politician.

But coming back to the idea that the politician can step out of the flow of history and devote himself to solely contemporary concerns as though he were living in a fishbowl—surely this is nonsense. Can one imagine a generation of leaders in our highly developed Western civilization deliberately turning their backs on the past, unable to answer questions like where do we come from? what are the roots of this or that predicament? and so forth. Surely one cannot. Such a generation would be a generation of blind men and their decisions would be nonsensical. Needless to say, such an attitude would have nothing to do with Marxism. Marx was, after all, an eminent historian who thought and fought in profoundly historical terms.

Urban Taken a step further, the retreat from the past leads one to futurology, and I am especially struck by those variants of future-research which do not stop at treating the past with contempt, but have little use for the present either.

Mann A great deal of futurology is plain arrogance. I am not against serious attempts at planning the future. We must, as best we can, try to make our history consciously and not allow *it* to make us. If futurologists are out to confound Marx's judgment that "men make their own history but they do not know what they are making," then I am all for futurology. At the same time we must recognize the limitations of future-research. It is not a science—it is a combination of practical research drawn from various fields of study. If seriously conducted, it can be useful and I support it, but if it encourages us to feel that we are encapsulated in some kind of an ahistorical module which has "Present to Future" written on it, then I feel we are up against intellectual fraud and arrogance.

Urban But if you *are* convinced that the old generation has made a mess of the world and the burden of the past has become unbearable, are you not entitled to agree with Sir Lewis Namier that "it is then that people come along to brush 'the clouds away of precedent and custom' and to live 'by the great beacon light God set in all'; the Puritans called it conscience, the French of 1789 called it reason"? It is this kind of impotence in the face of mounting problems that is running high in young people and urging them to make a fresh start.

Mann As Namier says, the call for a tabula rasa is far from being new; the French revolutionaries started "history" with Year One, and the Bolsheviks tried to abolish history after the October Revolution, with the result that eventually both went neatly back to the legacy of the French and Russian past. The past isn't so easily erased. I often wish it were, but I know that it isn't.

When, in 1946-47, the Czechs expelled the Sudeten Germans, the Czech Communist leader Gottwald said, "We are undoing the policy of the Premyslid dynasty."* Gottwald thought the Czechs could go back to pre-Premyslid times—of which we know very little—and pick up the threads which were let drop a thousand years ago. But you cannot abolish eight hundred years of symbiosis between Czechs and Germans

*The early Czech dynasty which goes back to the eleventh century and which invited, in the reign of King Vaclav I in the thirteenth century, German colonists to settle in Bohemia, where they stayed for eight hundred years, living in close symbiosis with the Czechs.

with a stroke of the pen. Of course the forms in which these two people lived together may never come back, but the two communities will go on being neighbors; the traditions which have been built up between them over the centuries will not cease to exist. There will be new contacts and relationships.

But the problem of abolishing the past is real in the minds of people—not only of the young. I have just read something the distinguished and aging American anthropologist, Margaret Mead, has written about this problem. Miss Mead claims that there is an unbridgeable gulf between the younger generation and the older generation—from which she most probably excludes herself—using the same kind of arguments you have just put to me. In other words, young people feel that the whole history of mankind has been a waste and a mess and that they are therefore entitled to have nothing but contempt for it. Well, there is a little mystification here: Miss Mead is desperate to show how young and "with it" she is—that she understands what those who are ten or twenty years junior to herself cannot understand. An old lady in a hurry.

In any case, I am not sure that I understand what Miss Mead and a lot of other people mean when they talk of "generations," because children are born not once every thirty years but every minute of the day, which gives us every possible nuance. There are (if you can dissociate yourself from trendy talk) no "generations," and therefore there can be no such thing as a generation gap. Moreover, it is my personal experience that there is no gulf; when I meet people thirty or forty years younger than myself, we communicate quite happily. Of course, if you go to a mass meeting of students and mistake their reactions to the harangues of their demagogic leaders for their real opinions, you may very well come away with the impression that you can have nothing in common with these people. But if you meet them privately, you can argue with them and at least understand what they are trying to do.

Let me give you a small example: I recently published a rather learned and very long book on Wallenstein and the Thirty Years' War—it runs to thirteen hundred pages, has thousands of footnotes, and costs more than forty Deutschmark. It deals with a period that can be of no intense interest to the young—or so one would have thought if the stories about the generation gap and the retreat from history were true. The book has sold unexpectedly well in the rather short time it has been out in German. What is more interesting, it has sold in large numbers to university students, schoolboys, and school-girls, who wrote me letters, which I have, and from which it is quite apparent that they have fully read and understood the book—often better than my professional critics. If the young were really an abyss away from us, as Miss Mead is claiming, this book of mine, and the ten years of work I had put into it, would have been wasted. But they have not been wasted. My young readers have formed a very shrewd opinion of the contemporaneousness of that wild and confused part of the early seventeenth century in the center of Europe with which my book deals.

We must not allow ourselves to be fooled by publicity, sensationalism, simplifications, television journalism, and especially talking too much about things that have no real substance. It is possible to talk a subject to death—*zerreden* is the rather fitting German word for it. The alleged loss of our sense of history is one example of how you can pick up a problem, air it in the press, radio, and television, blow it up into an issue, and launch it as a trend until the sociologists get into the act, write learned articles about it, and make it the subject of some expensive conference in a pleasant part of the world.

Urban But surely you have yourself recognized that the loss of historical consciousness is a problem. In "The History Lesson" you say that being unconscious of the historical past is also a form of alienation: "the . . . alienation of the past that has for so long been a dimension of European life. . . . And naturally this alienation is intimately connected with the other one, to which sociologists refer. A person to whom his past is alien, who despises it or loses the memory of it, becomes alien to himself."

Mann I am not saying that the neglect of the study of the past is unimportant. It is very important, but I increasingly feel that it is less important than we have been made to believe and that it is a passing phase. Interest in the future and in history do not really contradict each other—past and future belong together, subsumed under the concept of time, and if you know nothing of the past you will be unable to grasp any future.

When I connected the alienation of the past with the alienation sociologists talk about, I had in mind my impressions, for instance, of the city of Munich and its new suburbs as they strike the visitor who has been absent for some time. When I stroll through the center of Munich and see the Elector Maximilian still astride his horse in the Wittelsbacher Platz, and then see the concrete jungles that have sprung up in the outskirts, I cannot help asking myself: What is that foreigner still doing there? Out of thousands of people who drive past him every hour, how many know who he was, what Bavaria was in his days?

Urban What exactly is it that alienates you in this break between old and new?

Mann Those huge, cold, monstrous, badly constructed, and cheaply built satellite towns alienate me from the present because they dwarf me, because they depersonalize me, because they offend my sense of proportion. They are inhuman. I feel also alienated from the past because here the whole history of Europe is denied and mentally betrayed. The two alienations merge, and, as you know, there are many more suicides in these satellite towns than in those parts of the old cities that have been preserved by some miracle.

Urban "Denied and mentally betrayed"—what is one to understand by these words?

Mann I am, of course, not deploring the lack of monuments or old buildings—in a new settlement it would be unreasonable to look for such things. But it is a matter of experience that these new structures do not give you a real home—they do not provide protection and psychological security, and this is something the European settlements of the past always provided. You live in a concrete desert—lonely and anonymous.

Do the Young Reject the Past When They Reject History? 235

You are not part of any neighborhood, you belong to no community; there are no *Gasthäuser*, pubs, or cafes you could call your own; your life has no geographic or psychological center. Significantly, the student upheavals at Nanterre started under such conditions. Such conditions are not only inhuman but directly antihistorical.

Urban Antihistorical?

Mann Yes, because features which have been central to the peculiar feel of European life for a thousand years have been suddenly abandoned. We are being physically and psychologically uprooted, and that is alienating as well as antihistorical. So much in European literature is centered on the home surroundings: the bell tower, the church, the high street, Viktualienmarkt, Petticoat Lane, Abbey Orchard Close, rue-du-Chat-qui-Pêche, and so on. All these are vanishing from our townscape.

Urban It seems to me we are looking for some golden mean between an exaggerated sense of the past and a rejection of the wisdom of the past, both of which are likely to inhibit us, in their different ways, in the present. But this happy medium isn't easily come by. As Namier pointed out, the regular condition of human communities has always been that of the Freudian neurotic: They have been dominated by unconscious memories, fixated in the past, incapable of overcoming them.

Mann Freud certainly did not mean to say that we should not have a past we can remember. The neurotic for him was the man who could not assimilate the past and suffered from it unconsciously, and the task of psychoanalysis was not to erase the past, but to dig it out, bring it to light, and free the neurotic from his suffering. That, I would say, is also what the historian does. He digs out the past, he shows us how this situation has come out of that, he makes us conscious that in our lives forces from all spheres of our past are at work, and so forth.

Urban If you were asked by a group of students what kind of historical awareness you thought was good for them—what sort of historical knowledge they should assimilate or reject—where would you draw the line between a consciousness that suffers from too much, and one that suffers from too little memory? J. H. Plumb said, "Ninety percent of historians believe that the subject they practice is meaningless in any ultimate sense." If this were to be accepted, you would have to tell your students just that and send them home.

Mann I am a little more optimistic about the historian's dilemma than Professor Plumb is. I *would* talk to the students, and I would try to help them see, broadly speaking, two sides of the human past and, by implication, of the future: that which is serene, hopeful, and satisfying, and that which is blind, infamous, and diabolical. I would show the sicknesses of the human mind as well as the healing serums—something of man's great achievements as well as his crimes and follies.

I would insist that they have an inkling—no more—of the human past generally. H. G. Wells's *Short History of the World* would do. This would give them an overall idea of how we have arrived where we have in the twentieth century. Then I would ask them to concentrate on a single area and study all the details. History affords a series of neatly self-enclosed complexes. For example, the Roman Revolution from the Gracchi to Augustus and Cicero's letters and speeches are something like a compendium of politics on their own. I would encourage students to look at the original texts and then I would advise them to read at least one great book such as Ronald Syme's magnificent analysis, *The Roman Revolution*.

I would emphasize the importance of consulting the original texts, for it is above all through these that we can feel both the otherness and the similarity of the past. They teach us that every historical situation is unique and yet shares features with others. By disclosing the similarities behind the otherness, history sheds light on the present.

At the same time, I would warn against comparisons—they are always crude and inartistic. Yet, once it is accepted that all history is actual and present, comparisons with earlier periods often almost force themselves upon us, and with those are linked the sort of questions we have touched on throughout this conversation: Can we learn from history? Was everything bound to happen as it did? Does causation exist in history in the sense in which it is still uncontested in mechanics? And so on.

Urban You quoted Croce's view that "all history is contemporary history." This idea has weaker and stronger variants. One weak variant is that of Marc Bloch: "It is always by borrowing from our daily experiences and by shading them, when necessary, with new tints, that we derive the elements which help us to restore the past." A strong variant is what has been called the "Abominable Snowman Fallacy."* The Snowman walks backward with his feet pointing forward, thus evading his pursuers. The historian who imitates him may blind himself to what existed in the past but he will be able to derive lessons for the present—it is the sort of historical interpretation that is widely practiced by intellectual and political movements looking for a pedigree. If Croce's dictum is a middle ground between these two variants, and if we take his meaning to be that "each age writes the history of the past anew with reference to the conditions uppermost in its mind," why are we upset when the young claim to have discovered precedents and symbols in the past which legitimate their rebellion? Even if this does turn out to be a case of the "Abominable Snowman Fallacy"—have revolutionary movements ever prospered without it?

This is the second leg of the question with which we started this discussion, and perhaps we can try to answer it now.

Mann All history is, of course, selective. The historian selects his evidence according to the standards imposed by his time. Simply to identify a past situation with a present situation may be a harmless (if grotesque) kind of folly, or it may lead to misunderstandings and even fateful confusions. For instance, to believe (and we have already touched on this example) that

---

*A. W. Simpson, quoted by J. D. Heydon, in *General Education*, ed. Michael Yudkin, London, 1969.

Hazards of Learning

what Lenin did in St. Petersburg in 1917 can be repeated in Frankfurt today is absurd. It cannot be done, because Lenin attacked an archaic, primitive society which was physically and economically collapsing under the blows of war. By contrast, the German Federal Republic is a closely organized, well-functioning state with a great many achievements (not the least of which are economic) to its credit. Nine-tenths of its inhabitants back the state, especially when it is a question of defending it against force. That is the difference; hence one cannot play at Lenin—one cannot deploy the cunning, the deception, and the brutalities of Lenin in Western Europe in the 1970s. This is, again, a case of how not to learn from history.

When the French Jacobins played at being Romans during the French Revolution, imitating their customs more than anything else, that was a very harmless affair. Everyone knew that the Jacobins were playing at it, and I would say the same about the beards and haircuts and gear of the present student generation. Modeling yourself on Che Guevara is a bit childish and quite a bit silly, but if you desperately need a figure to identify with, go ahead and do it for a while. This isn't very tragic—it is a variety of hero worship, and that need not have awesome consequences.

Urban It is grotesque, though, when you consider that one of the purposes of the student rebellion was to repudiate the "great men" theory of history—the people alone make history.

Mann As an old man, I can afford to smile at your surprise that human nature is inconsistent. These brave young people are a little contradictory in their longings, without probably realizing that they are. This goes, of course, for the whole Communist "cult of the personality," too. After all, Marx abolished the great individual in history, yet where are great men more fulsomely worshipped than in Communist Russia? Human beings have seldom managed to match their deeds with their words, or to separate their judgments from their delusions. This is another thing one can learn from history.

Urban There is yet another student critique of history which has perhaps more appeal than most. The students claim that the axe-grinding type of history, while always foolish and mischievous, has become intolerably dangerous in the nuclear world. "What," they say, "do we find in the history books but history as national epic, history as national literature, or history as hero worship—each represented by scores of famous names?" Not being able to find their way through all the confusion, the students call a plague on all traditional approaches to history. They feel the world has become too small for a parochial account of the human story. They want a reading that speaks of peace and brotherhood and does nothing to prolong traditional feuds between nations and races.

Mann I share that sentiment—the history of the nation state as it is still taught in France, for instance, is indeed obsolete. I say the "nation state" as distinct from the "nation," because the two are by no means identical. Take Marc Bloch's famous book on feudalism. He deals with the broad phenomenon of feudal society between the ninth and thirteenth centuries and makes very clear distinctions between feudalism in the various regions of France, Germany, etc. He sees nations as characterized, for example, by a common language, but within these nations he identifies many local, self-contained complexes ("subcultures" would perhaps be the word for them today). The nation state has been a short-lived phenomenon—or so we must fervently hope—in the European context, anyway.

About twenty years ago—well before the first ideological student protest—I wrote a modern German history, and one of the ways in which I tried to eliminate bias from my account of the Franco-Prussian war of 1870 was, first, by not writing very much about it, and, second, by not going into the thorny and highly counterproductive question of who was responsible for the war. I did not investigate the niceties of the plan to put a Hohenzollern on the throne in Madrid, and I did not so much as mention the famous Ems Despatch. I confined myself to saying that very silly and very controversial reasons had been given on both sides.

I felt I could not bore my readers with going over the whole hoary question of responsibility again, nor did I want to keep nationalistic recriminations alive. There had been nonsense and misunderstanding between these two peoples and states—a lot of it anachronistic even at the time of the 1870 war. Undoubtedly, hard national interests, too, were involved, and the story had to be told, but my general feeling was, let's get over the question of who started what—and the war itself—as quickly as possible and talk about the consequences, for *these* were unfortunately long-lasting and nefarious.

Urban   Weren't you attacked for your views?

Mann   Oh yes, by the old guard of national-liberal historians, but most of these have now vanished or are in a pathetic state, so they have done me no great harm. Some of them said condescendingly, "What do you expect? That is the way history is written today," and they condemned me for having left out or demoted some of their familiar landmarks.

But while I cut down on the Franco-Prussian war, I was very conscious that I could not unduly economize on Bismarck. I did a portrait of him because I felt that Bismarck was, despite certain brutal traits in his character, a highly original and indeed fateful personality. Whether one liked him or not, one could not deny him greatness. Without him German history and the consciousness of the German nation would all be very different. So he warranted a few pages in my book.

Therefore my response to the students' critique is that their attacks on history as national epic or hero worship come thirty or forty years too late. The battles have been fought and won. The students are knocking on open doors, and if they do not realize that the doors are open, they have nothing but their ignorance to blame. They should read the books.

Urban   One of the curiosities of the historiographical debate is that, while in America and Western Europe there is this general questioning of the uses and credentials of history, and historians have been put on the defensive, history has retained and even strengthened its hold on East Europeans. The old-fashioned, Communist version of national history—history depicted as a long preparation for the triumph of Communism—has found no acceptance. The East European peoples like to think of themselves precisely in terms of national epics and national wars of liberation, with the appropriate landmarks—1830, 1848, 1863—uppermost in their minds. In Hungary, the 1956 revolution was modeled on 1848, and in Poland, Mickiewicz's anticzarist (and potentially anti-Russian) play *Dziady* is playing to packed houses again, although at the time of the 1969 student disorders it was ordered off the Warsaw stage. One could multiply the examples. What is interesting to observe is not only that the people are asserting their national past as a demonstration against the Communist variety of history and the Communist regime; more and more frequently the regime itself seeks to establish, or to reinforce, its legitimacy by identifying itself with the leading themes of the national, and often nationalistic, saga. In some East European countries, such as the Soviet Union and Rumania, this is, of course, more easily done than in others, but the tendency is universal throughout Eastern Europe.

Mann   The East European nations have always had to fight for the survival of their identity and they need the past for that. One of the most moving and significant acts of reconstruction I can think of is the rebuilding of Warsaw. The Polish capital, which, like Dresden, was virtually razed during the war, has been reconstructed, at enormous sacrifice, doornail by doornail, from old plans and sketches. Why did the Poles do it? Why did they not build a city of steel, plate glass, and concrete? Exactly because they felt "we need our great past—we need the external symbols of our history." The same goes for the Hungarians and the Czechs and the other East European nations. The Soviet Russians' increasing, and now openly encouraged, loyalty to the Russian past is well known; the further they move back in time from the controversial nineteenth century, on which Soviet historical judgments are still heavily loaded, the more openly they can invoke the Russian past and identify with it.

Urban   Warsaw was rebuilt by successive Communist governments. I wonder whether the Communist regime would have rebuilt the city brick by brick if *legitimacy-building* hadn't been its real purpose.

Mann   I am sure that, too, played a part. But why does the regime want this identification? Because the people are longing for national symbols—so the men in power give them those symbols. We must not think all this is a stratagem; we must not believe that all Polish Communists are traitors; many of them are sincere patriots and the past is part of their patrimony.

Somewhere there is a lesson in all this. The East Europeans are less spoiled than we are; they are much more threatened as nations and as individuals than we are; they have less time and fewer opportunities to get bored than we have. They are certainly not bored with their past.

We are bored with work, we are bored with affluence, we are even bored with rebellion—we are bored with our past too. We have twenty-five years of good living and an absence of any serious pressures behind us, and that, in the historical experience, breeds dissatisfaction, restlessness, loss of identity, and, at the same time, cynicism and utopianism. Or so it seems to one student of history.

Richard Hoggart

Making Contact
Beyond National Cultures

Richard Hoggart taught at the Universities of Hull and Leicester, and was Visiting Professor at the University of Rochester in New York. He then became Professor of English and Director of the Centre for Contemporary Cultural Studies at Birmingham University. Between 1970 and 1975 he was Assistant Director-General for Social Sciences, Humanities and Culture, of UNESCO. His many publications include *Auden; The Uses of Literacy; Speaking to Each Other*; and *Only Connect*, the BBC Reith Lectures for 1971. Professor Hoggart has served on many committees concerned with higher education, broadcasting, youth service, and the arts, and is a governor of the Royal Shakespeare Theatre.

Urban   "The number of those who need to be awakened is far greater than that of those who need comfort." These are Bishop Wilson's words, and you use them to give an *aperçu* of one of the most penetrating chapters of *The Uses of Literacy*. Bishop Wilson's dictum, you say, is just as true today as it was two hundred years ago.

What exactly was the point you were trying to make? My own first reaction would be to doubt whether Bishop Wilson's words do apply to our situation. Seeing the amount of awakening that has been done in the last few decades and the amount of anxiety it has caused, I should have thought we were badly in need of a period of stocktaking and stability.

Hoggart I think Bishop Wilson's words have as much force now as they had several decades ago. It is a commonplace by now, but is nevertheless worth repeating, that while our societies tend to produce greater prosperity and comfort, they are reducing the quality of the lives we live as human beings. Much of this deterioration is owing to a false consciousness generated and maintained by modern communication techniques. Our roles are structured for us by the press, by radio and television. People hardly know what alternative lives they might live, because they are kept in the dark about the alternatives. They do not know what alternative values there might be for them to enjoy and to respect, because they are not aware of their existence. If consuming things, having things, holding things, being constantly on the move to attain things, are the virtues held up as the only worthy social aims, obviously a great deal is lost. If you make fun of intellectual life, if you reduce the imaginative life to something you bow to on occasion, and give prizes to now and again but largely ignore, then you may feel comfortable but are denied any knowledge of the intellectual and spiritual unfreedom into which you have been manipulated. If you ran through the list of the things which are held up as of good repute and those which are laughed at or simply ignored by our communications media, you would find yourself looking at an all-embracing assumed world. We have to try to speak not just to those who have already seen through this assumed world but to others, to break through the plastic casing which is being presented to us as life by the media.

Urban In the eighteen years that have passed since you wrote your book, do you feel this assumed world has spread its tentacles?

Hoggart Yes. When I was writing that book I was concerned about the "entry of the working classes into society." The working classes were literate, they had money, and they had to be, as it were, looked after and catered to; and I was concerned that, in an age of centralization and technological development, working-class literacy should not end in cultural debasement.

The biggest single difference in the eighteen years that have gone by is in the emphasis we now put on making the world fit for meritocrats. Wherever you go—whether it is London or Paris—you can see that the drive, the focus of attention, is toward creating a world to which one can aspire because one is a rootless meritocrat. It is the world of the more expensive houses advertised in the Sunday papers, it is the world of the motorcar that has something slightly different about it, it is the world of the airport departure lounge, of the expensive luxury flats with swimming pools, and all the rest of it. This lifestyle is one of the great images of our age and is held up for admiration throughout the world. One of the British Sunday papers was complaining the other day that Paris is not what it used to be—that it has been taken over by the rootless bourgeoisie on the move. One can see what was meant. But it is true not only of Paris.

Urban But should one not welcome the meritocracy as a sign of democratization? Meritocracy means the leadership of those who have merit, and merit shows up only where there is equality of opportunity.

Hoggart Any society that would not give merit a chance would be a wrong kind of society, and I would not want merit to be held back on the grounds of a false conception of democracy. But democracy goes beyond that. Certainly, democracy *is* about giving people equal opportunity to develop their talents, but it is also about fellow-feeling, about community life, whether we are thinking of the social services, local government, or whatever. I am suspicious of the meritocracy and of the new world which is emerging as a result of the meritocracy, because meritocracy takes a society that may, in varying degrees, have had some residual sense of community life left in it, and drains it. It changes that society into one made up of large numbers of isolated, itemized, ambitious individuals, each trying to get on according to his likes.

One of the best reasons T. S. Eliot ever gave for being a conservative and not a democrat was that if you reward power-pushing, intellectual merit to the exclusion of all else, you create a world more naked and brutal than the world you are replacing: every ambitious man grappling upward and kicking others behind him. The world of the people one meets riding high on the meritocratic bandwagon is a loveless world.

Urban Community feeling and the warmth of the working-class milieu are things stressed by you throughout your writings. If the erosion of class consciousness deprives us of these qualities, what will take their place? You said that the media were largely responsible for surrounding us with an assumed world. Could they not also act beneficially by instilling in us a wider feeling of social solidarity that would go beyond class and nation?

Hoggart I am very doubtful whether we can do much to instill a wider community feeling by public means, although I recognize that in periods which move as fast as ours, attempts to create good public communication are certainly not to be derided.

What sort of consciousness is being lost? Working-class people I knew in the north of England—with all their limitations, which I do not underestimate—had a powerful sense of being part of a neighborhood and of having duties to one another that were rarely if ever made explicit but existed in practical ways. You knew what to do if somebody was dying, if somebody was having a baby, if you had to go to hospital and the children had to be looked after. There was no question, it was just done. This is of course true of many communities—peasant communities, tribal communities, and so on. But when you strain or filter a society, when you give it predominantly monetary incentives, you break up its cohesiveness. You break it up physically when you rehouse people, unless you put an enormous amount of care into thinking about how you rehouse them. I'm not saying that rehousing people in high-rise apartments will suddenly make them become brutal—it will not—but the community spirit begins to go. You have only to drive with a visitor from Asia around Birmingham—somebody will point out to him with pride, "That's the old people's home," and the Asian is as likely as not to be shocked. "Fancy putting your old people there! What old people need is to be in the heart of the family, and what we need is our old people with us." Now that seems to me a very civilized attitude, and it did commonly exist in my boyhood, but it is disappearing. The pressures of the consumer society, the pressures of work, the pressures of restricted space in vertical living have seen to that. Now this is one way—the negative way—in which institutions and public authorities (as well as other forces) can help to accelerate the disintegration of community feeling.

But institutions can also be necessary for the good of society. Take a linguistically diversified society that has several cultures in it. One of the interesting features of the late sixties is the rise of the small cultures and of groups inside larger societies—French Canadians, Welsh, and so on. Sometimes they will be oppressed and violent, as for instance those in Ireland and Belgium, but in other cases—and Switzerland is a good example—the public authorities are trying with some success to bring society into the twentieth century without destroying the cultures of the small communities. The Swiss have put immense thought, not only into removing causes of friction among the various cantons and languages, but into building on the fact that a variety of cultures is interesting, yet maintaining all the time that, for certain purposes, Switzerland has to have a single culture which is the nation. I am not saying Switzerland has entirely succeeded, but what success has been achieved shows that the authorities have a remarkable capacity for sitting down patiently and thinking about how to make connections and how to move an old form of culture into the modern era without brutal loss.

I'll give you another instance to illustrate the destruction of traditional cultures. I know one particular community in Asia which is remarkably unified. Its religious life (based on the village temples), its family life, its neighborhood life, its artistic life are all integrated. The members of this community don't know much about money; they spend a great deal of their time obeying their gods and doing them honor through the arts and observances. If a stranger walks into the village, he is received by a senior man at the outskirts and welcomed, given something to drink and a place to sleep. There is never any question of payment. It is beautiful, but clearly it will die. It is dying already and with extraordinary speed. Hotels have gone up, the tourists have rolled in, wanting to buy not only the material exotica but also the exotica in attitudes. The vernacular community architecture, which was marvelously adaptive, is changing into rigid modern forms. Legal institutions are changing—there used to be no techniques for litigation in this community, because there weren't any litigations. Now the techniques have to be learned.

Dancing in this society was an unselfconscious religious celebration. The dancers were totally wrapped up in the act of the ritual, and those who came to watch would often hang silently from the trees. It was as though they weren't really present as an audience but had been drawn by natural attraction to a celebration.

Now the dances have become a tourist attraction. The villagers will tell you that the dances are much more sophisticated than they used to be. There are even competitions. The dancers have turned outward, to audiences, to rows of tourists who clap politely. That society is at risk now. From being a culture of communal attitudes and relationships, it is becoming a buying-and-selling, giving-and-taking, consumer-commodity society.

I recognize that it could not stay as it was, but can't we take more thought about the way we want to carry forward?

Urban I wonder whether your pessimism is quite justified. Working-class communities arose on the ruins of peasant communities, and perhaps we should not exclude the possibility that the breakup of the working-class culture will be followed by yet another form of cohesion and fellowship. It is difficult to foresee what this might be, but it would be very surprising if there were a vacuum.

Hoggart One cannot tell. I have a respect for people's resilience—not only their capacity to resist but their capacity to kick back and defy some of the things offered them as part of the rat race; or to use them in their own way. In *The Uses of Literacy* I talked about the antibodies people have. I have also written about this in relation to motorcars; you could say different classes use motorcars in different ways. Does the fact that a working-class family has a motorcar make them into a middle-class family? Do they take over the attitudes with the object? I don't think so. A secondhand car in the working-class streets of the big cities is more a tool than a status symbol.

On the other hand it is also true that if people are exposed, year after year, to the pressures of hidden persuaders, if they are educated to feel at home in the assumed world of the Sunday supplements, something will go. I cannot prove it, but if you talk to some of the people who are caught up in that life, you will find that they are just not happy. They inhabit an ersatz world, their values are straw values. Looking for an apartment recently in Paris (it had to be in a bourgeois area for reasons that could not be escaped), we ran into this problem time and again. Some of the people we were sent to see by the estate agents—and at that level of apartment you are not usually dealing with the French but with a floating population of foreigners—were quite clearly living a life of hectic emptiness. They were members of a hotbed community which has few automatic assumptions to work from day by day. It is an environment without signposts.

Urban You say in *The Uses of Literacy* that this emptiness, this "skepticism without tension," is now an almost classless phenomenon which affects the ordinary man at all levels of his existence. Outside his personal life he believes in reducing and destroying things, but not in assertions of positive worth. "All these attitudes," you write, "can feed upon themselves, and so spread a nerve-killing effect over other areas. There is then a loss of moral tension, a sort of release in accepting a world with little larger meaning, in living in accordance with its lack of internal demands."

How do we change this attitude?

Hoggart One should try to change it by, first of all, being open and honest about its existence; and this can be effective so long as we are not living in some form of totalitarianism.

Can it be done by the public media? Let's take the classic instance, the uses of broadcasting. In broadcasting you start by having to decide what structure you will set up, and that is a public decision. According to the structure set up, you get this or that kind of broadcasting. The structure decides, within very broad limits, what is possible, and even more what is not possible.

It is the case, especially in commercial societies such as ours, that most media narrow the range of available choices. I'm not complaining that they do not give people what I think is good for them. I'm saying that the world is very rich and diverse, and if we have been lucky enough to travel and have a good education, we know that this diversity is worth exploring. But if you look at the uses made of television in some countries, you are struck first by an extraordinary focusing on things that are known to be popular for the sake of getting big audiences. What is wrong with this is, not that we are being "stufffed with virtue" for its own sake, but that we are, all of us, limited in the opportunities we have had—and of course inherently limited also by a predilection to go back to the things we know. And yet here is an exceptionally lively medium of which society has the right and duty to say, when it sets up a network, "We must find a structure for broadcasting that will allow it to recognize that most people have more potential interests than we or they know." I've had this argument with [British] Labour Party politicians—most of them, like most politicians, are caught up in the false dilemma that, since broadcasters have no right to "push things down other people's throats," they must "give people what they want."

I'm saying what I said at the beginning of this discussion: How do we know what we want until we see what is available? If you don't make a positive effort to provide what you think are worthwhile experiences across the whole range of human life, then you *will* be caught in the trap of ever narrowing choices. Broadcasters must, therefore, be given a structure which allows them to experiment, and I am not talking about experimenting with "highbrow" as against "lowbrow" programs. I would want them to experiment with programs that they, as professionals, believe to be interesting and good. They must be allowed freedom, money, and opportunity to experiment with frank news programs, with comedy, satire, and any other genre they think worth exploring.

Structures are often abused in radio and television. You can have a state structure which will try to keep people quiet by pushing out mainly recognized soporifics. Now and again, this kind of broadcasting will bow to culture by putting a cultural program (with a capital *C*) on the air. However, the general tone of this broadcasting will be ideological or at best anodyne. That is a fairly precise description of the broadcasting organizations in some countries. In the commercialized Western world you can have a structure that so ties broadcasters to commerce and advertising that they are chasing each other's tails for audience ratings at peak hours every night.

But you can avoid these pitfalls by giving broadcasting a structure that is flexible and diverse and encourages high professional standards right across the board. You can do a "cultural" program which is high-minded in name but trivial and patronizing in fact; and you can do a so-called "lowbrow" program and yet make it lively and creative.

As I say, each of us who tries to teach or write has to take stock and say what he believes. A good instance of this is the debate about the universities. I spent much of my time on the side of the students in the battles that developed at Birmingham in 1967-68. There were the usual sit-ins about democratization of the university structure, student participation, and so on. The students had a very good case, I think, and nobody was in any doubt where I stood. But it would be wrong to take that position always, as some people do, and to claim that teaching is a totally open situation in which nobody ever knows more than anybody else. We as teachers may make bigger mistakes because we are older and know more, but then we are not bullies and our opinions do not have to be accepted. The real danger comes from the sort of staff member who is so anxious to avoid appearing to stand on any issue at all that he will *always* agree with the students for fear of seeming old-fashioned and out of touch. You may have to say to the students sometimes, "I don't agree with you, and these are my reasons and my principles."

But you asked me how one works toward a wider recognition that some things are better than others, have been harder fought for, and still have to be harder fought for? You do it by trying to express them in your own life, and if you are teaching, your life has to be, or should be, a continuous stocktaking. In public affairs you do it by making sure that this recurrent stocktaking is built in as a primary consideration.

Urban I should have thought that the trivialization of Western culture is, in some measure, owing to a lack of real issues. We suffer from a certain lack of hardships. In Eastern Europe, where daily life is much tougher and the state and party surround the individual with constraints, sensibilities are more acute. As an East European poet once put it to me: "The land we are allowed to cultivate in Eastern Europe is much smaller than yours, and therefore we must dig deeper on the small patch we have." This intensive cultivation of a small area makes for powerful responses, whether in the arts or vis-à-vis the official ideology. The confrontation with ideology has at least the merit that it forces the East European citizen to think of a number of profound issues with which the ordinary man in the West is seldom confronted. Priests who have worked in Eastern Europe or visited it tell the same story. They are impressed not only by the keenness of practicing Christians, but by the sharpness and sensibility of the general public. Therefore the East European critique of Western culture isn't necessarily a Marxist critique, although Marxists are loudest in condemning the bourgeois culture for its commercialism, its triviality and toothlessness.

Hoggart I am interested to hear you say that there is this increased sensibility in Eastern Europe. I do not know enough about the East European countries to make an informed judgment. However, many of their criticisms of our culture are right, although others are wide of the mark and not as well founded. Democracies are at a disadvantage, because if you are democratic you want to leave things open to the play of human impulse and the market, and that must mean that you are prepared for some people to be crooked or to make mistakes and for decisions to go wrong in ways that you personally would not wish.

But this brings us back to your original question—if that is so, what is it that we as individuals and states should do to redress the balance? I am especially interested in the role of governments, partly because, being very Western, I always suspect governments, but also because I believe that if governments don't play a positive role in these matters, if they don't initiate, nothing will be done. One of the issues to which every government in the world is now giving attention is the "cultural development" of society. This is new. I was brought up in a world where the artist, the creator, was largely alone, and the contract between a writer and his reader or the playwright and his audience was a contract between individuals, and I still believe that it is best that this should be so. Now, however, governments, and especially Western governments, are taking a direct hand in shaping the "cultural climate" of society. In France, for instance, under de Gaulle, and with Malraux as Minister of Culture, it was felt that something had to be done to preserve "culture" at a time when a previously technologically backward France was becoming rapidly industrialized. Malraux produced an ambitious cultural plan with the clear aim of forestalling the loss of "culture" through the emergence of a mass, technocratic society.

The British don't formulate their problems in the same way, but they too are getting bothered about "culture." The size of the Arts Council grants keeps going up; there is a consciousness that the provinces have to be made more habitable, that art should be decentralized from London, and so on. It is in fact the same problem the French are grappling with, and the Arts Council is acting as a kind of ministry of culture in almost all but name. We find a similar situation in virtually every society in the world, each state spending millions on community projects with a cultural and artistic bias. The state has it in its power to make sure that certain things which are valuable shall have a chance to stay alive and develop. The private patron has gone, so it is the state that has to take good thought about the structure of community affairs as it affects the culture of society. The state has to ask questions about what kind of institutions, what kind of schools, what kind of community centers, what kind of theaters, what kind of musical life it should sponsor. There is no getting away from the fact that the state has to do more.

What worries me is that the argument at the state level is undernourished. For instance, a debate in the British House of Commons or in the Lords about broadcasting can be on an extremely low level. The knowledge displayed is poor and the thinking poorer still. Also a great many of the people who make cultural policies in some of the developed Western countries think in terms of criteria which, though they aren't necessarily politically biased, are simply old-fashioned. They are bound into their own high-bourgeois assumptions, and they believe that the cultural development of society is fully and best served if the simple transmission of received culture is encouraged. This is not so. Bourgeois culture, important as it may be, is the product of a certain time, place, and class; it isn't something that was for all time fixed and set so that we can now give it out to people like stamps or their wages. The exciting and interesting thing about culture in modern society is that it is open. So when a state assumes such a degree of responsibility for a society's cultural development, it has to defy the inertia of its own institutions and the resilience of established tastes and values.

Urban Sensitizing the public to the kind of values you are talking about is very important. But don't we run the risk of upsetting a great many people who would, if they were left

Hazards of Learning

within the constraints of a received culture, not be so upset? You speak (in *The Uses of Literacy*) of the "uprooted and anxious" members of the proletariat. These are people who have opted out of their class and lost contact with their environment without, however, being able to put down roots elsewhere. It seems to me that sensitizing the public to too many unorthodoxies would increase the element of uprootedness and anxiety in our society.

Hoggart This has links with several questions we have already touched on. Yes, there is a risk of alienation—there is always that risk. If it is right, as I believe it is, to take a critical view of society, then it is our job to be sure that our case is made as well as possible. In the course of that, we are bound to feel that we stand apart from society, and this can be disturbing. But then all self-awareness is disturbing, if it is properly entered into. Yet if we want to be men trying to stand on our own intellectually, then we must get out of the cocoon of the wholly enclosing set of attitudes that family and work and the newspapers and television try to provide. There is no way out of that. Conversely, an intellectual critic who has been turned so sour that he feels contemptuous of the great body of people and alien from them seems to me to have mistaken his way. We can criticize as savagely as we like, but if we look around and listen, we can also see that there is a lot of goodness and decency and kindness in society with which we should learn to make connections. It is a matter—to come back to a phrase I used before—of having a sense of fellow-feeling. What I am saying is: taken sloppily, this process of critical self-awareness may produce sloppy dissidents; taken thoroughly and well, it will produce serious dissidents. But the price of the dissidence need not be a loss of respect for Tom, Dick, and Harry—that is, for all of us.

Urban Would you class the student protestors as "sloppy dissidents"?

Hoggart Some of them, yes. They made a critique of society which was mainly rhetorical and which allowed them to adopt a certain amount of self-dramatization, based on a histrionic view of society. That is not the sort of thing one is asking for; one is asking for considered criticism which will, without blunting its sharpness and without blunting its rejection of many undesirable features in society, firmly rest on a sense of fellow-feeling.

Urban I'm struck by a phrase you use in your Reith lectures, and I wonder whether it has anything to do with this sense of "fellow-feeling." You speak of the need to connect, to place our arguments in the ribs of "a universal human grammar."

Hoggart Let me first tell you what I do not mean by that phrase. It *is* true that the world is becoming a global village— more and more people will no longer be able to live in small local communities and will have to become citizens of the world in very practical senses. Wider and wider areas of society will have to have contacts with people from other communities, other regions, other nations, and other continents. It is part of the whole traffic of modern society and it will increase. It is easy to say that, if peace is to be served, the resulting interdependence requires a profound understanding of other peoples, nations, and cultures. But it is much more difficult to evaluate exactly how this is to be done, because the political realities of the world are harsher than the fact that we are stretching hands across the sea and saying, whether in Moscow or New York, that we all love peace.

In other words, I am again struck by the thinness of the debate and the simplicity with which it is assumed that people can enter into so-called meaningful relationships with one another.

Let me give you an example. From my experience of international organizations I am struck by the fact that discussions there so often become forms of a rhetoric of general intent. That is not communicating at all. To this it may be objected that scientists, for instance, have established relations on an international level and that they do meet and talk to one another in their professional bodies. It is claimed that when scientists get together they are not meeting as politicians or diplomats—they are not jockeying for position but discussing science, and that there is therefore real conversation.

I do not accept this argument. It is true that scientists communicate when they talk about science; but for the rest their communication is confined to what one might call the level of fraternal acquaintanceship in the tea rooms and bars of convention centers. This is not what I mean by a "universal human grammar."

To be more positive: If I try to look at different cultures I am impressed by the similar echoes one hears from them, even when they are spread apart by many thousands of miles. Go to some Asian country and you will find that local cultures embody certain phrases about the nature of one's relationship to a neighborhood which have an exact echo in northern England. What, then, I mean by the use of a universal human grammar is that we would know better what sorts of foundations we could build on for international understanding if we knew more of the way in which our differing experiences have created overlapping ranges of attitudes. The danger of saying this is that the notion might become wishy-washy, and we might end up with only a couple of phrases to the effect that understanding, community, and so on, are good things. That was not my meaning. I meant that different people have different patterns of feeling, but there are enough similarities within the differences for us to realize that human beings in different times and places have recorded their experiences and made out of them art, thought, and ideas which do not merge into a common whole but which, though different, do reinforce and buttress one another.

Urban Until quite recently religion was the common grammar of mankind: Christianity for the white races, Confucianism for the Chinese, and so on. Now that these religions are less than universally accepted, I should have thought technology and the human experience of technology would be the universal language of human understanding.

Hoggart No, my meaning was that if we really want to understand one another we have to begin by understanding a culture, preferably our own, more fully than most of us ever try to do, and by seeing what are its virtues and what its limits. This is the culture we feel to be in our bones and that is our basis for understanding *other* cultures. If we do decide to move out from that position to try to understand other cultures, we must take them as seriously and sensitively as we can. In many ways there will be differences but in some ways we will hear common music, common sounds, common phrases, and common assumptions, and if we compare several of these with each other, we will find that we can begin to make connections by recognizing the differences and therefore also by recognizing similarities. This is what I meant by the universal grammar.

For instance, French attitudes to the British and British attitudes to the French have always been very mixed and very ambiguous. Living in France, I find that the differences are still there, very sharply. Yet what impresses me now are the similarities—the sense in which we are European, both of us, although each in his special way. One example is the French and British attitudes to the mind. The French are said to worship the mind; the British are said to be anti-intellectual. There is some truth in this. Yet if you stand back and look at Europe from a distance, you will find that the European countries' respect for reason is very much a common one. What I'm saying is that there is an identical common European grammar.

Urban You don't think that the cross-cultural echoes you mention are simply signs of regularities in human nature? After all, cultures are the work of human beings, and it would be surprising if the fruits of their creativity didn't show certain similarities.

Hoggart I am assuming that, but I mean more than that. The differences—and these are the things that first strike you—are extremely complex. Every culture has its special personality; its history, its art, its attitude to nature, and so on, are in many ways idiosyncratic. My point is that the universal grammar will not appear to a closed mind or eye. There is no easy way to understand a culture. The understanding has to begin with the recognition of the intractability of the differences, and it is only out of that that a stronger sense of the common elements will arise.

Urban This leads us directly to your idea of the exchangeability of experiences. In the concluding pages of your Reith lectures you say you are assuming that communication matters, and that one *can* communicate, adding "as yet another unprovable assumption that experience is exchangeable."

Hoggart Yes, "experience is exchangeable"; in another place I called it representativeness. What I mean by these two notions is this. We live our lives as individuals and we have a constant succession of experiences. At certain moments we say to ourselves that the experience we are just having is significant to us and representative of more than itself. We feel that it transcends our person, that it can be significant for others, that it can be "symbolic." It may sum up a whole period of our life, a typical stance, a characteristic attitude, and from then onward perhaps we will always remember it as a moment of representative significance. That moment is at the base of a great deal of art—much in the novel revolves around it, and there are words for it in many languages. Exchangeability means, then, that art, and especially writing, rests on the assumptions (a) that certain moments are typical and significant, (b) that they have more than personal significance, and (c) that they can be shared. Without these, there can be no art.

These are immense assumptions—yet everybody makes them. We all make them even if we've never read an essay on art.

People will remark to you at a certain moment, "That's just the sort of thing you would say." This may seem to sum up a situation very precisely; but you notice it is based on the assumption that people can communicate. Yet I don't think this should simply be taken for granted.

In my Reith lectures I looked at the basic assumptions behind the whole business of reading, writing, and talking, and what I was doing in the passage you quoted was to point to some extraordinary assumptions we make as a matter of course.

Let's take the one about certain moments being representative; that is not accepted by many people—it is not accepted by many social scientists. "On what grounds," they might ask, "do you decide that one moment is more representative than another?" And if I were to answer, "Have you noticed how, in our society, people use a curious gesture with the left hand that does this, etc.?" they would first counter by saying, "We don't know; we would need to have a survey, we would need some test to see whether people really are using such a gesture." I would then try to explain what the gesture might mean: "There isn't only this gesture that I find significant, but I notice throughout this decade a series of gestures all of which seem to me to have a common source and to signal that more and more people are feeling in such and such a way." This kind of explanation would make some social scientists furious: "How do I know, how *can* I know?" they would ask. Yet I do feel sure that my reading of these gestures is true, because they fit in with other "evidence" I've gathered about the style of a society. I can't prove this. And even a series of very elaborate surveys can prove only that these gestures are coming much more into prominence. But one cannot, as a social scientist, automatically make a leap from there to reading and interpreting the gestures.

Nor can we produce a slide rule of externally verified values and measure a society against them. A culture is a picture of the world, and to recognize that picture one has to look and listen, and that means listening to much more than words and manifest assertions. One should try to interpret a culture's attitudes to schooling, to ambition, to old age, to death, to self-improvement, to privacy, and many other things, including the gestures people make in different situations.

A sympathetic person might agree that XY, who writes about such things, has done justice to those gestures in his writings. He might say: "I didn't myself notice all those gestures until now, but since I have had them described I agree that they exist, and what is more, it rings true to me when XY says that these gestures mean such and such."

"All right," says a social scientist who objects—"All right, but what has really happened? You have found someone else who has an impressionistic mind, as you have." And there is no easy way round these differences. Yet communication cannot be wholly quantified. Passing on information from one place to another is not communicating.

We pick up signals, usually without being aware of it. We use words, tones, pauses, and gestures for speaking to each other. Most of these are part of common experience and they point to the fact that communicating depends on the assumption of close relationships. When you think of the different meanings that a phrase such as "Who do you think you're talking to?" can have, depending on which word receives stress, it is easy to see that tone is more important than the precise meaning of the words you use. Much talk about communication today is shallow because it has found no way of doing justice to the subtle inflections with which people and cultures talk to one another.

One of the most depressing experiences is to see how these fundamental difficulties and subtleties in communicating have been ignored for the sake of bowing before modern technological marvels. There is behaviorism, laced with a sort of gimcrack, smart, public relations, ad man's approach compounded of some social psychology and some neurology and some technology. I repeat what I said in my Reith lectures: Pangloss is reborn in every generation.

But those who believe that modern communication techniques will, as if automatically, create "significant contacts" are not the only offenders. There are also those who blur the outlines between a disinterested statement or analysis and all those other kinds of trimming which outnumber disinterested work: low-level proselytizing, doctored history, high-level intellectual acrobatics, everything which is publicly offered so as to tickle our fancies, or arouse our feelings for their own sakes, or hammer our emotions for the sake of some ulterior purpose.

Urban And yet we communicate.

Hoggart We do, but uncertainly and not all the time. I have argued that communication starts with speaking more honestly to oneself, that we can then, if we wish, move out to trying to speak to others, and that we sometimes succeed. But all those are acts of faith. There is no proof that either side finally communicates anything accurately. We are like the insects called pond skaters. We assume that there is a skin over the water of our shared experience and then set out across it and hope to meet, because if we assumed otherwise, we would sink without trace.

Urban I still wonder about the exchangeability of experience. It has not always been taken for granted that experiences are exchangeable even between countries culturally as close to one another as France and Germany. When we talk to nations across a political and ideological barrier, as we do in these broadcasts for instance, the exchangeability of experiences runs into obstacles more formidable than those you have shown to exist between cultures and individuals. If you were to say to yourself, "I wish to sensitize people beyond the political barrier to certain ideas and values which we regard to be good and worth having," how would you go about telling them about these values?

Hoggart I don't think much can be done at the institutional, political level. Governments and institutions can best help by getting out of the way. The best lingua franca is the arts, because it is through the arts that a society expresses itself most profoundly. If societies were serious about communicating with each other, they couldn't do better than let their people have a chance to feel the full force of each other's arts. What has most impressed me, and stood me in good stead in my attempt to understand the Soviet Union, for instance, has been my love of nineteenth-century Russian literature. I read it and taught about it and I think it one of the great creative achievements of the human mind. If I now try to think what my approach to things Soviet would be if I didn't have that complex texture to refer to, I am sure that approach would be much thinner.

But understanding society through its arts requires patience. The speed of modern life and the pressure of communications have made it harder for us to make the patient effort—to have that quiet, deep, soaking experience which is the only way to begin to understand what societies are like. I do not underestimate the advances we have made. I know that more people have a chance to learn more and understand more than ever before, that education is cheaper, that books are cheaper, and so on. However, there is a pressure on us to use these things as objects and tools, and not to surrender to them in a way you have to surrender before art if you want to understand it.

What I am saying is that anything which provides a firsthand human experience is the beginning, and the essential beginning, of an understanding of the sort we talk about; and that the arts are the key to all that. So, oddly enough, although I am at the moment in a highly institutionalized and very large organization, I have come to see more and more that the work I did in the early part of my life, that is, as a teacher of literature, had the germs of the truth in it even more than I thought—and I was never modest about the claims I made for it.

Urban There is a tendency in politically closed communities to blur the lines between culture and ideology. Your view is that "ideology is always less than a culture." The tendency to equate the two is widespread in the world today.

Hoggart This tendency is dangerous. Cultures are extremely rich phenomena. They give us the whole patterns of societies—their attitudes, their styles of life as they have evolved over the years in certain climatic, historical, and economic conditions. Even quite small cultures can embody complex responses to the conditions of life, and their richness is remarkable. If you spend six months reading deeply into the history of some small tribe, you will be struck by the fragile and yet tough creations with which human beings try to make sense and order of their worlds, whether in their marriage rituals, their barter trading, their initiation ceremonies, or what you will.

An ideology is that picture of the world which any given state has said *is* the world for its people. A totalitarian state also has it in its power to give its people an ideological picture of the "truth" about the world through the media, through education, through its refusal to air serious criticisms, etc. You raised the question interestingly when you said that there is a tendency to equate culture with ideology. This is perfectly true. It is in the nature of ideological governments that they always speak on behalf of the history of their culture, fusing it, and confusing it, with their own ideological interpretation of the world: "*We* are the people, *this* is our history, and *this* is the story of our relationship with the outside world; *these* are the virtues of our men, *those* are the virtues of our women, and *those* are our heroes back in time." Governments go in for this ideologization of culture because they know that by doing so they can draw upon considerable reserves of loyalty and credulity. But this is a travesty, a dilution and thinning out of the reality of culture which is always more complex and acts in more directions than ideology.

The ideological doctoring of cultural history can assume grotesque proportions, even though you can often see why the distortions come about. There are the new nations desperate to create a sense of national identity, especially those which had their national identity broken by colonialism; they want to get back over the gap, but at the same time they recognize that they are facing the late twentieth century. In some of the developing countries the promotion of national identity is hotly political and deeply challenged—if an opposition is allowed to exist—because some of the governments in power present a picture of the nation's history which is obviously selective. It is usually the sort of history in which everything that happened in the past points to the just emergence of the government in power. It shows that a people as virtuous as the one in question was bound to arrive at a government just like the one it has. I know oppositions who complain bitterly that, by pushing this image of the culture of a new country, the government is using education and history as a means of reinforcing its power.

Urban You were saying that at the institutional level little can be done to encourage the exchangeability of experience. I am reminded that it is precisely an international organization, UNESCO, that has taken the lead in sponsoring an unbiased, team-written history of mankind. Do you think that this kind of enterprise can remove some of the suspicions and misunderstandings from national cultures and further the exchangeability of experiences?

Hoggart It had to be done and the work is valuable, although I think its value is of a different order from what I was describing when I spoke of the supreme importance of the arts. So I go on speaking up for the arts, especially since it is always easier to settle for second-order solutions. That said, there is a great deal in favor of institutional undertakings such as the one you remarked upon, and I think it is going to be interesting to see how, for example, in Europe the history books are rewritten. There is no question at all that most of the textbooks should be recast, because the history taught to schoolchildren in almost any European country is scandalously one-sided; and part of the job has already been begun. In a sense the rewriting is, of course, performed by every intelligent student as soon as he realizes that his history books are silly and one-sided. To realize the sillinesses is, one might say, part of the process of self-education.

I was educated in a local authority grammar school, and the vision I was given of what other countries were like and what Britain was like in relation to them was ludicrous. I was given an equally ludicrous view of what Britain was like internally, and I had to write my own book about it eventually. Anything that removes unnecessary obstacles and biases is to be welcomed.

But let me repeat: Nothing is as good as the impact of art. You may say, "Surely something could be done by providing many more fellowships, longer stays abroad, exchanges, international seminars, and the like." I am not so sure. Let us imagine workmen spending three months abroad in a factory similar to their own, observing and learning how other people do their jobs. This may have its uses, but by and large people take away only what they *can* at that moment take away, and we all have highly selective perceptions. The great thing about the arts is that they invite us to face things as honestly and dispassionately as we can.

Urban If the arts are the vehicle of your universal human grammar, can this grammar enjoy wide understanding? You were saying in your Reith lectures that the pressure to trivialize serious things is built on the unspoken but clear assumption that most people are capable of responding to very little. Art is *par excellence* not accessible to a great many people. Isn't there, then, a danger that your language for cross-cultural communication will be understood by only a small minority who may well coincide with your meritocracy?

Hoggart That most people are capable of responding to very little is not *my* opinion but my summary of the assumptions behind many people's thinking when, for instance, they defend trivial broadcasting on the grounds that broadcasters should not set their sights above the lowest common denominator. It is the argument which holds that quality, thinking, understanding, are peculiar to perhaps ten percent of the population, and that you don't throw pearls before swine. I do not accept that. As I said very early in this discussion, I am sure that (to stick to the example of broadcasting) most people are capable of responding to more than they get from most broadcasting systems in the world. There is evidence for this, and yet we go on making crass assumptions. When the BBC's first Saturday night satire shows* were put on they were broadcast at a late hour because the planners thought they would appeal only to a small minority who understood irony and satire. Yet from early on they got very large audiences.

What is interesting here are the faulty assumptions and the preset, reach-me-down notions about how people split into categories and what they will understand and enjoy. Yet it was possible to have been more informed about the nature of British audiences, because there was plenty of evidence to tell us what sort of people we are. Of course most British people haven't read T. S. Eliot and many don't even read books, but

That Was the Week That Was, broadcast in the early 1960s.

one thing that has been common in British working-class life for a long time is a mocking, ironic strain. You will find it in Dickens: Sam Weller dances rings round most people by a style of ironic backchat and mickey-taking. When the BBC's satire shows appeared, many working-class people responded to them at once. They may not have understood all the references, but they got the gist and the style of attack. What I am saying is that here is a very precise instance of a quality—a very powerful quality—in people. The kind of irreverence that is found among British working-class people is a valuable quality, especially against governments. This quality was not recognized by the BBC planners and they were taken by surprise. That the broadcasters didn't notice is a relatively minor matter. It is a cause for more concern that politicians and teachers tend not to recognize it either. If we, as politicians and teachers, do not understand enough of a society's complex web of attitudes, of its richness and dialectics, we will miss a great many opportunities and will fail to make important connections. The capacity of people to respond to experiences is far wider than we usually recognize. We must bank on potentialities, and not settle for some preset notion about what each of us is capable of achieving. We are always capable of more than we imagine.

Lord Ashby

A Hippocratic Oath
for the Academic Profession

Lord Ashby is Master of Clare College, Cambridge (England), Chancellor of Queen's University, Belfast, a former Vice-Chancellor of the University of Cambridge (1967-69), and Chairman of the Royal Commission on Environmental Pollution, 1970-73. Lord Ashby's publications include *Scientists in Russia*; *Technology and the Academics*; *African Universities and Western Tradition*; *Masters and Scholars*; and *The Rise of the Student Estate* (with Mary Anderson).

Urban In a lecture you delivered at McMaster University in Hamilton, Ontario, in 1970 (later published in *Masters and Scholars*) you spoke of an "educational contract" that should govern the relationship between university teachers and students. Your conception of the university is that of a corporation in which, in addition to academic staff, graduates, and administrators, undergraduate students should also enjoy de jure status as citizens of the university. Such, as you point out, is at any rate the official framework in which British universities operate.

The contrast between this liberal view of the student's place in the university and that represented by Professor Max Beloff earlier is striking, for whereas Professor Beloff forcefully argued that the correct analogy for a university is a hierarchically organized community such as an ocean liner or an aircraft or a hospital, your view is that university students are "not customers in a shop or patients in a hospital or passengers on a ship," but members of a corporation with appropriate rights and responsibilities.

That said, I am curious to know what kinds of rights and obligations teachers and scholars assume in your view when they become citizens of the university, and more particularly, how you would define your concept of a "Hippocratic Oath for the academic profession"—a phrase you used in a lecture at the Association of Commonwealth Universities Congress in Australia in 1968.

Lord Ashby Until not so many years ago anybody who went into a university to teach knew that his main job was teaching and transmitting a culture and a moral code, because universities were all religious foundations—even those attached to the Muslim and Oriental world. So there was a built-in, unwritten obligation to teach and to be loyal to your institution, and your main focus of attention was the student.

I am not denying for a moment that this is still true for thousands of teachers in a great many universities; but my worry is that this educational contract is now being seriously diluted, because the university teacher has other claims on his loyalties. What matters to him most, if he is a young man, for instance in physics, is not whether he teaches physics well, but whether he publishes papers that his peers in physics will appreciate and will regard as good enough to elect him to an academy or give him some kind of honor. Even a professor in physics, and certainly a successful research worker in physics, depends often on criteria outside the main job that he is being paid to do inside the university. "Star" professors in one American university, for instance, expect to be away from the campus two years out of three. There are universities where it is not uncommon for some teachers to opt out of undergraduate teaching altogether. And we all know that when an academic talks about "getting back to my own work," he does not mean his lectures or his seminars.

In the case of a great many men—I would imagine most teachers in this country—this clash of loyalties can be, and is being, reconciled. Also, sometimes there may be good reasons for making exceptions, and I have no quarrel with justifiable exceptions. Nevertheless, while the majority of university teachers in this country have a great sense of duty toward their students, the temptation is there to neglect their teaching functions and to act as though they were workers in a research institute. And that is where I see a need for restating the contract a university teacher enters into, as contrasted with the contract a pure research worker in a government laboratory would have.

At the moment there is no declared code of professional practice to which academics have subscribed, and my purpose (in Australia) was to put in a plea for a code. If we had such a code, it would stabilize what I fear is a schizophrenic and disintegrating profession, and it would provide a basis of authority and example to the students. That is what I meant by calling for a Hippocratic Oath for the academic profession.

I have for years had to sit on committees picking people to work in universities, and I do not remember a single case in which any of us turned to the man we were thinking of appointing and asked: "Will you devote your time to the teaching of young students?" In fact, when I got my first professorship many years ago, my contract was to do research and to further the subject; there was nothing mentioned in the contract about students at all. Although the conscience of many university teachers does, in fact, prod them to look after students, and they do it very well, their written contract may not oblige them to do so. The result is that very distinguished research workers are tempted to neglect their students in favor of work that enhances their own prestige. One of the several causes of student discontent is the impression that, in many universities, the undergraduate is no longer the primary interest of the university. The ethical code I advocate would be similar to that which regulates a lawyer's duty to his client and a doctor's duty to his patient; it would set out the duty of teacher to pupil.

Urban When you speak of a Hippocratic Oath for academics, what—apart from the teacher's physical and mental presence—would be the articles of your code? I should have thought physical and mental presence were the necessary but not sufficient conditions for a teacher to fulfill his duty to his students and profession. There are surely qualities in the integrity of learning that lend themselves to translation into the culture of undergraduates.

Lord Ashby Scholarship has an inner integrity that should be of some help to the student in search of a moral content to his academic studies. The correct transmission of a subject involves a deep moral commitment that can lead to complicated questions. Let me illustrate the point by some of the hysterical talk now going on about the environment. It is wholly legitimate for publicists and politicians, and lawyers, for that matter, to advocate a point of view, and therefore to highlight certain facts and give less emphasis to others, in order to persuade people. But one of the unwritten laws of scholarship is that you must give no more emphasis to one fact than to another if your purpose is (as it must be) to convey an accurate picture of how things really are and not how you would like them to be. To give you a specific example: Everybody knows that cars emit a gas called carbon monoxide which is poisonous in large quantities, and everybody would agree that there ought not to be more of this about than is unavoidable. But a lot of people— including university teachers in science—alarm the public, claiming that this carbon monoxide is going to build up to a great threat to the health of humanity and will eventually choke us. But the facts simply do not bear out this statement. Carbon monoxide is not increasing in the air, because it is being eaten up by bacteria. Even in the streets in New York, among the skyscrapers, it does not reach concentrations that are likely to cause more than temporary discomfort. Yet you will find professional scientists being just as guilty as other people, picking out the facts that will back a case and keeping quiet about others.

One article in the Hippocratic Oath would therefore make it incumbent on the scholar in his official life (whatever he may want to do or say in his private life as a citizen) to preserve a rigorous integrity which does not permit him to hide some facts, or even to blur them slightly, and to bring others out into the open in order to make any kind of point. In other words, scholarship has an inherent morality—a very limited one—which must come over in the way any subject is taught.

Then I would go on to say that the Hippocratic Oath would involve more than that, although this is implicit in what I have just said, namely that you do not ever take into account, when you are assessing a man's scholarship, whether he belongs to the same race or the same religion or the same political party as yourself. If an inexperienced worker who is entirely unknown to me, who is of a different race from my own and holds political views contrary to my own, produces a piece of scholarship which confounds something that I hold to be true, I have to take his work into account: I have either to say that I do not believe his results to be true and explain why, or I have to alter my views in order to fit his results. Thus there is in scholarship a built-in internationalism that automatically eliminates all intercommunity, interracial, international prejudices that divide us so seriously in other ways. These are the kinds of ethical signposts one implicitly tries to build into the duties of a university teacher.

Urban   It is a fairly tall order. Has your proposal for a Hippocratic Oath fallen on receptive ears?

Lord Ashby   Alas, no. In the discussion that followed the publication of my rather provocative assertion, it emerged very clearly that two of the large professional organizations of university teachers that I am familiar with—the Association of

University Teachers (AUT) in England and the Association of American University Professors (AAUP) in the United States—had never managed to get any kind of statement of the obligations of their profession. The American Association had tried as long ago as 1919, but their code was so watered down by a querulous insistence that academics must have safe jobs, that nobody must be in a position to sack them, and that they must have unlimited academic freedom, that the statement had become a charter of the rights of the academic profession, with very little being said about academic obligations. The Association of University Teachers had not even tried to do that. It concentrated a good deal too much on the right of university teachers to say what they like and not to be interfered with for their political views or prejudices; nothing was said of their obligation to speak the truth and attend to their students.

Urban You said that scientific work implies its own, though very limited, ethos. I wonder if this ethos is universal enough to satisfy the moral expectations of students. You recognize the difficulty very clearly in *Masters and Scholars* where you say that nowadays students are not satisfied with the repertoire of moral principles carried by the techniques and conventions of scholarship. "Students want a moral compass to guide them in their self-imposed responsibilities to society and in their search for their own identity."

What you say about the limited range of the moral effectiveness of scholarship and the students' desire to go beyond it are statements of fact. But you are treading on controversial ground when you then make certain assertions about what the university can, and what it cannot, do to provide students with a moral compass. You write: "It is essential that he [the student] should become reconciled to the fact that the university's contribution is limited. Its contribution is to provide an education, not an identity. . . . Scholars can legitimately expect the masters to ignite their intellects, but not their consciences."

Let me speak up for the students and say that their expectation to be able to distill from the accumulated knowledge of mankind, of which the university is the unique depository, some vital wisdom that will nourish them later in life, is a fact of our time and surely legitimate. They have observed that the integrity of scholarship is a feeble light, easily extinguished by the exigencies of national policies, ideology, considerations of prestige, vested interests, and the like. Modern students want a broad beam they can follow with tolerable certainty.

Lord Ashby You may well be right, but it would only be honest of me to confess that the statement you quoted from *Masters and Scholars* was made as the only alternative left open to us with the present organization of our universities. It is a point one cannot make too often that universities have, for seven-eighths of their eight hundred years of history, been religious organizations where the morality was built in. Until just over a hundred years ago you could not graduate from this college (Clare College, Cambridge, England) unless you were a member of the Church of England. More than that—you had to agree, before you could take a degree, that your views were consistent with the doctrines of the Church of England. All that is now gone; we are left with a vacuum, and I entirely agree with you that the young want more than a sterilized, aseptic knowledge of science and the facts of history. The difficulty that I find myself in is a purely practical one. If you believe that it is a purpose of the university to give philosophical and moral background as well as training in rational thought, then your first problem is to appoint a teaching staff who can do this. As I say, this used to be the case—you could not have got a job in this university two centuries ago unless you satisfied the Fellows that you were a devout Christian. Now we put people into academic jobs solely on the strength of their skills in particular subjects. If we are going to provide the moral background as well, we must first appoint people who have the right moral attitude, and we have to decide what that right moral attitude is.

But before trying to answer that question, let me give you a small example of the nature of our dilemma. We have in Britain today a far more permissive attitude toward sex than we had when I was a student, and it would be a very unwise college that made it a rigid rule that no student could have a girl in his room at night. On the other hand, we have a much less permissive attitude about hypocrisy than we used to. It was only ten years ago that everybody knew that a Cambridge college shut its doors at night but everybody could get in by climbing over the wall. The modern student would say, "This is hypocrisy—if you don't want me to get in, keep me out. If you are going to make rules like that, I shan't come here, and if you know we are going to get in after the gates are shut, why don't you leave them open?" This attitude is one of the symptoms that the permissive society is no less moral than my generation was, but that it has changed the order of its moral priorities.

Coming back to the question of offering students a moral and philosophical background, I do not see how any university in Europe or America could appoint an academic staff on the strength of their moral attitude, because we do not agree what the moral attitude should be. Personally I would rather have somebody who detested hypocrisy than somebody who was modern in his ideas about sex, but then some of my colleagues would be horrified at that suggestion. So what I think we are feeling our way to is watching the young develop their own standards of morality and then giving them what help we can.

I end up in a very weak position as far as your question is concerned; namely, I agree that the young want more from the university than aseptic knowledge, that some guidelines ought to be provided before they go out into the world, where they will certainly have to make up their minds about moral issues, and that the university is the place where they should find the guidelines. They do not get them at home—more and more parents find themselves incapable of dealing with these problems, leaving them to the professional teachers at the universities. But whether there will ever again be a consensus about moral attitudes at the university and the will to enforce them is a question I would hesitate to answer.

Urban Let me come back to a question you have already partly answered. How far can the ethical code inherent in the scientific method be stretched to provide us with a substitute for the moral signposts we appear to have lost, or certainly lost sight of? We have both said that the ethical implications of scholarship are a kind of strip mining—the deposits are all near the surface and easily exhausted. But is this, in fact, a valid analogy? Distinguished scientists like Jacques Monod, the French biologist, believe that the scientific method is the only paradigm on which human morality can be legitimately modeled, and that moral codes of any other provenance are at best fanciful.

Lord Ashby The moral signposts of science are too limited. We have already briefly discussed what they are: integrity in the pursuit of truth, the recognition that error is merely an approach to the truth that has been found to be inaccurate and has been improved on, and the tolerance that goes with it. Then we spoke of the built-in internationalism of the scientific method and its rejection of any hierarchy and authority.

These are good things, but when we come to the difficult problem of compassion, of justice, of the ordinary loyalties that you want a family to show toward one another if children are to be brought up in a stable atmosphere—I am not sure that you will find guidelines for these in the ethos of scholarship. I once said, in trying to work this problem out for myself, that you can expect a man to have certain moral principles if you know that he is a scientist and believes in the Second Law of Thermodynamics. But the set of moral principles that you could depend on him to follow would be much narrower than those of a man who had faith in the Sermon on the Mount. I would agree that Monod hasn't the complete answer. He has a better answer than nothing, but it still falls very short of what we would ideally require.

Urban Today those who believe in the message of the Sermon on the Mount are themselves scared of saying "this is morally right, that is morally wrong." They appear to have lost confidence in their ability to adjudicate, not because of moral cowardice, but because many sincere Christians believe, in the words of the Rt. Rev. Trevor Huddleston (Bishop of Stepney) that the moral theology in which they were trained "no longer seems to ask, let alone answer, the questions that mankind itself is asking. It has largely ceased to be credible because it is concerned with an ethical system that does not *appear* to be relevant in a world of such revolutionary and rapid technological change."

But Bishop Huddleston is not content to state the dilemma. He pleads for establishing an "ethical think tank"—a committee of wise people, not limited to Christians—because he believes that "in our fluid, plural, mobile society we desperately need a body of people to help us, who are wholly committed to the truth that this is God's world and that, as a consequence, there are immutable ethical principles and a moral law which express ultimate meaning and purpose."

You have said that the morality of scholarship is too narrow; we now have an authentic view stating that the morality of the Sermon on the Mount also appears to be irrelevant and ineffectual. Where I see a connection between Bishop Huddleston and your proposal for a Hippocratic Oath for academics is in Huddleston's suggestion for an "ethical think tank." Personally I doubt whether either an oath or the conjoint wisdom of a committee can equip us with those dos and don'ts, the principles of which we no longer instinctively accept. The problem is by no means new, but its relevance to our situation is striking.

That your confidence in the spillover effects of science into the moral field is limited seems clear also from another aspect of your thinking. You suggest (in *Technology and the Academics*) that technology could become the cement between science and humanism, because, unlike science, technology does not eliminate the human element. This is a surprising assertion, for many of us have come to believe the fashionable thing, that technology is a soul-destroying and depersonalizing, rather than a humanizing and integrating, activity. Perhaps you are thinking of technology on a higher level of application than the one on which technology affects us in our practical affairs, for you are asserting, not only that technology is inseparable from humanism, but also that technology could become "the core of a new twentieth-century humanism."

Lord Ashby   I certainly believe this to be so. When you look at a scientist working at science, he is creating in his mind problems within his discipline. The whole thing is somewhat artificial, for it is the essence of the scientific method that the human element is eliminated—science concerns itself only with phenomena upon which all qualified observers agree. It describes, classifies, and measures in such a way that variation due to human judgment is excluded. When a chemist poses himself a problem, he is looking for a solution consistent with the rest of chemistry, but it will have no relevance of itself to the social life of the world outside.

Now technology, unlike pure science, concerns the applications of science to the needs of man and society. You design a bridge not merely in order to solve some problem of mechanics, but to provide communication between one side of a river and another, and therefore the whole social purpose of the work technology is doing immediately comes into the picture. This changes the social obligations of the men engaged in it. Once you are solving social problems by the use of science, you must know the social purpose of what you are doing. And as soon as you have views about the social purpose, you have got to make up your mind whether it is a social purpose consistent with your view of what is good or bad for society. The technologist is up to his neck in human problems, whether he likes it or not.

I can give you an example which may strike you as being light-hearted to begin with, but does not end up being light-hearted. It has to do with the consequences of learning to make beer. If you are going to be a brewer you must, as a first condition, be quite sure in your own mind that you genuinely want to make beer. From this it is a natural step to the study of biology, microbiology, and chemistry. You have then got to learn something about the technology of actual beer production, because once you begin to operate in thousand-gallon vats instead of test tubes, entirely new techniques have to be applied. But if you are going to spend your entire life making beer, then it seems to me necessary that you should reconcile in your conscience just what effect on society you are having.

Well, in Britain, you are selling beer through public houses—institutions that are almost unique to this country because the public house is a club where the same people meet night after night, have their drinks and talk together. The pub is the nursery where political ideas that change whole governments occur—it is the pub-talk that makes the vote in most constituencies when there is an election, and therefore the whole design of the pub, the way in which it brings people together, its social milieu, are decisive for the social and political fortunes of the country. The social consequences of your work as a brewer are therefore an integral part of your profession.

You also have to face the problem that some people drink too much and that drunkenness is a very old and dangerous shortcoming of mankind, which in these days of cars leads to serious criminal offenses and slaughter on the roads. This takes you into the whole problem of the morality of drinking—what do you say to a temperance league which is out to prevent any alcohol from being consumed in the country, or to legislation that would prolong opening hours? Do you agree with this or that?

You have to make up your mind. You are doing a kind of cost-benefit analysis without money being involved but with values being put in the scales instead. Without beer (and this is my own frank view), we would not only be short of a very pleasant beverage but, in England, we would also be short of one of the most important forums for forming public opinion. Also, in a country that hasn't got a lot of sunshine, where you cannot often sit in the garden to enjoy your drink and talk to people, public houses provide one of the happiest places for social intercourse.

On the other side, you have to realize that a great many people do waste money, neglect their families, and even get into criminal trouble because of the effects of alcohol. Someone has to make a balanced judgment between these two sets of factors, and you can't make balanced judgments of values without working out your own sets of values. If you are a technologist, you have yourself to make a decision as to where you stand on this particular kind of issue. Anyone who goes in for brewing has to do this; anyone who goes in for civil engineering has to do this.

Take the example of the civil engineer who builds a road into some remote territory in Africa. He may assert that it is not his business to take into account the effect on primitive villages upcountry. Nevertheless his road will transform the whole society at the end of that road. This might be a calamity. One of the mistakes we have often made in carrying what we call civilization into these countries was that we had not followed through the social and moral consequences of simple engineering ventures like building roads and having telephones.

Urban This would speak for an interdisciplinary element to be built into university teaching, so that the man who designs the road or brews the beer is not utterly ignorant of the social and anthropological implications of his work.

Lord Ashby You are quite right to bring me down to earth, for one has to ask, "If all this is true, what does the university do about it?" It seems to me there are only three solutions the university can offer, and one of these is wrong. The first thing it can do is to give short courses on the moral attitude you ought to have when you build a road into an African state. That seems to me to be indoctrination; but the days when you could say, "This is the kit of beliefs, and you jolly well accept them or get out" are over. The second possible solution is to have seminars from people who have had to make value judgments of the kind I have mentioned. This could be done in two ways. One is to mount a fully multidisciplinary training, so that a student can follow all technologies to their social consequences. Unfortunately this would not be practical, since there isn't the time for it in a university curriculum, nor are there the teachers to do it. That leaves the third alternative, which I personally favor: You take a typical case study and follow it through in depth. An intelligent person, if he is really concerned and interested in what he is doing, would then be able to work out a great deal for himself. So I'd like to see every technology student at universities taken through a crash history of a particularly illuminating case that begins with facts and statistics and then illustrates for him how you make political decisions. For between the analytical understanding of a situation and the political decisions made on it, there is a complete jump.

You begin with the facts, but once you are airborne, you are working on ideologies, prejudices, self-interest, and many other irrational factors which are all part and parcel—and I would say the principal part and parcel—of the political decision-making process. The student would thus get used to the idea that when he is himself launched on a technological project, these elusive and irrational factors are the ones he will have to take into account when he calculates the social spillover of his work in technology. This is an entirely pragmatic program for equipping the student for the social responsibilities he must be prepared to shoulder as a technologist, and I think it is workable.

Urban Your idea of how one ought to pursue a general education at the university is, I believe, closely linked with the point you have just made. You say in *Technology and the Academics* that "the path to culture should be through a man's specialty, not by bypassing it," and this, you feel, could be achieved by making specialist studies the core around which are grouped liberal studies relevant to these specialist studies—an idea I also encountered in my conversation with Lord James earlier.

Lord Ashby Yes, I once quoted Alfred North Whitehead to underline my point: The habit of apprehending technology in its completeness—this is the nub of technology as a humane pursuit, and this is what education in higher technology should try to achieve. I would like to see this education in technological humanism come at the end rather than at the beginning of the university curriculum. Some American universities, Harvard for example, have a very sophisticated general education system, but they run it in the first two years of a four-year course. The University of Keele, in England, runs it earlier still, in the first year of study. I would like to see it come at the very end of the course, when a man's enthusiasm over becoming good at one subject has been more or less satiated. It is at this point—before he goes away—that we should say to him: "Now you'd better think of the consequences that are going to follow from the expertise you've got," and put him through the kind of seminar I have described.

Urban You are very emphatic in your writings that the university student, having become familiar with the orthodoxies of his subject, should then begin to look with skepticism upon all present knowledge, with the intention of purging it of errors and false assumptions. Now this is an appealingly liberal attitude to scholarship with which I personally very much agree. The nice question is, at what point is the student satisfied that he has absorbed and understood enough about his subject to dissent from received knowledge, and how does he then go about challenging it and the people who have handed it down to him? In Eastern Europe, for example, all legitimate knowledge is, by and large, orthodox knowledge; dissent is, at best, suspect.

Lord Ashby At the beginning of an undergraduate's life I would expect him to be prepared to listen to orthodoxy, because until he understands the conventional point of view—in other words, until he understands my generation's axioms—he cannot begin to doubt them, challenge them, and change them. My quarrel with a lot of the young now is that they do not bother to learn the conventional. They want to break straight into dissent without really understanding what it is they are challenging. Not only that, but they also argue— perhaps not unreasonably—that they want the university to produce "not a book but a man." Then they silently point to me as a teacher (although they do not put it in this simple way): "But not a man like you."

This immediately raises the difficulty that if that is what the students have in mind, then it is very hard for us to ask them to accept our conformity even as a starting point. My answer to a student who says to me, "But I don't want to be a man like you," is to tell him, "But you must know what a man like me does believe before you start building your dissent from what I believe. Therefore be patient and listen until you understand my point of view. Then I shall encourage you to differ from it—but don't sweep it aside without listening to it."

My understanding of the totalitarian regimes is that they would, as you say, expect you to go along with the first leg of that argument but not encourage you to go on to the second part, except in certain specified fields. Clearly in science it is encouraged, otherwise research would not be as good as it is in many of the totalitarian states. But in the politically more sensitive subjects, the art of dissent is not encouraged, let alone taught. We are supposed to teach it, and I think we do.

But I am in the perennially weak position of the liberal on this sort of point, for the liberal can encourage so much tolerance that the rigidity, which is the precondition of any serious political thinking, breaks down. This gives us sanity and pragmatism, but it robs us of the comprehensiveness of thinking and purpose that is perhaps the outstanding demand of the current student generation.

Urban You said a minute ago that true scholarship is free from any bias of race, religion, and political allegiance and is therefore international *par excellence*. But you are taking this point a good deal further when you claim in *Technology and the Academics* that the new cement of mankind is not a common religion or a common language, but a "common way of thinking about nature and a common stock of knowledge." I wonder whether this is really so. My experience of East-West international conferences is that the more scientific the subject discussed, the less real the détente, the less real the broader understanding which issues from it. And this is not so surprising if we bear in mind the point you made earlier in this conversation, namely that it is of the essence of the scientific method that the human element should be eliminated. If that is so, we can have conferences on abstract scientific topics without re-creating anything like the medieval situation you describe in *Technology and the Academics*, where a scholar arriving on foot at a distant university would be as much at home in Italy as at St. Andrews, because he and his hosts spoke the same language and knelt before the same cross. If your implication was, as I think it must have been, that the "same language" and the "cross" stood for Latin and a shared ideology, I think the scientific method offers a poor substitute.

Lord Ashby I am not sure that my experience is quite consistent with yours. I would agree that the community feeling scientists carry away with them when they have met at an international conference and then go back to their own countries may not change the relationship between the countries politically, because scientists are politically not very powerful. But the experience I have had in actually living in the Soviet Union, as I did for a time during the war, was that from the understanding two scientists have when they start talking about scientific matters there can grow a good deal of mutual trust, and this can lead to the discussion of other problems about which they differ and which do divide the nations as a whole from one another. But my experience was that you could cross this bridge quite easily on the basis of your earlier scientific conversations. This sort of contact can make for a very real détente as between, for instance, Soviet and British individuals, but I think I would not be able to sustain the thesis that all these individual détentes added up to make a great contribution to a major détente between one nation and another. I am sure, though, that individual contacts do a lot of good, and without them the whole process of airing ideas between Eastern Europe and Western Europe would be much more difficult. My feeling is that the cohesion of the scholarly world holds these nations together in ways which may not be very visible, but are perhaps more important than we think. I am more optimistic about it than you are.

Coming to your question whether the ethos of the scientific method offers an equivalent to the common language of Latin and Christianity, well, it is the nearest thing, and of course it is a very pale and flimsy substitute for the enormous imposed faith of the medieval Church, which put you in jail or tortured you if you were a dissenter. International discussions on very sensitive points like nuclear disarmament, for instance, would not have got very far without scientists taking part in them at the lower, technical, level and having gained a great deal of respect for each other before the politicians got into the act. So these contacts are better than nothing. Whether they are going to help détente in any important sense is another matter. Given time, they may; I am an optimist.

Urban I would have thought that mankind's common concern with the environment, population growth, the finite nature of our energy resources, and the need to plan ahead for common contingencies connected with all these problems would create another shared language for understanding one another's problems and for furthering a sense of cooperation in fields that go beyond those immediately within the scientist's compass.

Lord Ashby Here we are talking about a different kind of cementing agent—not so much a shared way of thinking embodied in the supranational commonwealth of scholars and universities, as the practical concern of keeping the seas unpolluted, economizing with our water resources, and the like. It is perfectly true that these common concerns are another powerful source of understanding and possible cooperation. Most of the environmental issues are not politically sensitive—not within the Western world anyway. There is a large degree of agreement between East and West on what ought to be done. That the Baltic should be kept cleaner, to take one example, is highly relevant to the interests of the Federal Republic of Germany, the USSR, Denmark, Poland, and other countries. Once this is realized and agreed—as it is—you have removed one, admittedly neutral, kind of obstacle to international understanding, but this may well pave the way to removing tension in other, and politically less neutral, areas too.

Another field in which I found from personal experience that it is easy to get good cooperation is meteorology. When, at the time of Stalin, I was representing Australia in the Soviet Union, the Russians were very anxious to get news about the weather from the Southern Hemisphere, and it proved quite easy—even, as I say, under Stalin—to get an Australian-Soviet agreement on exchanging meteorological data. So there are certain areas where political détente can be aided by technological and scientific cooperation, but they are, I agree, limited.

Urban I want to take you back, if I may, to the problem of social morality, for on that, it seems to me, hinges the whole troublesome question of student unrest. We have seen that—rightly or wrongly—the young are looking precisely for those qualities which have so far eluded our grasp in this discussion: guidelines for a worthwhile life, a personal identity, norms for social justice, and so on. Wouldn't a certain paternalism, unfashionable though that may sound to us, be preferable to the moral cluelessness that is our condition today? I was struck, during the Watergate inquiry, with how often the investigating senators went back, not only to American law, which would be expected of them, but also to Biblical axioms of right and wrong, as though they were no longer satisfied that the contemporary ethic could furnish a worthy interpretation of American legality, and therefore recourse had to be found to an older and firmer set of ground rules. Of course, this puritanic tradition has old roots in America, but I was, nevertheless, surprised to see it surface quite so strongly and with so little sophistication.

Lord Ashby   This takes us back to the old problem of having a benign totalitarianism, and the question I would want to ask is, who is going to impose it? If it is going to be imposed by our elected democratic leaders, then our criteria for electing members of Parliament have to change. I don't believe it can be imposed by the churches, because confidence in them has been reduced in many ways, largely, perhaps, by the way they squabble among themselves. The failure of the attempts in England to get even the Church of England and the Methodist Church to combine has convinced a great many devout and basically religious people that organized Christianity, as found in this country, is not a very generous movement. One wonders, therefore, where one is going to get this agreed moral code.

As I said earlier in this discussion, what we who teach the young are watching for is to see any signs of what the young themselves want. One of the things their moral code would certainly include would be an elimination of injustices caused by poverty, by being unlucky in having been born to under-privileged parents, injustices between and within nations—particularly toward minorities—making sure that color ceases to matter, and the like. These things are building stones of pragmatic and rather superficial principles of morality, but they all add up to an immense respect of one human being for another, irrespective of his birth or even his mental capacity. There is a certain distrust of intellectualism, which looks offensive when you give it that label, but if you consider the label from another angle and find that it denotes, in fact, a faith in the human being irrespective of his abilities, it looks very attractive.

One sees this attitude in action with highly intellectual students who get into a university like Cambridge. Quietly, without ever getting into the press, they help the underprivileged. Some students for instance go out every Sunday to a home for the mentally handicapped. This would have been almost unthinkable in my student days.

In brief, the big change we are experiencing is the search for a morality that does not measure people by their success, by their money, by their intellectual ability, or by any other endowment. We have got away from the false measuring rod—people are measured only by their humanity. This is awfully vaguely put, because I am trying to give expression to a set of values that I can sense to be stirring in the background but which I cannot as yet identify.

The biologists may be able to help toward an answer. Animal communities haven't a system of morality—each community presumably has its own, elementary, intuitive principles and behavior which we cannot understand. If you watch birds feeding their young you realize that the birds have arranged their social life in such a way that they minimize interference with one another. What the young are beginning to produce is something in which each individual has his own system of morality, and the effect of the youth culture on him is to see that his system does not impinge on other people's. This is, of course, a very elementary rule of thumb, and I wonder whether we shall get a whole spectrum of moralities, limited at one end by the law and at the other end by the amount of freedom young people want to leave to one another. I am still feeling my way.

There is another approach which I find very attractive; I heard it explained by one of our own graduates, who is now an economist but is a very distinguished exponent of Christianity as well, in his spare time. He gave a talk to the students, in which he took the line that all achievement depends on self-discipline. Just as you would not expect to row in a boat race if you were not prepared to accept the discipline of rowing in the boat, so you can't expect to live the life of a successful citizen unless you accept discipline. But then, in the discussion that followed, we drove him into just the corner you have driven me into. We said, "O.K., what is the discipline that makes for a self-respecting and successful citizen?" And his only answer was the Ten Commandments. Now I was quite prepared to accept the Ten Commandments as a reasonable guide, but I was surprised to find that one of my companions, a distinguished professor of theology, wasn't at all satisfied. That wasn't a good enough answer, he said—the Ten Commandments were very mixed. What about "Thou shalt not kill"? Is everyone to be a pacifist? I myself felt that the Ten Commandments were a start, and I would say the same in answer to your question, but some theologians would not even accept that.

Urban I do realize the enormous difficulty of finding even the beginnings of an answer to this problem—a problem as keenly felt in the Communist East as it is in the West. The Rumanian pastor Richard Wurmbrand, writing his *Sermons in Solitary Confinement* in a cell thirty feet below ground in a Bucharest prison, tells of his grievances against God's "unjust laws" in a way that reminds me of what—*mutatis mutandis*—your Cambridge theologian may have had in mind:

"Thou shalt not kill" is said to a Swede or a Swiss whose nation has known no war for centuries. We Rumanians have the same commandment, although our country has been invaded by foreigners in every generation, and we have to defend ourselves.

"Thou shalt not steal" is said to a billionaire, who has more than he will ever need and has no reason to steal. I am terribly hungry, and would steal bread if only I could find it. But in doing this I would be breaking one of your unjust laws. . . .

"Thou shalt not bear false witness" is a law for a man who has no reason to lie . . . ; it is also for me, who have to answer the Communist interrogator. If I tell him the truth, as he asks me, appealing to my Christian obligation, many other arrests will follow.

But coming back to our search for a morality, it is sad that we should have so little faith and firm guidance to offer to the young. The admission, and the fact, that we depend for our public ethic on the whims, fads, and instincts of very young and often untutored people is unprecedented. That does not automatically make it wrong, of course.

Lord Ashby You are right in saying that we have not strong enough faith. Men who have that faith antagonize a lot of people, but at least they provide great comfort and strength to those who will follow them. But to give you a shred of optimism: We may be in a temporary phase in which the young are rejecting all help from older people on these ethical questions, but I am confident that this will pass.

In my student days a student respected his professor to such an extent that he was prepared to listen to his professor's views on all sorts of questions that had nothing to do with his expertise. My own professor, for example, was a very great man, and looking back now I find myself still trying to imitate him in the way I deal with human problems.

When one of his technicians was ill, I remember hearing quite by chance that the professor had sent him money to go away for a holiday afterward. This is something that has stayed with me all my life—this is how you should treat people who work for you in your department, and my admiration for the man was built into my immense respect for the professor as a teacher in my own subject. If this attitude were to come back, it would not only give the young an anchor to hold on to, but it would also encourage us to live by our best moral principles, in order to set an example. At the moment, the ethics of my generation are at a discount, but if I were to be on show all the time, I am sure I would be encouraged to be a better person.

Urban The crisis of morality concerns the aims of university education perhaps more than any other kind of education. You remarked yourself in *Masters and Scholars* that "a generation ago Walter Moberly lamented that a university will teach students how to make bombs or cathedrals, but it will not teach them which of the two objects they ought to make." Has the university lost some of this neutrality?

Lord Ashby Moberly's complaint is less and less justified. My generation, and that of people twenty years younger than myself, has been immensely affected by the great protest movement of youth. It has done us good. Today, anyone teaching the technology of either bombs or cathedral building would have to justify the making of bombs and, for that matter, the building of cathedrals. I was in Manchester when Moberly wrote his book, and talking to my students at the time I remember very vividly that they did not very much want to be told which of these things to make. Today the student is demanding to be told just that, and he will not do any work that will lead him to making the bomb. Mind you, Moberly's plea has not been answered in the way Moberly hoped—which was to reintroduce Christian traditions into the university. But at least now the teacher knows how to pursue Moberly's dilemma, because the students won't let him run away from it. To that extent we have shifted a little way in a good direction.

Urban To conclude this dialogue, I feel we ought to say something about giving the young an "identity," bearing in mind your warning that you regard this as being outside the scope of what the university can provide. The question is inevitably posed in rather vague terms, especially where it is most pressing—among the rather spoiled sons and daughters of well-to-do Americans and West Europeans. In Eastern Europe, for instance, where a student's landscape is filled with material problems such as housing, grants, adverse political conditions, and the like, a student's first concern is to survive, and the identity crisis takes its place at the bottom of his priorities.

Lord Ashby You can see this with black Americans too. The black protest is never against the quality of life. A black graduate will never do what a white Harvard law student often does when he takes his degree—becoming a poor man's lawyer instead of taking a profitable job on Wall Street. The whole aim of the black student is to get himself into a successful career. He is not hunting for an identity; he already has one only too clearly.

We have the same experience here in Cambridge with students whose parents never went to a university and who may be the first from their schools ever to come to Cambridge. They do not have an identity crisis. All such a student wants is to get a good degree and to make a contribution to the world. I think you are right—the man with an identity crisis is the man who has had such a comfortable start that he has to ask himself, "What am I that has not been given me by my father?"

This is the question students find it so difficult to answer. We cannot answer it for them, any more than we can set the present generation of students a moral compass. But we can encourage them to set it themselves, and we can help them by challenging them to succeed.